DATABASES
FOR
NETWORKS
AND
MINICOMPUTERS

DATABASES FOR NETWORKS AND MINICOMPUTERS

Dimitris N. Chorafas

PBI

a petrocelli book

new york   princeton

Designed by Diane L. Backes
Typesetting by Backes Graphics

Printed in the United States of America
1 2 3 4 5 6 7 8 9 10

Library of Congress Cataloging in Publication Data

Chorafas, Dimitris N.
  Databases for networks and minicomputers.

  "A Petrocelli book."
  Bibliography: p.
  Includes index.
  1. Data base management. 2. Computer networks. 3. Minicomputers.
I. Title.
QA76.9.D3C46   001.64   81-21140
ISBN 0-89433-136-1   AACR2

Table of Contents

Introduction

One of the leading subjects of the 1980s is database technology. The planning, organization, implementation and maintenance of distributed files and their integration into a comprehensive, company-wide database constitutes the pivotal point of information systems design for this decade. Only after the database has been properly integrated can we talk in a meaningful way about segmenting and distributing its contents at the user site—where the work is being done.

Whether within the context of a private system, or by having access to public utilities (such as Tymnet, Telenet, MCI, SBS, ACS, and Interactive Videotex), *distributed databases* (DDB) will increasingly be connected to networks; be accessible from a diversity of end user machines; communicate file-to-file; and be subjected to the requirements of office automation relating to subscriber equipment and to large database systems.

A functional and accessible database is one of the most critical elements of growth and survival in modern business. The advent of small computers has allowed the storage of valuable information in a distributed manner, thus broadening the possibilities for management decision making. Furthermore, while data was our main preoccupation in the past, office automation underlines text storage and retrieval—management information systems point out the need for both voice and image handling.

Properly accessed databases result in personnel cost reductions, higher productivity and, most importantly, control of communications cost. This is a different way of looking at databases than was utilized over the past ten years. It brings into perspective the steady update of knowhow, the impact of text and data entry, and the roles of the data dictionary and database administrator.

This book focuses on prerequisites: the necessary organizational steps to prepare the text and data assets of the firm for the coming online distributed environment. The audience is expert in data processing, data communications and databasing who are at the crossroads of critical choices—choices that will position their organizations for information systems challenges of the 1980s.

This is an action book. The advice in its pages has matured through years of practice. It has been critically evaluated by professional people through seminars which I have held since 1978 in Chicago and, more recently, special programs at the University of Florida and George Washington University. The basic message is the impact of the cutting edge of technology on databases and databasing at large.

We all know that technology is moving fast, but we do not always appreciate that organizational and procedural aspects often lag several years behind hardware developments and capabilities (as we will see in Chapter 1). There is a new breed of end user machines: intelligent terminals and mini- and microcomputers that contain text and data derived from database management systems. Such equipment is being linked together via an information network, and this calls for much more in terms of organizational perspectives than simply providing the datalink. To prepare for the distributed environment of this decade, users must develop valid procedural solutions for handling text, data and, eventually, voice. Processes are interrelated in many aspects. Technology has broken down the boundaries of formerly separated markets and equipment such as: copiers, word processors, computers (maxi, midi and mini), reprographics and so on. Former individual domains are now constituents of a new generation of computers/communications devices, and concepts are flowing freely from one solution to another.

This book points up to the reader that it is now time to standardize database concepts and their implementation. It offers one concrete approach based on experience: a solution which has been successfully implemented in industrial companies and financial institutions. The suggested database design bypasses short term goals, and helps the specialist plan for the longer term.

The proper choices start with the database architecture; the priorities to be set in database integration, segmentation, distribution and maintenance; and the adoption of the proper protocols. A database is not created in a vacuum, design considerations should pay attention to the starting point—text and data entry. If there is something we lack in our profession, it is the recognition of the high cost, design impact, and overall importance of this activity. As a topic, input is often glossed over by authors; even managers of data processing fail to appreciate the vital role a solid data entry system plays in their operations.

Yet, if data entry is one of the "musts," the modern enterprise should focus on several others. We should have a good data dictionary that applies to all corporate data. It makes sense to develop a single database design tool that serves the firm as a whole. We should establish the function of the database administrator; someone able to evaluate user needs and interpret them into database design approaches. We should adopt a classification and identification scheme able to name all entities reflected in the database uniquely and efficiently. (Three chapters have been devoted to the description of a system the author personally developed to this end.)

The benefits to be derived from a properly designed and implemented database are both operational and decision making in nature. Whether or not they realize it, managers at all levels have become increasingly dependent on computers for the information they need to plan, evaluate and control the activities of their organizations. As business expands and markets become more competitive, communications and databasing requirements intensify. New standards and guidelines promulgated by professional groups must be observed in the design of computer based information systems. Unless our data assets are properly planned, in a few years it will be impossible to exercise effective control over them.

The premises of this book start with the fundamentals: What is the difference between data processing, data communications, and databasing? What sort of lessons should we learn from this layered approach? What is the difference between mini- and mainframe databases? How can we plan a database? How can we project an architecture? Then, having outlined some of the problems presented in the study, design and implementation of databases, the book looks into the background issues of priorities, protocols, communicating processes and interactivity.

From a user perspective, setting the right premises at the planning stage is the only valid way of achieving simplicity and better service. We should not forget that, though we talk of microfiles, the dedication of equipment to one application and eventually to one user (even with dropping semiconductor prices) can have economic shortcomings. Memory usage often increases when the work is split. Complexity may do the same; and the answer is virtual memory.

Database distribution might also constrain the user to a limited set of data. Solutions are available through a data dictionary accessible to all users. Then comes the problem of coordination, synchronization, and optimal resource utilization. The cost many companies are willing to pay to satisfy such requirements is to install database administrators. We will hear increasingly more about these administrators in the future.

There are other requirements which need to be met. For example, identification and classification, pivotal points of database streamlining to meet increased demands for interactive access while maintaining response time and availability. Without these, decentralized databasing will show the disadvantages experienced in the pre-database period when uncoordinated requests and galloping error rates brought many systems toward disintegration. For data quality control, we need standards against which to measure the quality and content of the data. Such standards have a crying need for a modern, lean and effective identification methodology. Then comes the subject of database integration, segmentation and distribution.

Data are a corporate resource. Designers must focus on the access methods to be adopted to the database and the ability of several end users to cooperate. This implies rules to be observed right away within a distributed environment, while meeting immediate and long-range requirements. Part and parcel of this approach are organizational issues, managerial needs, economic considerations, data communications, systems security, the existence of different (often dispersive) locations, access authorization, journaling and the effective distribution of processes, information elements and applications.

These subjects are treated in the last four chapters of the book. The learned reader will notice that one key is missing: that of DBMS. The original intention was to include it under the same cover, however, space did not allow doing so. Hence, rather than cutting short the different issues, an alternative path was chosen: a second volume, covering operating systems for distributed database, database management systems, the hierarchical, network and relational models around which the DBMS have been designed, rearend engine, logic over data approaches, and the recent advances in memory support media on which is stored the database.

Let me close by expressing my thanks to everyone who contributed to making this a successful book. To my colleagues, for their advice; to the organizations I visited in my research, for their insight; and to Eva-Maria Binder for the many typings of the text, the drawings and the Index.

Valmer and Vitznau, January 1982

Prof. Dr. Ing. Dimitris N. Chorafas

1 Communicating, Processing, Warehousing

INTRODUCTION

We live in an age of specialization: each system component (like each man) should have a function to accomplish. This function should be properly defined, supported and interfaced to other system faculties. Specialization clearly calls for a separation of functions between the *transport* activity (text and data communications, image, voice); the *processing* capability (of text and data); and *storage* or *warehousing* (involving text, data, image and voice).

In the past, the attributes presented by the processing system were intermingled with others, like communications and access to databases. However, years of experience acquired by leading users since the early to mid-1960s, gives evidence that this is an unwanted practice, one which leads to considerable confusion, project delays and high costs.

Misunderstandings have resulted because these three functions, while separate by their own nature, are nevertheless complementary. Databasing capabilities are inseparable from the faculties the datacomm supports. Furthermore, this interaction sees to it that there is a trend to higher speeds, higher numbers of messages per transaction, more bits per message, and more bytes to be stored and retrieved from memory. It is most important to outline clearly the existence and the specific mission these partitions should fulfill, as they constitute the three fundamental layers of a networking system. This is a fairly new concept that points up the fact that many information systems experience difficulties because current efforts in data processing, databasing and communications tend to apply:

> 5th generation hardware, with
> 3rd generation software, and
> 1st generation images and system concepts.

The confusion which persists about the functions involving computers and communications has led to many failures. A rational approach would divide these functions into three distinct entities to be served by specialized engines. Each one of these engines is, in itself, a pillar in the evolving concept of using minicomputers within a distributed information environment. Each can serve *office automation, factory robotics* and *executive information services* equally well. These are expected to experience an unprecedented market thrust during the decade of the 1980s. To make a successful application, management must have a clear vision on orientation; systems potential; and the products and services needed to meet that potential. As always, a success story starts with some simple, basic facts.

THREE FUNDAMENTAL LAYERS

To help clarify this issue and to encourage meaningful discussion when policy and plans must be formed, let us define communications as constituting the transport of:

> voice
> data
> text
> image

Whatever is transported remains unaltered. To support communications requirements in an able manner, we need logical faculties such as: protocols; lines (physical or logical); store and forward software (S+F); low bit error rate (BER); error detection and correction capabilities (EDC); and acknowledgement (ACK) disciplines.

Other problems regard physical facilities such as: efficient lines (coaxial, optical fibers, satellites, radio links) and storage capacity (for S+F). Other issues are of an administrative nature such as directory assistance, statistics and billing capabilities.

We also need communications experts, and these are classically in short supply. First, communications specialists are not readily available in the market. Second, management does not always appreciate the need for data-comm skill. As Figure 1.1 suggests, a study done by SBS in the United States found that, while communications costs represent twenty-five percent of the data processing budget, the personnel assigned this task are minimal, however, a large staff works in the more settled data processing lines.

The classical processing gear concerns mainly:

> text,
> data.

However, new developments involve:

> image,
> voice.

The needed faculties for the coming years are logic; arithmetic; ability to change semantic content; controlled collection of supported issues; and presentation of output as a programmed response to input. Whatever is processed is (most likely) altered.

To process the data, we need to store and retrieve them. This calls for physical supports (like discs and tapes) and logical faculties (file access, DBMS, recognition memories). Today's concern is mainly about:

> data (databases).

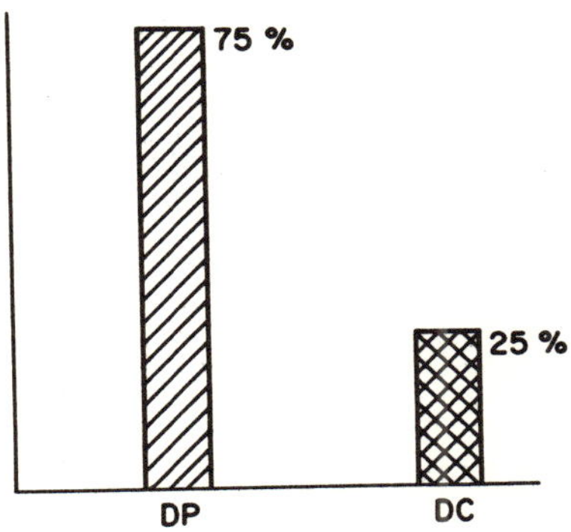

FIGURE 1.1

But in the coming years, our interest in "warehousing" will include:

    text
    image
    voice.

To do this work in a punctual and accurate way, we need: protocols; memory supports; recognition capabilities; and access mechanisms (for storage and retrieval). Whatever is warehoused remains unaltered. Thus, we can clearly draw the lines between communicating, processing and databasing. Each layer is assigned a specific mission.

It is most important to observe that each one of the three large layers described is itself divided into sublayers. The latter are functionally oriented and intended to answer a specific goal. In databasing DBMS (Database Management Systems) and file access are examples of layering within a given layer.

A communications example can be more explicit about sublayers than one on databasing, because in terms of a formal discipline, data communications have been around longer and have attracted more work in terms of formalization and standardization. Within the broader datacomm layer four functional layers are distinguishable: the data link, routing, virtual circuit (in X.25 discipline) and flow control.

Whether in databasing or datacomm, a layered approach holds implicit the notion of *Protocols.*[1] A protocol is a formal set of conventions governing the format and control of text and data. It comprises well-defined procedures clearly understood by all parties—whether human or machine. These fundamental principles are what any message system management needs to support operations. Let us recapitulate: *projecting and running successful information systems requires a clear distinction between the three fundamental layers* described: *data transport; data processing;* and *databasing. It also calls for the establishment and observance of protocols.*

ORGANIZATIONAL PREREQUISITES

The developing knowledge in the handling of information aggregates now treats the message as a file in the database. Therefore, files and messages must

---

[1]See also: (1) COMPUTER NETWORKS FOR DISTRIBUTED INFORMATION SYSTEMS and (2) DATA COMMUNICATIONS FOR DIS; same author, same publisher; 1980.

4

be designed interchangeably. Furthermore, text, data, and images must be classified three ways:

1. *Vital:* should be immediately updatable and available at all times.
2. *Necessary*: should be available to management and operations, but can be delayed without interrupting operations.
3. *Simple Useful*: if need be, we could skip them.

A major English bank, for example, sorted all text/data assets into categories of one hundred percent, seventy-five percent, and twenty-five percent classification. The twenty-five percent are "vital"; the following fifty percent are two levels of "necessary" information; the last twenty-five percent is simply useful. An American bank found after study that only five percent to ten percent of all documents handled have legal value; fifteen percent to twenty percent are needed for operations, the other seventy-five percent could be eliminated without much harm. Still another American bank established that only ten percent of all paper printed flows outside the bank, the rest is for internal consumption, and could be accessible online.

Such findings are behind the developing policy that, for immediate access purposes, computer resources should be brought as near to the end user as possible. The overall structure should be simple.

> Input should be captured at origin;
> Output presented at destination.

Electronic capture is the first evolutionary stage toward a dependable database structure. Because the dependability of a system can be no better than its weakest link, protection against human error should be provided.

The more computers are spread around, the greater the possibility of accidents due to human error. But machines also have failures. If something can go wrong, it will!

The time out of computers, databases, and communications systems should be classified as:

> *catastrophic,*
> *major* (problem),
> *minor* (inconvenience).

Backup facilities should be provided accordingly. To assure better overall availability, maintenance (for both hardware and software) should be done online. Remote diagnostics must have a dedicated database and lead to quality histories.

Drills should be conducted periodically so that management and employees know what to do in time out. Contingency planning and disaster recovery are basic responsibilities. Audit trails, journaling, statistics, security, authorization, and authentication are vital elements of any information system.

Furthermore, since nobody can afford building a totally new information system, particular care to:

> provide interfaces,
>
> assure the back-up files, and
>
> set the groundwork for expansion and transformation should be taken in all evolutionary projects.

Software costs are staggering. In the typical case the total AP library will stand at six hundred to seven hundred K statements. This represents quite a significant financial investment. As we will see in a subsequent section, we must also cope with software maintenance problems.

The importance of layering is underlined in these few words: the more layers we construct (whether in the basic software or in applications programming) the more limited the maintenance work needed since we will be working within the confines of a single layer.

But layered approaches also have limits due to the cost of the *interfaces*. The idea of an interface is valid in datacomm, data processing and databasing. It is a shared boundary of logical or physical components, implemented through software routines. Such routines handle the set of rules governing the relationship among dissimilar functions within two adjoining layers of an information processing system.

This is true both of the finer layers and of the more macroscopic ones. Yet, until now, most managements (and computer specialists) have paid relatively little attention to the importance of coordinating databasing with data communications in their plans for the development of the systems which concern them. The situation will change rapidly during the 1980s as companies accept the need to take account of these facts from many points of view. That is why, prior to looking at databases, we will briefly review developments in datacomm.

BACKGROUND IN DATA COMMUNICATIONS

No *new system* is invented from scratch or composed of only new components. Usually, we apply known facts and change one of the key ingredients: this may be the system concept, the way we proceed to integration, a vital engine in the system, or the physical principle used in building up that engine.

It is, therefore, not surprising that, when data communications became of age, what was known from telephony filtered through the new discipline: at the beginning, we made no distinction between the line and the end station—the same way the telephone set is usually taken as being the line's end.

Though every researcher of data communications has his own ideas on the origins the most likely beginning was 1940. In the course of a meeting of the American Mathematical Society, at Dartmouth College, Bell Labs presented an online link to a relay calculator. An operator sat down at the modified Teletype 26 keyboard, depressed a key, and opened the door to the computer communications age.

The first incidence of terminal-to-computer dialogue was duly noted, and then forgotten. Years later, in 1950, computers were still built of vacuum tubes (the transistor had been developed in 1948), and we only spoke of mainframes and batch processing. Operating systems were still some years away—so was the art of online terminals.

By 1960 we had some rudimentary forms of OS and multiprogramming, but no multiprocessing, multiple access, and time sharing. Yet, 1960 is significant for another reason. AT&T started operating the dataphone service. Digital transmission could be sent over the switched telephone network at speeds of six hundred BPS (bits per second); and its product introductions carefully explained the need for a modulator set at one end of the telephone line and of a demodulator at the other (modems).

Off to a slow start, data communications trailed computer systems in applications, leading them in basic discovery. By 1963, Dartmouth presented its time sharing system; a binary data link was announced; and we began to hear careful remarks about sending data over leased voice grade lines. Within the same timeframe, at the Rand Corporation, Paul Baran was given the assignment of conceiving a reliable, errorfree communications system that could survive heavy damage during war. His solution shifted attention from time-sharing to networking.

Baran's design called for an all-digital, computer controlled, nationwide network using packet switching. It was a logical development, and from that point on, some specialists began to think of computer communications in broader terms than what happens between a mainframe and its terminals. First a new concept, then a new industry was born.

What we have available today in computer communications services, can be highlighted under three main headings: The first is *media*.

1. *Microwaves:* becoming (and will probably remain so for some time) the preferred solution for medium to long distance communications, although not necessarily for local services due to bandwidth congestion problems.

2. *Satellites:* expanding in usage, in capacity and in sophistication—though there are several limitations to overcome: spectrum congestion, inherent delay, vulnerability.

3. *Fiber Optics:* the wave of the future; both local.usage and cross-country networks can profit—the former being the most likely.

Transmission of any nature over lines is based on observing rules of conduct called *protocols.* They can be simple or quite complex, depending on the facility supported. Each layer has its own formal rule, and the functional usage of this layer makes the protocol's observance mandatory. When we build a network, we must choose the *technical solution*:

1. *Packet Switching:* (Baran's approach) is favored, and will become increasingly welcomed particularly in applications where transmission costs are high; text, data, voice and image get integrated; and the work-flow justifies the money invested.

2. *Message Switching:* has gone through phases. An aged telegraph era technology revamped with telex (TWX) could see a revival of interest in office automation as terminating equipment becomes more intelligent.

3. *Circuit Switching:* is the way the telephone system works for voice grade lines. This, too, may see a revival as transmission facilities become better and cheaper, and the system converts to intelligent lines.

Regardless of the technical solution, no network can function without *supported services.* Three main issues come under this heading:

1. *Network Population:* number of nodes; line capacity; admissible term-inals. A significant growth is projected in the number of networks in response to user needs, with a trend towards design able to support both synchronous and asynchronous devices as well as digitized voice, facsi-mile, and text.

2. *Internetworking:* Different networks need to talk to each other. This has not always been easy because of diverse protocols, but developing inter-national standards will insure that internetworking becomes a reality. Another challenge is device incompatibility above the interface level.

3. *Network Control Centers:* will support increased levels of diagnostics, fault-isolation capabilities and quality histories. The trend toward decentralized control of switching and value-added functions will be complemented by centralized control of network management.

To better explain the reference made to *Value Added Functions*, let us first recall that (as with so many other developments) necessity has been the mother of invention. Tymnet was at odds with AT&T (for having sold line services) and someone suggested that if this offer presented an added value, there would be no problems. Today, value added services include any or all of the following subjects:

Protocol Conversion

Error Detection and Correction (EDC)

Message Storage and Forward (S+F)

Speed Conversion

Formatting

Communications Processing.

They are all characteristic of the transport function, applicable to data, text, image and voice—allowing devices to be both physically and logically intermingled over the same network.

NETWORKING

The traditional environment before integrated, horizontal, balanced, value added networks were built was composed of separate star type networks for each application. These were synchronous or asynchronous, rather cumbersome and overlapping: in addition, users somehow accepted the idea that a new network had to be configured for each DP job that posed data communications requirements.

What is more, the star-like, hierarchical structures of the 1960s and 1970s worked independently, yet carried jobs which often presented data exchange needs. Typically, with star type networks, there was no ability to interconnect the broad range of processors, databases, and terminals needed within a modern information system. To help in fulfilling this requirement, the *gateways* were invented.

All this presented a number of problems and challenges. Costs increased while less than optimal service was derived from such a fractional set-up. Each time new equipment was introduced, we were almost sure that it would only work with part of the system. New technologies integrated badly with the old; modifications and upgrades became more expensive as the star networks grew.

It is no surprise that horizontal, applications independent packet type networks evolved as the reasonable answer to the interconnecting problem. They featured a standardized architecture, and an effort was made toward the construction and implementation of networks open to future development:

1. *Applications independence* has been assured through the packet concept which carries information (data, text, image, eventually voice) without opening the envelope to look into its contents.

2. The *layered concept* permitted specialization and functionality. Each layer is dedicated to one facet of the overall service, and can be changed to benefit from technological advances without impacting the entire structure.

3. The *separation of functions* (which over long years were intermingled) led to the functionality of datacomm, data processing, and databasing. This permitted a better understanding of each one of the issues in terms of better implementation.

4. The design of *distributed databases* has been greatly assisted through networking, and this has, in turn, implied the support of data dictionaries able to automatically handle a directory assistance.

5. Another key design element has been *transparency*, enabling the network subsystem to transport any bit stream through nodes and links without modifications.

The separation of functions and the specialization which followed removed the communications control activity from the computer's operating system (OS), which was not designed to do that job in the first place. In turn, this relieved applications looking after flow control, access capabilities, and other functional issues all in one setting.

Availability, the measure of the ability of a system to accept and respond to requests through continuing service (uptime), has been increased. By separating the functions, the probability of a fault that causes the system to work in a degraded fashion was brought under control; we have been better able to follow the extent to which a system is degraded by such a fault; and the length of time for which the system remains degraded has been shortened.

Systems integrity has been improved: specialization supported in a significant way the ability of computers and communications systems to maintain this state accurately. Integrity is contingent on the probability of the occurrence of a fault that causes loss of state; and the cost of recovering the state lost due to such a fault. As with availability, some tradeoff between these factors has been possible.

In short, modern network approaches, by separating each function which enters into play and by structuring this function through normalization allow a more efficient sharing of better maintained resources. Equipment can be used for multiple functions to a greater extent. The human factor can specialize, and the proper setting is established for a forward thrust to greater levels of sophistication, as technology and ingenuity expand.

Specialization, horizontal solutions, and the layered approach open significant capabilities to future developments when new layers are needed:

> to provide network-wide directions for database elements and applications programs,

to process network files, and

to assure reliable database management in a distributed sense,

they can be added through proper interfaces. The entire process of making changes in the network system structure is eased. This is just as true with hardware (adding or deleting nodes, lines, data terminating equipment) as with software (from routing functions to database management). The same is true about the need to provide the user with transparency regarding the fine mechanics of the network and assuring him that he can operate in a reasonably friendly environment.

FULFILLING DATABASING REQUIREMENTS

Within a competitive industrial environment, online communications can offer a significant advantage, but the transport mechanism delivers information from origin to destination. It does not alter the content. Arithmetic and logical operations will be executed by the applications programs (the processes) and here we face a different challenge.

Over nearly a fifteen-year period, from the late 1950s to the early 1970s, we rewrote applications software every time we changed machines. We don't do that any more; programming libraries have grown tremendously to represent one million statements or more for the medium to larger firm. Rewriting applications would tie down available system analysts and programmers for years. Even maintaining them employs eighty percent of the available programming manpower in the typical firm.

Because of skyrocketing software development costs, finding and buying packages is becoming increasingly profitable. But the use of packages also demands a certain discipline: the streamlining of procedures (both at headquarters and in the periphery) and also the standardization of software. This means that equipment should be standardized, all programs fully documented, program development and maintenance centralized. The software should be strongly built and designed for a long life cycle. All information system projects should abide by:

timetables,

budgets, and

quality standards.

If new projects are done, the computer should assist in analysis, programming and testing. The systems personnel should be uniformly and continuously trained because, otherwise, the professional approach is lost. Efficient applications of computers, databases, and datacomm rest on able brainpower—this includes the system architects, analysts, designers, system and application programmers and the end users.

Successful computers and communications systems imply coinvolvement: by top management in setting objectives and fathering the project and by the end user in actively participating in all the phases of analysis and babysitting. Good business sense is imperative. The existing programs are aging: many are poorly documented and, when they were projected, they had been written for batch, not online operations.

The evolution in concepts over a twenty-year period is shown in Figure 1.2. Usually, the aging programs do not support a database management and, the databases themselves have not been organized collections of data. As our experience accumulates, we appreciate the need to rethink the whole database facility:

1. structure the information elements (I.E.) included in the database

2. integrate, segment, and distribute the data resources included in the **DB**

3. provide for a data dictionary and, with it, for directory, data definition and link services to the applications programs

4. control the text and database through a **DBMS** (database management system)

5. avoid unwanted duplication

6. integrate communicating, processing and databasing into a coherent, comprehensive information system

The database must be available to all applications programs and no procedure should have its own database. To obtain integration of the text and database we must: identify all IE; make them homogeneous; assure authorized access to these elements; and, for safeguarding purposes, declare data a corporate asset. Employers, managers, even programs attempting to access unauthorized data should be subject to corrective action (some company regulations imply dismissal for personnel).

While we think and talk of major system changes, we must also safeguard the current supply of data. Within an organization, information should flow without interruption. As a medium size automobile manufacturer calculated: with line production facilities, a sixty-day "blackout" leads to fifteen percent loss of billed sales—while with job-shop type operations, the fifteen percent loss corresponds to a forty-day blackout. (Job-shops have to carry much larger inventories than line production set-ups.) Is our programming library measuring up to the situation? Time and again, management asks this critical question of specialists—and in the majority of cases the answer is *no*! Aging programs do not support the most modern requirements. What is the solution? Figure 1.3 gives an answer. Granted, no firm has the manpower needed to fully rewrite its library. Granted also that computer costs per operation and bit of storage

	CENTRAL	PERIPHERAL AT WORKSTATION
1965	ALL BATCH	————
1970	MOSTLY BATCH: BUT WITH RB AND RT DATA ENTRY AND INTEROGATION	PRIVATE LINES; POINT-TO-POINT; NON-INTELLIGENT TERMINALS, IN 2-DIGIT NUMBERS
1975	MAINLY BATCH: WITH RB + DE/INTEROGATION AND MINI LOCALLY INSTALLED	PRIVATE LINES BUT MULTIDROP BEGINNING OF INTELLIGENT TER-MINALS IN 3-DIGIT NUMBERS + MINI (DIS)
1980	B+RB + DE/I; LINKED BY PACKET SWITCHING NETWORK (E.G. CITIBANK)	PRIVATE LINES, BE-GINNING OF PUBLIC UTILITY (TELENET, TRANSPAC), INTELLIGENT TERMINALS IN 4-DIGIT NUMBERS, MINI
1985	POLLING THROUGH RB AND REMOTE DIAGNOSTICS AND SAVE (IMAGE) BY NETWORK	PUBLIC LINES (INFORM-ATION UTILITY) WITH CUG AND ACCESS BY PRIVATE AND PUBLIC USERS (INCLUDING HIS)

FIGURE 1.2

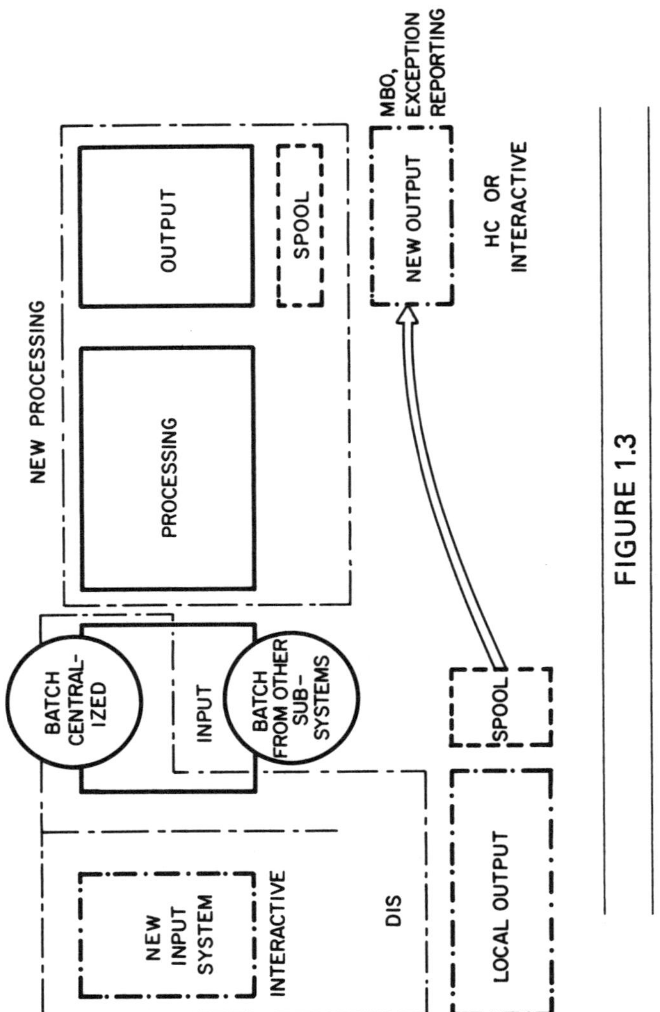
NEW PROCESSING
PROCESSING
OUTPUT
SPOOL
MBO,
EXCEPTION
REPORTING
NEW OUTPUT
HC OR
INTERACTIVE
BATCH
CENTRAL-
IZED
INPUT
BATCH
FROM OTHER
SUB-
SYSTEMS
SPOOL
NEW
INPUT
SYSTEM
INTERACTIVE
DIS
LOCAL OUTPUT
FIGURE 1.3

drop rather sharply as a matter of time and technology. Let's leave the processing aspects as they stand (or buy packages) and revamp the input/output components and the access to the database.

Processing will not change: neither will the output procedure—except that rather than printing tons of paper we should leave the data on spool. Then, a new output routine will screen this data and produce an interactive type of exception reporting based on management by objectives requirements. This is the sense of the Viewdata (Interactive Videotex) approach.

At the input side, the programs may stand as they are now except that an interactive new input system should be superimposed on the part presently belonging to centralized batch. The new input system should be established at the periphery, where text and data originate. If supported by intelligent devices it can serve the sales offices, factories, branch offices and other sites with a local output—and in case this operation is more complete than the old centralized information product, nothing inhibits its merge into the central new output. Let us not forget that data input requirements currently consume thirty percent of the DP/DE/DB budget. Ideally, output should be framed into pages and multipages. Transmitted through a datacomm mechanism, it should be stored on a mini- or microcomputer easily accessible by the user's workstation and involve a user-friendly protocol.

The suggested solution depends on program structure and robustness; the cost and benefit such interactive message systems offer; response times; the kind of terminals (the simplest the best); the memory requirements to be supported; and other factors. Still, great care should be exercised to assure that it becomes a *documented success.* Speaking from experience, I advise it as a good way to develop a networking system, without having to redo everything.

2 The Database

INTRODUCTION

Computer operations: their sophistication and complexity—have greatly evolved since the 1950s. This cannot necessarily be said of the way the data processing job is approached, and of the tools available to do that job. A precise example is the study, implementation and maintenance of the database (DB).

The right introduction to the concept of a database is much more important than that addressed towards other subjects connected with information systems, because everybody has his own idea about what is (or is not) a DB and thinks that his idea is not only the best but also the only valid one.

A modern, well organized, computer supported database is an aggregate of information elements (IE). This aggregate must be managed in a uniform way; projected and defined in a coherent and comprehensive manner; available for diverse applications; accessible to the users through data communications (DC, datacomm) media; and able to support housekeeping services such as recovery, security and the like.

The *information element* (data set) is the building block of the database. It is any object which we store, retrieve and generally address following a data handling request. Bits; bytes; fields; records; files; real or conceptual sections of the database (subschemas); schemas and eventually the database itself fit under this broad definition.

An information element can be a page or a string of pages (scrolls), in general, it is any format supported by real or virtual storage capabilities. The reference to an IE is totally independent of its content (and, eventually, of its location). It is dependent on the storage and retrieval (calling) faculty; and on the need to identify this information element for reasons relating to processing and visualization. Another recently advanced term is *encapsulated* information element. An element whose internal structure is accessible only to the machine. Some examples of encapsulated information elements are:

> pages (with virtual storage),
>
> scrolls (logical grouping of pages addressed as an entity), and
>
> objects (as used with IBM's System 38, which advanced the term *encapsulated* in the first place).

Thus, the handling of information elements can be both user visible, and user transparent (following system specifications). For user transparent solutions the machine needs a lot of software support. Such requirements, and the organizational prerequisites behind them at the user's site, lead us to the concept of database management (DBM).

Database management merges the user's need for system support (and for more sophisticated data manipulation techniques) with the technological capabilities of computers available to do our job. The identification of the distinct entities we called IE, and their management, respond to the requirement of handling all functions associated with retrieving, sorting, updating, and filing data that belong to a given data structure. This is an integral part of the application. The handling of data structures runs concurrently with the application on the same computer resource, contending with the processes (application programs, AP) for memory space, CPU time, and peripheral availability.

WHAT IS MEANT BY "DATABASE"?

A database is an organized, orderly collection of information elements designed (in an application-independent manner) to serve DP purposes. (An information element is the building block of the database.) Thus, the database includes all files, and constitutes a storehouse of information for all corporate data, for any purpose whatsoever (Figure 2.1):

>   settlements,
>
>   allocation/optimization, and
>
>   top management decision.

Orderly databases consist of elements stored in an organized, planned fashion. The correct structuring of these information elements is critical for both storage and retrieval purposes.

Furthermore, given the computer capacity available today for storage and processing purposes, data should be stored in original (crude) form and they should be free of errors prior to storage. Data will be manipulated as the need arises, by using the power of the computer.

The proper structure of a database presupposes considerable preparatory work. It requires an image of what is to be done; precise goals in terms of database integration; pruning of all unwanted redundancies and elimination of differences and contradictions at the IE level. The organizational effort comes after this preparatory work.

The following is an example of database reorganization from an oil company study. It involves two major phases: a logical database integration; and a physical organization of the mainlines.

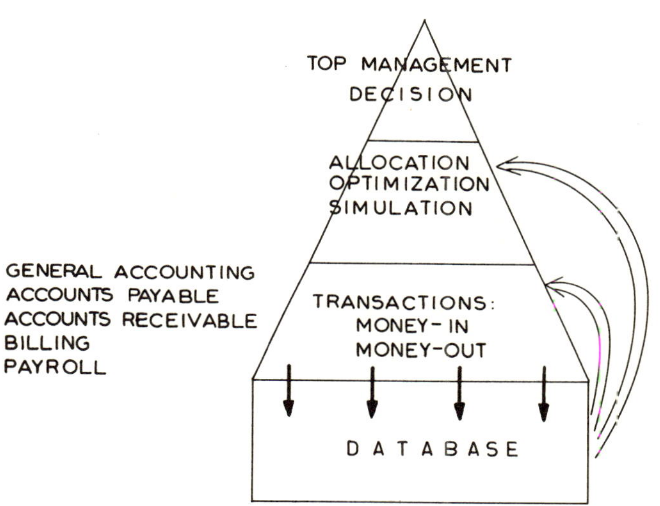

ALL DATA SHOULD BE STORED IN ORIGINAL (CRUDE) FORM.
THEY SHOULD BE MANIPULATED AS THE NEED ARISES, EVERY TIME THIS IS NECESSARY, BY USING THE POWER OF THE COMPUTER.

FIGURE 2.1

1. *Integrate the DB*

   A. Study content.

   B. Present a concise, understandable representation of the state of the art of the system.

   C. Develop an integration concept:

      * Study AP
      * Examine data structure
      * Streamline IE organization.

   D. Divide the DB into homogeneous groups (mainlines) regarding operation.

   E. Provide efficient access to information.

   F. Assure simple and consistent update procedures.

All matters regarding understandability, efficiency, and consistency must be studied and resolved. The proper programmatic interfaces must be established between the IE and the processes (application programs) they serve.

This is a different way of stating an organizational prerequisite: that of observing the evolving requirement for separating processing from I/O (and data communications) and DB handling procedures. A three-layered approach is presented in Figure 2.2. Portability, robustness and quality control (QC) should characterize each of the layers.

The next phase comes after this work has been completed, reviewed and thoroughly tested. This phase establishes organizational mainlines. These are expressed in terms of broad programmatic interfaces and impact on the integration of the database regarding the subsequent applications.

Again with reference to the oil company operations we examined in the preceding paragraphs, the following list outlines the methods used to organize the program inventory with a corresponding impact on the information elements.

1. *Organize mainlines*

   A. Production

      *Geological studies
      *Cost of research (dry holes, results)
      *Management of production
      *Imports

   B. Manufacturing

      *Budgets
      *Cost control

OLD APPROACH:
ONE PROGRAM
INCLUDING: PROCESSING PROPER
FILE ACCESS
I/O OPERATIONS
NEW APPROACH: LAYERED
I/O ORIENTED
PROCESSING PROPER
DB ACCESS
INTERFACES
PORTABILITY, ROBUSTNESS, Q C
IF ONE OF 3 MAIN PARTS CHANGES
(PARTICULARLY DB, I/O) THE OTHERS
WILL NOT BE AFFECTED.

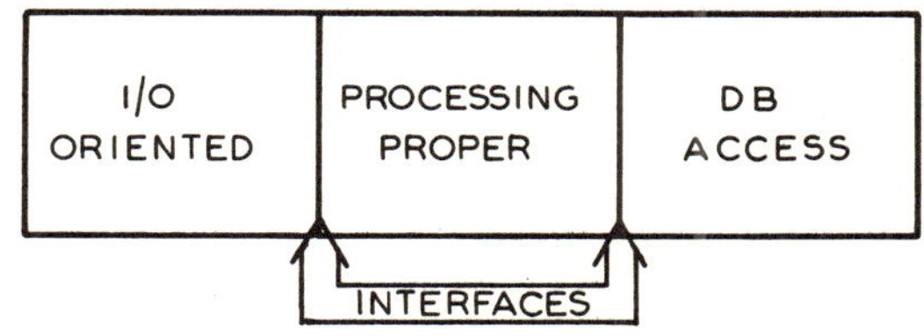

FIGURE 2.2

    *Delivery
    *Refining operations
    *Capital investment (new refineries, major work)
    *Maintenance
    *Personnel
    *General accounting
    *Inventories (machinery, SP, materials)
    *Inventories for ready goods and semi-manufacturing
    *Cash management

C. Sales/marketing

    *Customer file
    *Inventory file
    *Cost control
    *Sales statistics, sales orders, deliveries
    *Sales planning

D. Management information systems

    *Sales forecasts and plans
    *Capital budget
    *Sales statistics
    *Inventories
    *Cost control

To be implemented, such fundamental studies call for management decisions. Since this approach represents a major deviation from past practices, management decisions can fall in a vacuum without proper support by the specialists who will execute them. The support by the specialists has two prerequisites: training and conviction; the latter by means of practical examples.

USING DATABASES

Databases are accessed all the time for queries, upkeep, and data processing applications. Redundant and inconsistent information severely dilutes a system's capacity to deal with large amounts of data. The consolidation of information elements into a database should eliminate most data redundancy. Their integration should be flexible, contrary to conventional file structures which tend to be rigid and inflexible.

The nature of conventional file management systems requires that the logic of application programs be intricately interwoven with file design. But, as stated in the preceding section, this is an erroneous procedure. DB access must be divided from main processing and, main processing must be divided from I/O (and communications) handling. Design perspectives must be rethought, revamped and restructured. New approaches are necessary, and this is true whether we:

> use a physically centralized DB organization,
>
> centralize the central information file and distribute the applications-oriented DB segments (Figures 2.3), or
>
> distribute all data resources in a physical sense, supported by an equal number of minicomputers.

Whether a database system is centralized, partly distributed or fully distributed, a fundamental requirement is easy, well directed, reliable, but also protected access. Within a data processing environment, access to a DB is a steady job.

In the past, DB have *not* been organized collections of data. Therefore, we need to rethink the whole DB facility:

> structure the IE,
>
> avoid unwanted duplication, and
>
> integrate the IE into a coherent, comprehensive database.

This DB must be available to all AP—no program (process) should have its own database.

The issue of handling databases becomes complex as the database subject itself is in full evolution. Databases originally involved diffused data: a multiplicity of overlapping files which constituted discreet islands and rarely communicated with one another. The first basic effort has been to structure these databases into a coherent entity. Later came the need to partition, segment and then distribute them—with the prerequisite of a logical but thorough integration in the background.

As we will see in the appropriate chapter, to obtain integration of the DB we must:

> identify all IE,
>
> make them homogeneous, and
>
> assure authorized access to these elements.

For security and proprietary purposes, data must be declared a corporate asset. Employees, managers, even programs attempting to access unauthorized data should be subject to corrective action (some company regulations imply dismissal).

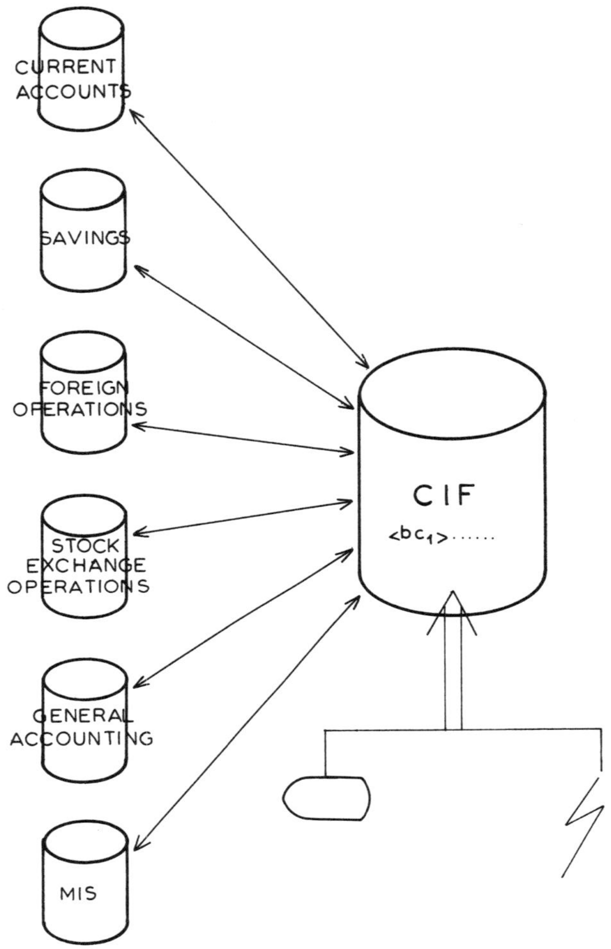

FIGURE 2.3

A corporate information structure must be built. Figure 2.4 identifies such a structure established by a leading financial institute. It outlines two distinct levels:

    detail, and

    consolidation.

Though both rest on the same database elements, each has its own prerequisites. Properly designed algorithms, for each of these levels address themselves to the same IE in the DB. Because accesses can happen in an overlapping, simultaneous, even conflicting manner, there is a need for procedures that are able to resolve deadlocks and handle problems relative to upkeeping and synchronization.

The user (man or program) is accessing a DB in order to obtain the information elements necessary for data processing. Hence, there is an advantage in

> bringing the most frequently needed IE close to the user (through a database (DB)),

> while keeping at a central or regional *data warehouse* (DW) those information elements which are rarely necessary.

The reason for distributing the database structure and content is a practical one. Data access increases exponentially with the number of online users, and we have reached the point where one machine, no matter how large it may be, cannot handle all data. Hence, a distributed DB becomes mandatory, and this brings with it a lot of requirements.

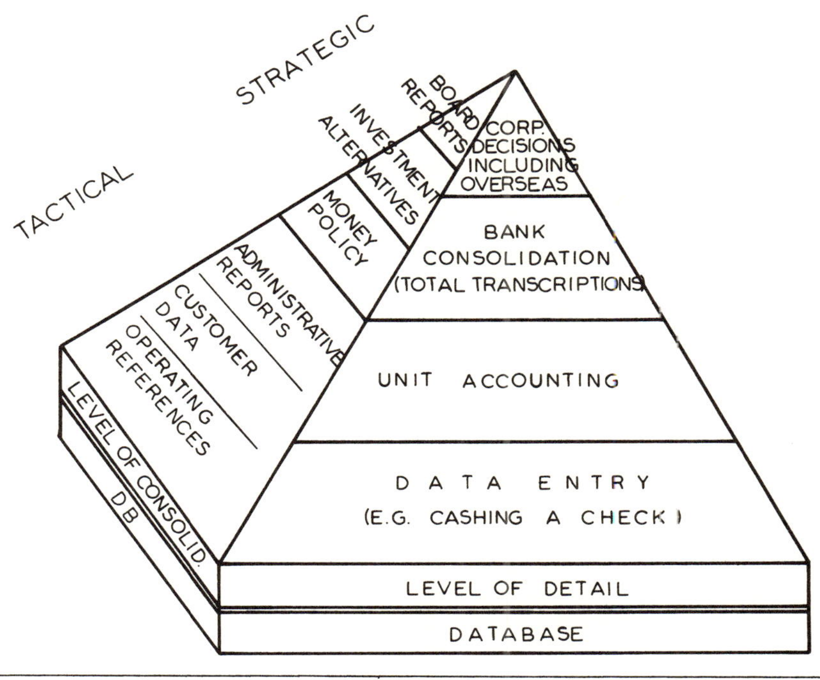

FIGURE 2.4

A DB DISTRIBUTION

When we talk of DDB we explicitly imply that we have a database to start with—that is: *one single logical level.* There is a great difference (albeit, not often appreciated) between:

> a database distribution, and
>
> the distribution of conventional files.

Distributed files are different physical and logical entities. A distributed database is an integrated logical structure. This calls for design prerequisites and also involves communications disciplines, diagnostics and housekeeping.

"Mirror transactions" are an example of the latter reference, born by the system to reflect a transaction happening at one host into others with the same DB/IE. Diagnostics, both remote and local; error logging and analysis on data transfers; read/write and so on, are but a few examples of the supporting understructure, which will also need to encompass:

> *line processing* (actual line supervision; interrupt status; process-ing queues).
>
> *interfaces to AP* (which also involve network messages).
>
> *communications protocols* (they really belong to data communica-tions but may also effect DB organization and structure).

It is no accident that ANSI, ECMA, ISO and CCITT occupy themselves with setting standards which affect both networking, and file transfer proto-cols. Though these standards do not yet tackle DB access, they are neverthe-less DDB oriented, and address themselves at higher levels than X.25.[1]

ANSI/SPARC set the session and presentation control standards which are still at the proposal level; no definite specifications have been published as of this time, but ECMA has a protocol proposal—backed by France and England—which applies at the byte level and settles the interpretation of the headers. More importantly, a standard on session and presentation control has been set by the International Standards Organization (ISO); it is the Open System In-terconnection (OSI).

Why is this activity so recent? Is the subject of the database a late 20th Century discovery? The answer is, of course, "no!" The first complex data-base was most likely that of the Library of Alexandria. The access to data has always required meticulous attention, and data are inherently difficult to

---

[1]See also "Data Communications for Distributed Information Systems", 1980; same author, same publisher.

access in cases where disorganization and masses of paper hide valuable information from view and easy reach.

A database has prerequisites. And these are the methodological and orderly procedures which permit an easy, cost/effective access to files. While access to files with discreet units, such as books, has problems and prerequisites—these manifoldly expand when we talk of:

> unified,
>
> computer-supported, and
>
> online accessible

information elements which can master trillions of bytes, then increase that number by another order of magnitude by pushing retrieval down to the bit level.

Database requirements today are indistinguishable from data communications perspectives. *A message is a file in the database. Each file in the DB can be a potential message.*

The prerequisites to any database/datacomm development (Figure 2.5) are:

> clear objectives
>
> sound organization, and
>
> a robust structure.

These have to be set against an environment which supports interactive approaches (man-machine); communicating with other processes and with IE stored in databases (job networking); as well as databases transmitting to other databases.

This system will necessarily involve the services of a data dictionary (for directory and data description assistance); of application libraries; query languages; and record and application generators.

Application generators impact on the choice of the communicating databases, and on the solutions to be given. They allow the description of an application through a system which maps the:

> parameters,
>
> functions

and allows us to spend little time in coding, instead of concentrating on generating the maps. These are basically interactive elements and may influence the DB structure and the specific solutions which will be adopted, particularly when choices have to be made among alternatives.

Design-wise, a critical decision concerns the policy to be followed regarding *synchronous* and *asynchronous* communications. A synchronous communication between processes and IE implies realtime access among processes

OBJECTIVES, ORGANIZATION AND STRUCTURE
DATA DICTIONARY
INTERACTIVE APPROACHES
DC
DB
JOB NETWORKING
COMMUNICATING DATABASES
ENVIRONMENT
DIRECTORY AND DATA DESCRIPTION ELEMENTS
SUPPORTING SOFTWARE
APPLICATIONS GENERATORS
APPLICATIONS LIBRARIES
RECORD GENERATORS
QUERY LANGUAGES
SOFTWARE PACKAGES AND FIRMWARE

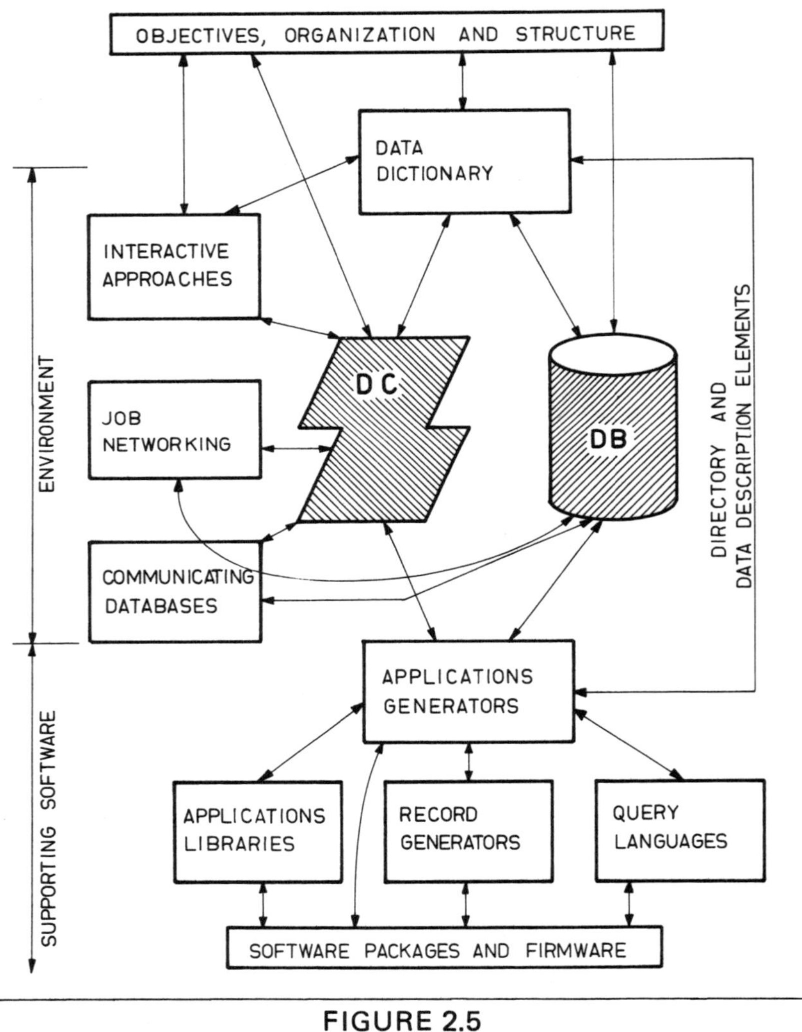

FIGURE 2.5

and by the processes on to the information elements. An asynchronous communication is characterized by deferred access.

In principle, synchronous communications must be those which, if not in realtime (RT), cannot be made effectively with current technology. For instance, updating requirements. If information handling is of the read-only type, then it can be done asynchronously. Among the questions to be asked are: is synchronism really needed? (Often the user thinks he needs synchronous handling; but this is not always true.) What is the cost? What is the technological complexity? How can we optimize the system under current operating conditions?

Concurrent access to the DB is, then, a basis of evaluation and in this process we must remember that there are performance problems to be faced. As in all walks of life (and of technology), if things are clustered skillfully, it makes a magnitude of difference in performance.

DATA SECURITY PROVISIONS

As databases get increasingly distributed; a micro- or minicomputer based at the work place; pulled and concentrated through mainframe supported power; transported over communications wires; accessed by hundreds and thousands of terminals; the problems associated with the security, protection and access authorization become immense and manifold.

The first step to protect a DB is its clear definition and identification. This calls for a hierarchical structure of command, even if the ultimate result is to distribute the IE among various means of support. The following identifies the mission and responsibility to be kept hierarchical or distributed:

1. *Hierarchical*

    A. Data and IE definition

    B. Logical structure

    C. Organization and management

    D. Security provisions

    E. Production and maintenance of software

    F. Decision on hardware to be used.

2. *Distributed*

    A. The physical resource

    B. The IE to be stored on the physical resource

    C. Implementation of the security provisions.

Once again we direct the reader's attention to the need for intensive preparatory work—and for new concepts. Conventional file management systems contain extremely limited data security provisions. Yet, access to computer readable data may be denied to individuals with system access only by providing physical and logical protection for the media on which the file is stored.

Apart from pruning the files, organizing and integrating them into a comprehensive pool of sensitive information elements; design problems connected to databases share the search for ways and means to: manage the requirement of accessing data by one machine out of the jurisdiction of the other machine handling this data. (Interestingly enough, ninety percent of all updates are not of a concurrent (multi-site) nature. But for the ten percent that are we must provide efficient mechanisms; and we can afford to do it.)

The work to be done can be divided into seven phases:

> defining the DB and its content (global information requirements)
> partitioning it into working segments
> distributing it where the job is to be done
> connecting the partitions through a data communications network
> accessing it
> updating it
> protecting it

We can capitalize on standardization by *rethinking* the whole process and reorganizing our approaches. Database utilization, efficiency and sizing are items that must be given the same consideration that was applied when the original system was designed.

The impact the new function may have on existing functions must also be considered. Does this new function duplicate any part of existing coding? If so, is the duplication required? Does the new function overlap or eliminate the need for coding elsewhere in the system, or does the similar coding serve another function for entirely different reasons? Does the new function use existing IE or only new ones? Are the new and the old approaches compatible?

To simplify, we should strive to separate DB access (including storage update and retrieval) from processing. Then, we should define the function of the DDB system; the geographic distribution of the data; the philosophy to be followed in the design; and the data security prerequisites. All these factors influence the organization of the distributed DB system and the communications requirements.

As we will see in the chapters dedicated to distributed databases, DDB organizations can be classified in different ways:

> One classification is according to the geographical distribution of databases, directories and security provisions.
>
> Another classification is by the amount of redundancy—the database is either partitioned or replicated.

Either of these may be centralized or distributed under this scheme.

A partitioned database is spread across several computers, perhaps with one large central portion and several remote subsidiaries. When a large, active file is divided among different processors in a distributed system, data accessibility increases at the cost of more control and communications overhead than is seen in a single data file in one computer.

Efficient network software minimizes this overhead, but poses other types of requirements. There is no free lunch with computers. To help the reader with some criteria in balancing complexity with nearby access, serviceability and efficiency, Table 2.1 presents a classification of DB management requirements.

We will return to these ideas, but first let us examine the difference in projecting, implementing and maintaining databases, when we talk of mainframes, mini- and microcomputers.

TABLE 2-1

Classification of Database Management Requirements
(In terms of increasing complexity)

---

1. Single general-purpose computer/small DB (least complexity).

2. Single special-purpose database computer (rearend).

3. One special-purpose DB computer combined with one or more general-purpose computers.

4. Two or more special-purpose computers (rearend) combined with one or more general-purpose processors. Single data structure.

5. Databases run within a homogeneous network (identical computers); one type of software and data structure.

6. Single software system, heterogeneous network (nonidentical computers).

7. Multiple software; heterogeneous network (hosts, minis, intelligent terminals) nonidentical in terms of logical and physical characteristics (greatest complexity).

---

3 Mini and Mainframe Databases

INTRODUCTION

Developments in databases and the evolution of the software support which is needed to run them, do not take place in the abstract. They reflect some goals: whether consciously set-up, or promoted step by step by developing needs and through daily practice. Yet, in a time of fast moving technology, clear policies are necessary to:

> reduce the high cost of AP developments,
>
> provide a common interface to the information elements, the files and the DB itself,
>
> assure new and interactive user facilities,
>
> and guarantee a user friendly communications capability.

Databases can be implemented on mainframes or minicomputers; they can be run through general purpose or dedicated machines. The maxi vs. mini contrast in DB handling is not only a difference in equipment and capabilities. It is also a difference in the organization of files and the implementation of support systems; a reflection of past influences.

Mainframes, for example, often work with sequential files because, from the beginning, tape-based record handling was sequential. To a considerable extent this structure has survived until today even though there are superimposed index sequential, random, and other organizations. With micros and minis we have the opportunity to apply homogeneity and rationality in file design.

Homogeneity and rationality are basic requirements for new projects whether we talk of maxi or mini supported databases. Data security and dependability are prerequisites in an implementation, no matter which is the moving gear; this is also valid when considering the interfaces provided the end user.

MICROFILES

The reason for distributing a database is to bring the IE close to the end user. Carried to the level of the personal computer (microcomputer), this will mean that rationalization in the DB design should consider the distribution of the information elements end-to-end. These personalized DB structures are called *microfiles*. However, it is not reasonable to assume that they will be of "micro" dimensions. Just as the microprocessor today incorporates the capacity of a 370/135—a good size system in the early 70s—microfiles will become of respectable dimensions.

During the last five years (and even more so in the decade of the 1980s) immediate access storage and logic costs formed a negligible proportion of total system cost. Such trends enabled computer manufacturers to primarily provide packaged system designs and maintenance services paid for by the price of the hardware; now even this is changing.

Furthermore, the evolution of new storage media will bring memories able to store and retrieve up to 500 million bytes, at costs which are within the reach of each user. Design and organization are the changes in the implementation of maintenance of microfiles.

Design, organization and easy maintenance are necessary to assure that some of the experiences with minicomputer supported files will not be repeated in the microcomputer era. Indeed, many users who came into computing through minis found that they needed much more extensive file storage if they were to exploit computing satisfactorily in the course of their businesses.

One solution is to provide excellent communications between small systems and mainframes. But there are many difficulties to be overcome before this can be brought about. These difficulties spring from the need to enable each end user to move smoothly towards a method of working which will be best for him in the context of communications and computing technology.

Design and organization objectives should detail both the current and coming policies of access to files—including the implementation of microfiles; dividing the latter into logical and physical structures.

Procedural studies should recall that microfiles will provide storage for desktop machines and for pocket computers—whose forerunners are the pocket translators. At the beginning they will be the equivalent of a floppy disc in solid state, holding up to one million bytes of information. The most likely implementation is bubble memory. But, eventually, microfiles will constitute fairly large memory devices, including video tapes and optical discs among the physical media used to support them.

Let us repeat what we have said on this issue. Just as the microcomputers currently provide a power equivalent to the mainframes of the late 1960s and the early 1970s, by the middle to late 1980s microfiles will constitute storage elements of respectable size and will require significant logical support for their organization and implementation.

The evolution of this new approach to personal archives will add to the challenges of the databases and databasing. Users will have to come to grips with the problem of determining which functions should be decentralized and which should remain centralized.

With microfiles at the disposition of anyone: including the smallest office or the single person, many functions that have traditionally been centralized should be decentralized and applications development will be done more closely to the user. This will underline the need for close coordination between:

> procedural work,
>
> databasing,
>
> datacomm,
>
> interactive approaches, and
>
> user and specialist documentation.

These references will call for careful preparatory work. Efficiency in a DB environment will never come as a matter of course. It must be embedded at the drafting board, with the basic service features being given full perspective.

BASIC PREREQUISITES

At the same time that central processors are benefitting from the silicon technology developed as a result of the struggle to reach the moon, the storage media have reached an unprecedented development in capabilities. But the needed understructure in methodology has not followed at the pace of the physical developments.

Larger organizations which have been making extensive use of small processors from a variety of sources are now beginning to appreciate this requirement. They have to create their own system design and allocate systems support, and they invariably reach the conclusion that things will be better and happier if standards are available and enforced.

The establishment of standard procedures and standard tools calls for detailed knowledge of the user's needs coupled with the ability to design ranges of compatible modules, together with building interfaces enabling these to be linked to other modules. The following new functions are necessary since the design stage of a DB:

1. Administrative aids, such as the data dictionary (DD), and the conceptual schema capabilities.

It makes no difference if the supporting gear is a mini or a maxi. These services are vital and have to be provided within an environment of multiaccess, and multiprogramming whether at one side or through a network.

2. The logical restructuring of the IE for online usage.

This is a highly demanding task involving the logical, online restructuring of the DB even if this means running the system for some time on a degraded mode. Just as demanding is:

3. The provision for management reporting and graphics aids to become primitives of a DBMS.

As the user works interactively with the system, particularly the mini- and microcomputer, it becomes quite important to incorporate paging, menu selection, and graphics commands into the primitives. This can help both in efficiency and in ease of use.

4. The making of a new, more efficient and secure methodology for

* Recovery,
* Backup,
* Communications, and
* DB access.

Distributed databases (DDB) and DB communications are a very difficult undertaking with current technology, and it takes a great amount of discipline to achieve success.

Here the mini vs. mainframe contrast can be exemplified at both the logical and the physical levels of reference. The maxicomputer hardware must assist the process of:

1. Segmentation for shared procedures
2. Segmentation for security reasons
3. Associative memory usage for:

* address transforming
* data value searches

4. Larger (mass) memory capability for first level page buffering
5. Virtual storage (paging) hardware features

The mini will be largely installed at the end user facility. Given its more limited power and special objectives at the place where transactions are being handled, the mini should be largely oriented in handling the: data dictionary (or, at least, the local directory); dialogue procedures; needed DB control system; a generalized report writer; and also the dialogue processing transparent to the user.

It cannot be too often repeated that the object of DB design at the free-standing mini level is the ease of use (on behalf of the man communicating with the information stored in the DB); the handling of nonprocedural approaches; and other user friendly characteristics such as exemplified by the absence of a complex data manipulation language (DML) capability.

The mini and micro interfaces should be tailor-made to the human user. The basic questions to be asked in projecting them are: who is sitting at the interactive terminal? how often? for what purpose? Nine times out of ten, the answers will indicate the need for a transparent structure of file organization.

ROLE OF THE MAINFRAME

As with the transition from maxicomputers to minicomputers in the 1970's, many people may interpret this approach as leading to a reduction in the role of the mainframe, which remained for many years a remote, inflexible, bureaucratic tool in the conventions it imposed on the users. But with distributed databases and simultaneous update requirements, we now appreciate the role mainframes may play in keeping the information system as one well-knit logical entity.

Maxis will support mass memory. This is no job for the minis. Their primary objective, in a given company, is to allow users to express themselves through computer-assisted facilities. To do so, they must guarantee easy, protected access and realtime data availability.

Many differences in DB implementation on micro, mini and mainframes result from the basic issues we have outlined:

1. A micro will not support a database management system (DBMS). Data organization must be simple.

2. A mini will support a DBMS but the system specialist will wisely choose one and only one data structure.

3. A maxi—because of poor past practice rather than rational choice and design—will most likely support not just one but a variety of DB organizational solutions.

Sequential, index sequential and networking (or hierarchical) systems have often been found working at the same time at the same mainframe.

Mainframes can afford to spend an inordinate amount of their computer power in running diverse and incompatible DB systems. Theirs is also an easier environment, as by and large (again because of past practices) the jobs running on them are batch.

A minicomputer will most likely be in interactive operation and, the relative power factor set aside, the complexity of the OS job increases by that much. This complexity will also hit the mainframes at the moment they get themselves integrated into a network—what we mentioned previously about predominantly batch handling is primarily valid with stand-alone equipment.

Consider the example of Figure 3.1, a network composed of mainframes whose files are sequential, IS and IDS. The programs written in the early 70's are in Cobol 68. This network drives a great number of minis. They are interactive, and their programs are in Cobol 74. How can we integrate these resources into a properly working aggregate?

Two types of prerequisites must be fulfilled, some oneshot, others continuous.

> *One-shot:* write a file translator program to put the mainframe files in format acceptable by the minicomputer.
>
> *Continuous:* account for the fact that the stream of data from other applications is still handled on the mainframes.

In other cases, protocol conversion may be the problem. There may be a considerable difference in the extent to which information is handled between data terminating devices chosen without concern for a homogenous structure—or even an impossibility for doing so. Like code conversion, protocol conversion is no simple local exercise. It is a major systems design task.

MINICOMPUTERS

MAINFRAMES

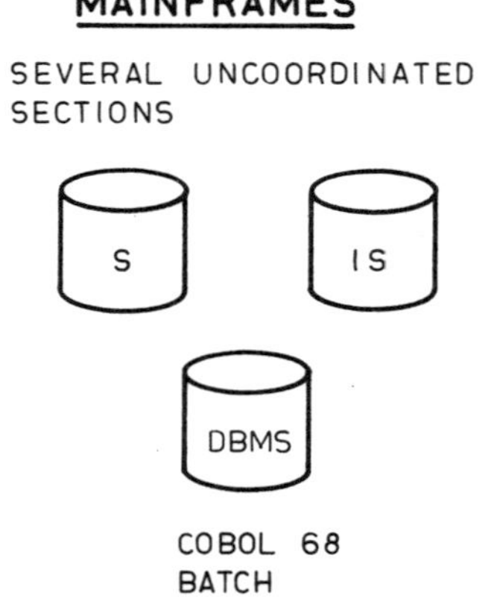

FIGURE 3.1

This reference does not underestimate the importance of standards to minimize and rationalize the proliferation of protocols. But it is beyond doubt that, until such standards are developed and enforced, we need computer power to drive the interfaces.

Alternatively, in a horizontal network dedicated to data transport and supporting several hosts and data terminating equipment, such interfaces can be provided through gateways or the support of a unique networkwide language and code. Still, however, computer power will be necessary to support conversion routines and the extraction type programs, though some manufacturers do develop software for their machines able to handle a dual environment.

It is evident that solutions to the question of minicomputer vs. mainframe DB handling have no universal portability; nor is there a profound enough body of knowledge to support them. Such solutions are situational to a large degree and have to be studied with skill and an open mind within a given applications environment.

A MINICOMPUTER LEVEL OF DB ORGANIZATION

The fundamental interest at the minicomputer level of DB organization is: "How is the user going ahead with the application? Can he use the projected organizational solution?"

The answer will most likely be "yes," if he handles simple problems (yes/no; available balance type) which are well standardized; "no," if he needs creative man/information communication which will involve major data warehouses.

The mini will not drive two digit billion byte memories, at least not in the early 80's. This is the job of the mainframe. But the mini should support the data elements which are capable of answering the local user's needs—or at least use the network facilities to fetch time.

The mini should do what it does in a user friendly manner. That is not necessarily true of the maxi. Today, the application program (and the user calling on it) has, for instance, to say: "Find Record A; then B." An easier man/information communication would be to specify "Payroll."

In this sense, the end user will neither know nor call upon a DML (data manipulation language). An extended DB control system will do this work for him.

In such a design, we should always keep in mind that people at the micro- and minicomputer levels are *not* as technically qualified as people working with the mainframe. Therefore, both the languages available and the DB structure must answer the user's requirements in an able manner.

Furthermore, people working on mini, by and large, work interactively. Hence, considerations on similarities and differences must observe not only mini and maxi but also the question of batch vs. interactive.

What does *interactive* mean? It means both a prerequisite and a result of RT update. It identifies any system ready to react to demands from the environment.

An interactive system may work in one phase—or in three (Figure 3.2). Memo posting, the old type of RT update is an example of the former.

> Controlled data collection,
>
> permanent DB update,
>
> management query

exemplify the triphase. This can happen both in a timesharing (TS) environment and in one dedicated to interactive usage.

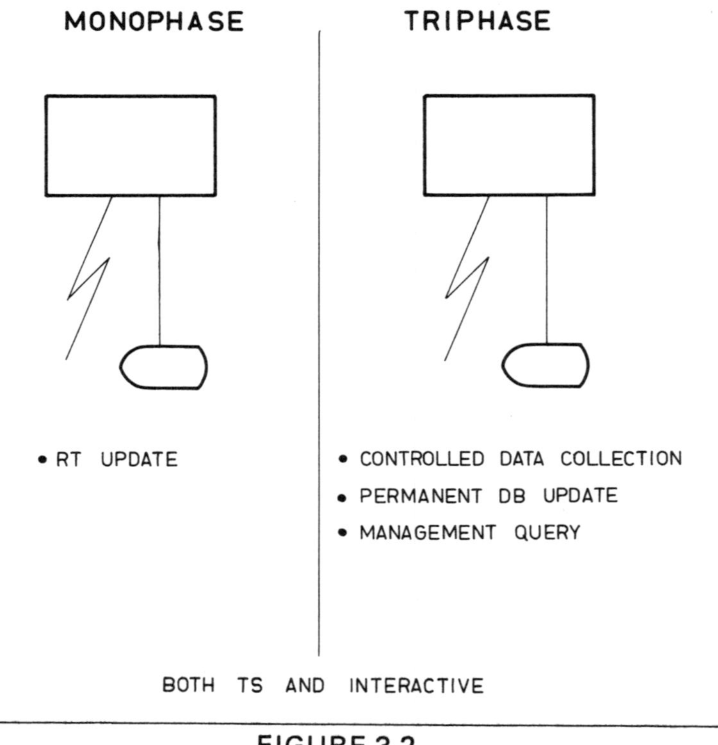

FIGURE 3.2

In addition, data collection and management query can be day-long; while the permanent DB update takes place once in awhile. Human factors enter this equation. What is tolerable? People working at a terminal sometimes get nervous. Are they willing to wait "x" minutes to get an answer only a complex, sophisticated database system can give?

There are other questions to be answered. What is a big computer? How do we define a small machine? The 370/168 used to be the biggest system. Then it became a "good size" system; still later a system of average dimensions; and, like the 370/135, tomorrow it may be on request for everybody's desk.

DIFFERENCES: REAL OR FICTITIOUS?

At any given time, differences in size seem to be fictitious, because the issue is elusive and changes with fast moving technology. To the contrary,

> synchronous vs. asynchronous DB operations,
>
> interactive vs. batch approaches, and
>
> data dictionary (DD) vs. no DD availability

are real differences. Sometimes these help sort out the big machines from the small ones.

Today, several minis do not have a DB structure. Depending on the application, this is not necessarily a limitation. However, as the applications environment expands, the difference becomes both felt and known.

And there is the case of other minis which have been given maxicomputer DB systems at a reduced level of complexity. Often, the user finds that these become too heavy to manage; eating up machine resources by themselves.

Similarly, the user at the minicomputer level lacks preparation at large, more so with DB systems, though the mini or micro in the hands of the user will better the latter's comprehension and communicating capability.

Compared to mainframes, online transaction processing through minicomputers has several advantages:

1. hardware is less expensive (acquisition price)

2. machines can work unattended

3. software development costs are lower

4. computers are located where the work is done

5. interactive capabilities are optimized

6. environmrents are easier to control

7. machines have been designed for maintenance

Simplicity must also be emphasized. Developing a mainframe transaction processing application can be:

complex,

costly, and

time consuming,

and these issues are better explained if we keep in mind that the origins of many mainframe transaction processing systems are in batch techniques (early 1950s; early 1960s).

It is no accident that the more experience users gained, the more they tended to move away from batch. Interactive applications started developing in the late 60s, and called for new types of machines.

1. The nature of online transaction processing requires an interactive architecture.

2. User oriented applications call for features not available on mainframes.

3. Man/information communications require that the machine is located near the user—not miles away.

4. The multiplicity of terminals—and their diverse characteristics—points to the need of mini and midi processors.

Mainframes (and their OS) cannot handle thousands of devices. They are slowed down, and this is quite visible in an online environment.

Let's recall that AT&T foresees 3.6 million terminals, in the U.S. alone, by 1983. Such large scale system handling cannot be supported through mainframes. On the other hand, the massive databases foreseen for the mid-to-late 1980s cannot be run through micro- or even minicomputers. Both mainframes and minis have their place in information processing. Table 3.1 presents some relative advantages and disadvantages of minicomputers.

Whether handled by maxi, mini or micro, the database task has to be studied in terms of the end user. The user oriented pyramid can be seen at three levels (Figure 3.3). At the top are complex people, facing equally complex problems and needing corresponding instruments. Things are much simpler at the bottom—but the risk of poor or even wrong usage of the tools tends to be somewhat greater.

TABLE 3.1

The Place of Minicomputers

ADVANTAGES

1. Economy through specialization.
2. No large, complex operating systems.
3. Smaller online databases.
4. Fewer costs for program development.
5. Less time for program development.
6. Simpler programming.
7. Separation programming/ database management.
8. Shared data through better, specialized interfaces.
9. Shared processors (different host computers) access to a multiplicity of data.
10. Physical separation frontend, rearend.
11. Flexibility to place rearend in remote/central location.
12. Data reliability and security (computer crime).
13. Machine reliability (less system drift).
14. Fewer problems in change-over to new host; better portability.

DISADVANTAGES

1. Cost of a special machine for a database.
2. Balance of resources. (The rearend machine may turn out to be overloaded/ underloaded. We don't know yet how to balance.)
3. Response time overhead:
   a. transmission time of the command to the rearend;
   b. transmission time of results to the host;
   c. task queuing delays relative to these transmissions;
   d. overheads related to incompatible character sets, data formats, etc.
4. Within a network, the need for protocols.
5. Used with DBMS, the need for control schemas and the overhead to handle the DBMS requirements.

COMPLEX PEOPLE
" PROBLEMS
" INSTRUMENTS
UNSTRUCTURED
ENVIRONMENTS
INFORMATION
STRUCTURED
SIMPLER PEOPLE
" PROBLEMS
" INSTRUMENTS

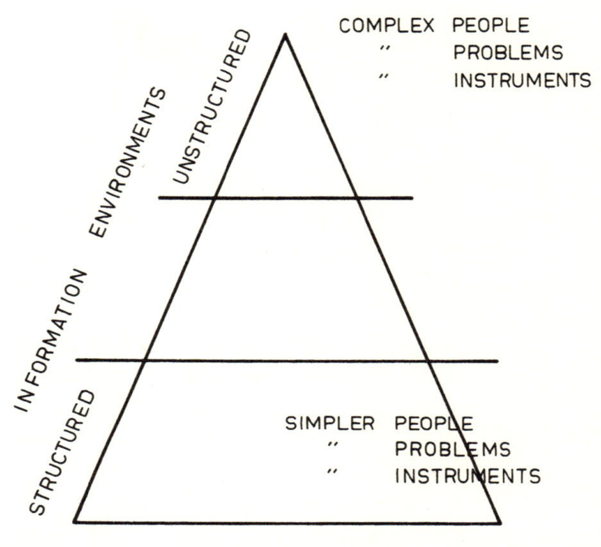

FIGURE 3.3

4 Planning a Database

INTRODUCTION

Several database functions are fairly repetitive and must be standardized. If not, they will require a large set of resources totally out of proportion with those of the application program itself. This is one reason why, instead of being under the control of the task that requested it, database management functions should be performed on a specialized processor that would have the sole task of efficiently managing data structures (a rearend machine).

This approach, like any other concerning the rational management of a database, has many implications. One of them is the definition of a language which can be used as an interface to the database manager. The other is the database planning operations which must take place.

For a rational and effective planning procedure, we should start by defining the objectives to be reached through an integrated database. Then we should classify these objectives according to their importance to the current AP subsystems and those to be developed in the future. Then, a basic action strategy should be developed, taking into account the best technology can offer.

It is a sound procedure to evaluate the database strategy for impact on the computer/communications structure and the terminal devices. We should look at the input and output systems as the mechanisms used to customize a data model, (database) and to specific operational requirements in terms of implementation.

A rearend approach might, for instance, be designed and optimized for a specific set of tasks. The processor should be specialized for logical operations, data moves, string manipulation and compare action. A technology is called for, suitable as a staging device without introducing an extra level of I/O activity getting the data in and out of central memory. These are planning considerations which bring into perspective both the logical structure and the physical supports which will be used.

There are rules to be observed, and experience challenges the idea that any business (industrial or financial) is truly unique. The underlying principles are common to all. One of the common denominators is the care needed in evaluating the DB strategy for potentially adverse consequences to current operations, providing for solutions.

Other common planning rules: state the DB strategy in terms of projects; plan for integration; provide for regular evaluations (design reviews); keep the procedures active for corrective action; establish and maintain a time-table; and train human resources to meet both the timetable and the planning prerequisites.

RATIONAL DATABASE ORGANIZATION

The best way to design a new database (or reorganize an existing one) is to think of the end user. Which facilities will he require? How should they be structured? What sort of compromises should be reached between requirements proper to man/machine communication and those pertinent to devices (physical or logical; terminals or programs)?

A properly organized database consists of a set of named DB segments. Each segment is a collection of named files. Each file consists of an ordered set of uniform records; each record is composed of a collection of named fields; and so on to the smallest IE which is addressable.

A file can be viewed as a table. Each record is a row in the table and each field is a column in that same table. Information about each field is kept in the database along with the data. This field description information consists of at least:

1. the name of the field
2. the data type
3. the data length
4. the semantic description

Among the data types to be supported, we distinguish: real numbers, integers, text strings, and bit strings. Since ordering is used to distinguish records, a file may contain duplicate records.

With online databases, a user must be able to interactively define a file by specifying the name of the file, the number of the fields, and their attributes. Before data can be read or written into a database, the source and target must be specified. The user can do so by *binding* fields of a file to program variables.

On an interactive man/information communications basis, *selection* of a record (or set of records) will be done either by record number, or by a match with some of the field values or ranges of field values—the *scan* points to the selected records. After binding and selection have been completed, a user may read, write, insert, update, or delete the selected records.

Data transmission requirements require special attention. Data transmission will be done directly or with conversion to the data type specified for the

46

program variable. The user should also be able to read or write a record from continuous memory with no conversion or binding.

These are the basic requirements imposed by interactive applications as far as database facilities are concerned. The planning phase should fully account for them because interactivity is the rule of the 1980's, even if we look into the late 70's we will appreciate that information systems have become increasingly database centered.

Originally, the focus in information processing was on computation; today i is on the generalized storage and manipulation of data. The typical state-of-the-art system for the coming decade will support online access to large databases shared by many applications and many terminal users. We should never lose sight of this when planning databases.

SUPPORTED FACILITIES

A significant range of faculties must be supported by an online database system. When we talk of micro- and minicomputer applications we talk primarily of online systems.

Figure 4.1 offers an overall view to the solution of the problems of database faculties. The approach that is taken, is divided into three broad classes:

> organization,
> integration, and
> software.

Particularly within an interactive environment, organization can be effective not only if it is properly outlined, but also (and primarily) if the established rules and standards are policed. This is the job of the database administrator (DBA). To do his work effectively, the DBA requires the services of a data dictionary and guidelines to follow in the new and expanding field of interactive solutions.

Database integration calls for the following basic images and facilities.

> concept
> structure
> meaning
> homogeneity
> partition (segmentation)
> distribution (in physical media or diverse topology)
> controlled duplication
> storage/retrieval capabilities
> query faculties

A DATABASE SOLUTION
DATABASE SOFTWARE
DATABASE INTEGRATION
DATABASE ORGANIZATION
DATABASE ADMINISTRATION
PARTITION
TOPOLOGY
MULTI – COPY UPDATE
OS
JOURNALING + STATISTICS
INTEGRITY + RECOVERY
DATA DICTIONARY
INTERACTIVE SOLUTION

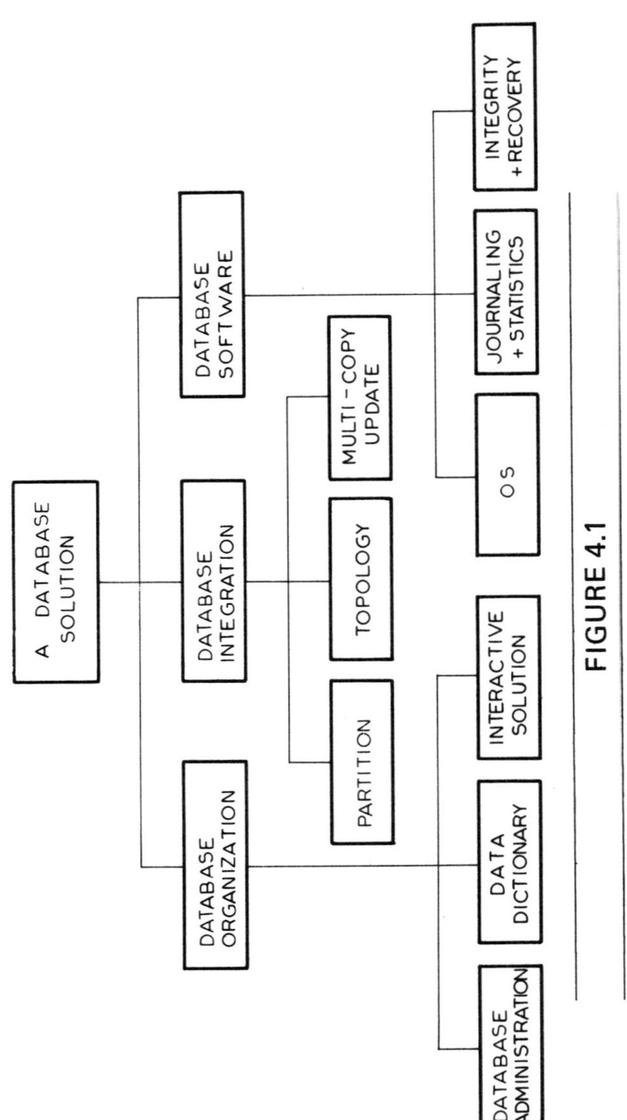

FIGURE 4.1

virtual storage (VS) solutions
DB management
data dictionary availability

Partition of the database elements into logical sets may not be required as a function of topology. It will, however, be necessary because of the diverse physical storage media used in a computer system. This is something virtual storage solutions aim to correct by making these different physical supports transparent to the user.

Partition, distribution and a certain degree of controlled duplication (to help bring the IE near the user, and for system recovery purposes) bring up the issue of the simultaneous update. As we will see, when we talk of distributed databases, good DP practice demands that a consistent image of the DB is definitely assured. Hence, the need for a simultaneous update mechanism.

These operations will be run by using raw computer power. But as with all DP activities we need software modules to drive the hardware elements. This is the role of the DB dedicated basic software which includes; the operating system (OS) functions (monitors, supervisory routines, I/O controls, and so on); the journaling and statistics faculties; and the integrity mechanism.

The acquisition, purification, storage, processing, retrieval, presentation and dissemination of information for operating personnel and for management (at all levels) are the first basic objectives of required facilities for the implementation of a DB. This is followed by the creation of organic harmony in the integration of man/machine systems into the day-to-day affairs of the corporation.

The latter point is a basic difference in database implementation between mainframes and mini- or microsystems. Because of working largely in batch, the DB of maxicomputers is accessible mainly during working hours when human operators are usually available. If work is done, say, in two shifts, for eight hours per day the database is often locked off by the simple procedure of cutting the power supply. (Though with large scale systems, it is recommended to keep power on during the night hours in order to avoid stabilization problems the following morning.)

With minis, power-on must be steady whether or not there are data processing operations in effect; and minis should in principle work unattended. These minis might be part of a network, and even with public lines they can be polled through central (or regional) locations by mainframes or other minis for data transmission requirements. Thus, interfaces must be contained within the DB system, and with them a planned implementation of security and protection.

As underlined in Chapter 2, data protection and security is necessary to supplement a primary mission with information systems. If a system is planned well enough, this mission will be subservient to and embedded in the overall management plans, procedures and objective established by the corporation. The role of a database in corporate environments is unique: we cannot create a "product" to be delivered to operating personnel or to management without dynamic and day-to-day response to the requirements of the various departments and divisions which this information product is to serve.

A database supporting multiple sectors of the organization will necessarily involve confidential data. These data have to be protected from intruders, and the security mechanism must account for all known ways of invasion existing today—from wire tapping to computer crime.

Figure 4.2 presents the prerequisites to a solid DB study in terms of the functions to be supported and the faculties to be provided.

Starting with the security provisions, these should include the identification of:

> author,
> sender,
> receiver, and
> person (or machine) responsible for operation.

The author of a message to be stored in the database may not be the sender. (We said that a file is a message in the DB, and vice versa.) Just the same, the receiver at the destination may be different than the person (or machine) responsible for the operation. There are also issues concerning annotations, operational data, distribution lists, and files addressed in the database.

The security section of the journal should definitely involve identifications which will permit reconstruction of the data exchange as it has taken place. Unusual events; time in and time out; exercised control (particularly stop action); restore operations; restart and recovery are examples of faculties which can guarantee that valuable data will be available when necessary. Evidently, these examples are pertinent to an online environment. And that is precisely what we mean when referring to minicomputer run microfiles polled by mainframe based DB.

END-TO-END EFFICIENCY

A good solid database planning study should reflect the aim of end-to-end efficiency. Over the last twenty years, computer systems vendors (and many users) created a situation not unlike that faced by supersonic aircraft. However short the flight, the door-to-door travel time can be longer than experienced with older transport technology more conveniently located.

Efficiency has many facets. Prior to engaging in a DB study, it is advisable to predict the time, cost and performance of the projected database. Let

50

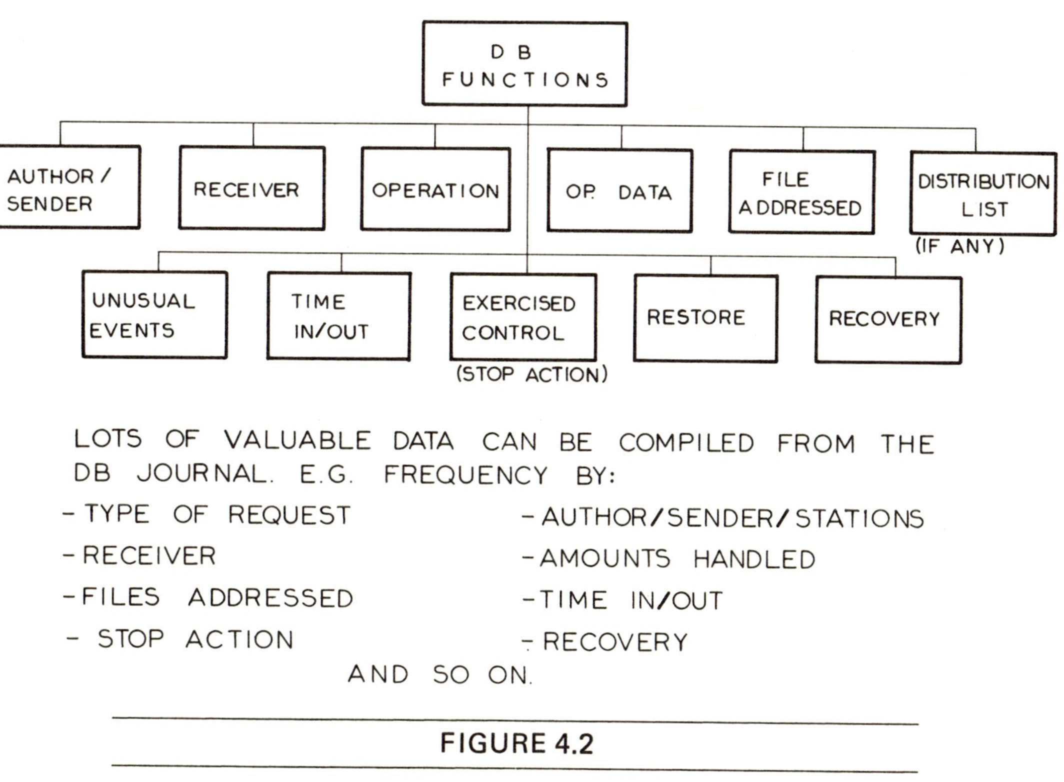

D B
FUNCTIONS
AUTHOR /
SENDER
RECEIVER
OPERATION
OP. DATA
FILE
ADDRESSED
DISTRIBUTION
LIST
(IF ANY)
UNUSUAL
EVENTS
TIME
IN/OUT
EXERCISED
CONTROL
(STOP ACTION)
RESTORE
RECOVERY
LOTS OF VALUABLE DATA CAN BE COMPILED FROM THE
DB JOURNAL. E.G. FREQUENCY BY:
- TYPE OF REQUEST
- RECEIVER
- FILES ADDRESSED
- STOP ACTION
- AUTHOR/SENDER/STATIONS
- AMOUNTS HANDLED
- TIME IN/OUT
- RECOVERY
AND SO ON.

FIGURE 4.2

me emphasize that this should be done prior to a decision to establish that project. The budget and also the timeplan must be evaluated. Shorter system development cycles are needed to avoid the long delays often required to progress from DB planning to implementation and operation.

Other characteristics have also been discussed. Easier access to data, making it possible to extract data and reports from the system without long delays. This means steering away from batch and towards interactivity.

Planning for an interactive DB is almost synonymous with looking for one which can support a reasonable freedom of output choices, e.g., the ability to use a display, color, graphics, hard copy printer, microfiche or any other output media. In turn, this will allow increased responsiveness from today's DP environment, and will relieve management's frustration over the inflexibility of the present complex batch-based system.

Database planning should relieve bottlenecks. A batch-oriented DB carried into an interactive environment will represent a bottleneck. The call for services will be constrained by the limited access capacity of the facility. The classical DB design is inflexible and completely out of control in respect to the purpose for which it was originally created: to serve the organization. Too many personnel look upon the database as an "end within itself."

There are other issues to keep in perspective. We will examine most of them in the following chapters. But to assure that the reader has a complete picture at this point, here are the headlines. They have to do with the storage hardware; the user interfaces; the formats; the accesses; the restart procedures and in general all issues concerning distributed database systems.

Storage design should be independent of the specific applications. The explicit data definition should be made independent of the AP. Just the same, integrity assurance is independent of application programs. It is not necessary for users to know the data formats or physical storage structures. Keeping a single copy of the data eliminates redundancy and inconsistency of multiple files. Recovery should be assured independently of the AP.

Current and projected communications functions should be given due weight. This means planning for the storage and forwarding of data; eventual switch monitoring; error detection and correction; response control; priority assignment; reliability and redundancy control. If the DB is partitioned into two or more modules, this will involve intramodule communications. If the modules are distributed into several centers, there will also be intermodule and intercenter communications. The latter will demand driver/handler routines; line control and task scheduling; message handling and routing of packages; DB load and unload software; and also a significant number of system support and utility routines.

Native commands should include the following types of control and monitoring: program and data file transfer; data file display; status interrogation;

DB statistics gathering and display; resource enable/disable operations; maintenance and support functions; system access faculties; and DB system initialization routines. Interest should be generated not only in DB architectures that are more efficient in information storage and retrieval, but in the many facets of design activity directed at database systems.

Finally, it is necessary to underscore the need for employing the highest level of human resources available when working with databases. A few talented people can be more productive in developing a top-notch DB system, with carefully thought-out interfaces, than large teams which are difficult to coordinate and control. We will return to this issue when we talk of the database administrator.

DISTRIBUTED DATABASES

Databases for minicomputers and networks mean distributed DB. A distributed database is one logical DB placed at multiple physical locations. These may or may not be geographically distributed. A local database:

> supports a "one system" environment;
> is independent of the equipment running in this environment;
> represents a collection of data organized to satisfy user requirements within prearranged application perspectives.

Whether we talk of functionally or geographically distributed databases, we should first make a unified system study and consider both topology and functionality. The structure of a distributed database should support the partition and separation of application processing to the degree necessary to satisfy IS requirements.

Typically, a distributed information system will be divided into three main subsystems. These are listed below and identified in Figure 4.3.

> A transport mechanism which assures process to process and process to IE communication.

> Distributed processing through computer based procedures.

> Distributed databases locally supporting the different processes but also remotely accessible through programs or terminals.

A network architecture must provide the needed routines to support multitasking; file access; file management; operating interfaces; communications control (including standard interfaces for device independence); terminal control (terminal handling, format handling, code conversion, list for supported terminals); network control (network configuration, recovery/restart, alter-

P6
P8
P7
DB III
DB II
PROCESSES
P5
P4
PORTS
PORTS
DATA
TRANSPORT
X.25
DTE
DB I
P2
P1
P3
PORTS

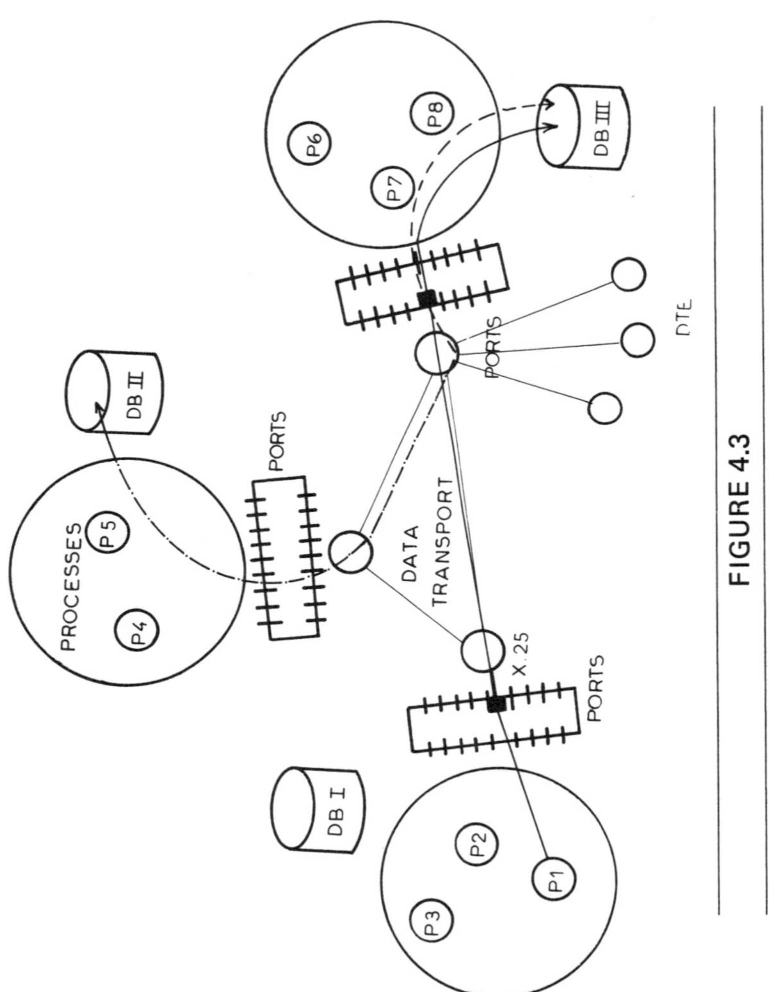

FIGURE 4.3

late routing); and network operation (network definition, dynamic control, adaptability).

Thus, in terms of basic components, a distributed database will involve: a transport network; the mainframe DB (one or several); the distributed data level (usually several); the transaction level at the work station (also distributed and multiple); and logical support activity which includes the backups and journals.

Like all information systems activity, distributed databases require a great deal of preparation and the documented answers to questions such as: What functions should be distributed? Where should they be based? How and where should they be distributed? How and where should the hierarchy of functions be controlled? How is DB integrity insured? How and where should the DB be distributed? How should reliability and security be enhanced?

This is a new philosophy in systems planning and a departure from past practices where information systems have been implemented using a centralized database, even when other functions have been distributed. Few organizations have implemented distributed databases, and these were obliged to develop their own systems. For long years, software to support distributed databases has not been available from manufacturers.

Distributed databases are now in evolution. The most interesting trend in terms of development is that they support data at many nodes. The nodes are assumed to communicate over communications links; and the latter can vary in bandwidth and delay. Local networks are definitely a part of this reference. The distributed database system may be located within a single building.

Let us first distinguish between distributed data processing and distributed databases; and then between types of distributed database systems. Whether local or spread over a wide area, a distributed data processing system consists of: a number of nodes (locations which may contain one or more computer configurations). A network architecture adds the significant capability of entering a job at one node and letting the system decide where to run the job.

The distinction between distributed processes and DDB can be logical, physical or both. The inclusion of a distributed database means that not only is processing power distributed to whomever needs it, but also the database is distributed along with the responsibility for its usage.

Distributing responsibility for the system to the end user is one of the main reasons distributed information systems will eventually become the dominant form of processing. The objectives especially relevant to the distribution of databases are:

1. local access facilities to assure reduced cost of data communications;

2. shared resources to permit geographically separated nodes to access different DB;

3. access transparency to provide uniform logical solutions for all locations;

4. fast response to user queries;

5. reliability, to assure that the system will continue to function adequately in spite of the loss of some of its components;

6. expandability, to accommodate changes in database size on existing nodes or by adding new ones.

(If the sites are widely dispersed geographically, the network must employ long distance communications media. But communications perspectives are just as valid in local networks, whenever intra-site processing environments exist.)

TRANSACTIONAL CAPABILITIES

User interaction is a critical design factor. Users interact with a database by entering transactions. These are implemented through online queries and access to the database. Transactions have important properties which must be studied within each applications environment.

Transactions are sustained through two basic faculties:

> system, and
> data access.

System access usually involves user authentication. Associated with it are login/logout time, at both the network interface message processor and the participating host system; and additional facilities to resolve conflict situations (for instance, in the event that two or more users request networking sessions involving the same target DB).

Data access may be enforced through discretionary or other systems. The former implies a system wherein the owner of an object (file, program) can grant access rights to the other users.

A nondiscretionary system would deny some or all of the other users such rights. Access to objects may be, for instance, granted through labels which specify the access class of the given object and the clearance of the subject requesting access—or, through tables.

The selection of the proper housekeeping functions will depend on the basic architectural design chosen. The possibilities are:

> partitioning,
> full replication, or
> hybrid solutions.

When a database is partitioned, it is divided into sets, with one set assigned to each node. Only one copy of each record of data item exists, and it is assigned to some node as its home location at any instant of time.

56

The rational choice is to assign a record to the node most frequently accessing that record, to minimize response time and communications. Accesses that cannot be handled locally are exceptions. But exceptions can grow in number.

To face a growing number of exceptions, it is necessary to keep statistics on the misses in local memory. Some studies concerning this are described in the following paragraphs. Such statistics might suggest the wisdom of replication for some of the IE. A very easy algorithm can be applied to this end, for instance:

$$\text{Exception ratio} = \frac{\text{number of misses}}{\text{number of records requested}}$$

It is necessary to identify the records missed by type of query (or AP) and comment on where (in which other node) the record has been.

When data are replicated, two or more copies of the same information exist in the system. As an extreme, every node could have its own copy of all data. The benefits of replacing data can provide substantial improvements in performance, cost (of communications links), and reliability. But the cost of storage media increases.

The most severe logical problem is, however, the greatly complicated update mechanism needed to maintain consistency in the several copies of the data. We will return to this issue.

5 Database Architecture

INTRODUCTION

We are presently faced with an increasing user acceptance of architectural approaches in database organization and control. Also technology is improving rapidly at the logical, physical and use levels in terms of goals to be reached and availability of IE assured to the end user.

In deciding among goals, we must understand the costs and the timing of the costs needed to meet specific applications requirements. DB costs are sometimes high, especially in the areas of personnel education and reorganization. That is why the corporation can look forward to profits from this effort only if a long range plan for the database has been established.

The greatest profit will come from organizational prerequisites, the streamlining of current procedures, and the intellectual work which will be put into these processes. The database engine will not provide solutions as a matter of course. In fact it may give no answers worth talking about, until the knowhow which should normally come with a systems study has been acquired. The study of prerequisites will offer the best insight for the establishment of architectural alternatives. It will also assure the subsequent multiplication factor of each DB element.

As the reporting structure moves from the elementary, settlement type DP operation to the top of the decision making pyramid, the span of information to be derived from each IE increases (Figure 5.1). But amplification has, inherently, the risk of distortions because of errors that infiltrated the database. A different way of making the statement is to underline the necessity for IE which is both correct and actual.

An excellent example on pruning databases and establishing priorities on DP handling is the thorough investigation (referred to in Chapter 1) made by The Barclay's Bank in England, to assert the functioning of the organization in the face of catastrophic failures in its information system. The rule applied can be expressed through four numbers:

100%; 75%; 50%; 25%.

These numbers represent the thresholds in management reporting with the corresponding databasing and information processing activity. Another signi-

SPAN OF INFORMATION
BASED ON THE ELEMENTS
OF THE REAL DATABASE
DATA-
BASE

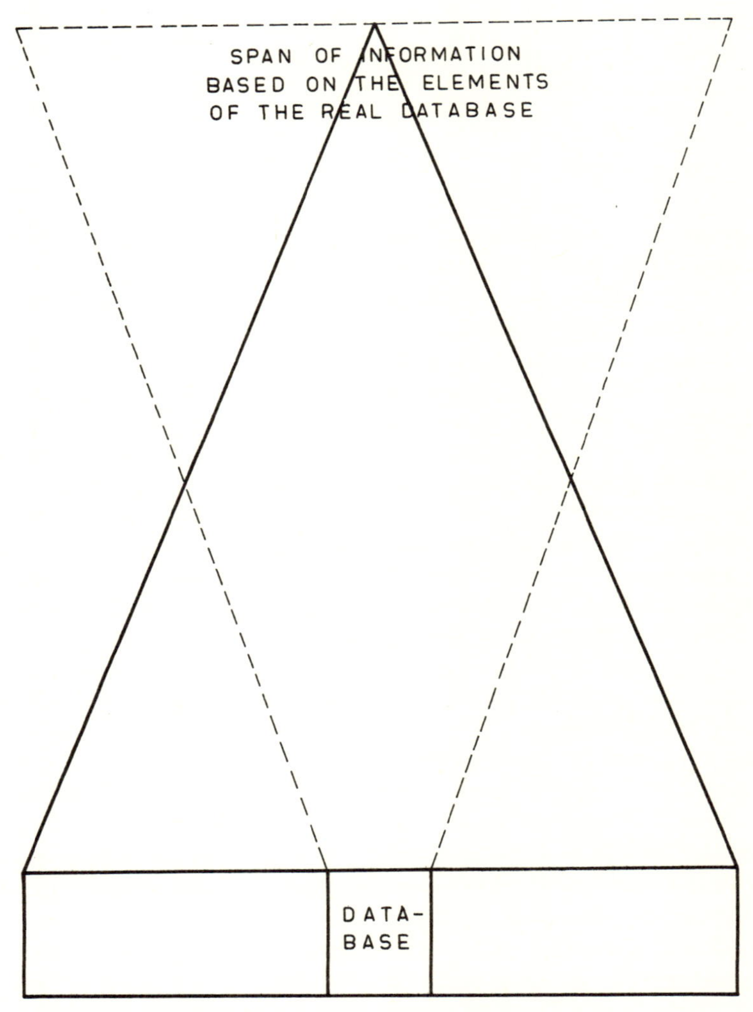

FIGURE 5.1

icant finding is that of Citibank—ninety percent of all printed paper in an organization is for internal consumption. (Studies among insurance and financial institutions confirm this.)

If management decides (as it should) that printed paper is out and documents of all sorts should, in the future, be kept in the DB, and be accessed interactively, the DB architects will be getting the most basic decision they need in order to proceed with their work.

FACTORS BEHIND A DB ARCHITECTURE

The availability of low cost direct access mass storage has encouraged users to move toward disc based random access files and away from tape-oriented sequential files.

Simultaneously, a growing market for database systems has spurred R&D to provide increasingly better technology. *The third vital factor is interactivity.* Man/information communications systems are becoming online with query and realtime update capabilities. This leads to an access of multiple files, which impose their own requirements. Storage design must be independent of specific applications; explicit data definitions must be provided; formats must be established; this impacts not only on logical but also on physical storage structures.

Multiple access brings other requirements into perspective. Both *integrity assurance* and *recovery* must be independent of application programs. A distributed DB augments the problem area because of multicopy update—though keeping a single copy of the data eliminates the redundancy and inconsistency of multiple files.

The role of databases in online, interactive transaction processing applications increases the demand for:

> high performance,
> system availability, and
> user friendly interfaces.

The trend toward distributed systems leads to remote databases, thus adding new demands to age old issues of data integrity, recovery, security and privacy.

Data sharing among programs is the first, and most obvious requirement of a DB architecture. Sharing implies:

> the existence of a centralized location for the organizational database;
>
> the use of a data dictionary, which carries definitive information about the database, and proprietary characteristics such as security or privacy; and
>
> a reasonable degree of data independence.

The objective of data independence is to insulate applications programs from the underlying database management technology. The way the information is stored and internally accessed, the file restructure, and so on, should be transparent to the user.

Data independence also facilitates data sharing by allowing the same data to appear *as if* organized differently for different application programs. The system performs the necessary conversions.

Resource sharing, data independence, efficiency and other prerequisites suggest a prominent role for the rearend machine. Any database architecture must consider the advantages (and possible constraints) dedicated database machines offer within a given environment.

Though database computers substantially improve the efficiency of accessing information, at the present state-of-the-art, the database application must be a large fraction of the total system load to make them effective.

In other words, only when the load is appreciable, say half the available computer power, does off-loading become attractive. (This is, however, the typical business application environment.) Likewise, multiaccess situations suggest rearend solutions so that the database computer can off-load the host.

The next requirement is to look carefully into storage technologies prior to making design decisions. Their use depends on three principal factors:

> cost per bit,
> access time, and
> storage capacity.

Reduced cost per bit in all technologies primarily derives from an increase in density on the material being used for storage. This reference is valid both for central memory (CM) and auxilliary devices. As a matter of fact, technology is a major influence on how other elements of the storage hierarchy are used.

CM provides the necessary buffer area to operate direct access or sequential access storage. As central memory has become cheaper, the optimum system balance has shifted towards larger main stores. With this, processor utilization has increased while the amount of I/O has decreased, as more data are kept in main storage rather than moved to a lower level.

Direct access auxiliary devices have traditionally been satisfied through disc technology. The capacity of magnetic discs has increased rapidly because of developments in recording density: an increase from three hundred thirty bits/cm^2 (2.000 bits/sq.in.) in the early 1960's to one million bits/cm^2 (six million bits/sq.in.) currently.

Because of the different levels of auxiliary storage used (both media and access time), logical solutions receive as much attention as the physical.

Storage spaces are organized in a hierarchical fashion, each with proper characteristics in: access time, cost and capability. Storage hierarchies depend on the overall concept, the logical media available, the storage access patterns and program behavior in run time environments. A hierarchy design involves making tradeoffs.

AN EVOLVING ARCHITECTURAL DESIGN

An evolving architecture will permit unification and simplification of the various approaches to database systems. In addition, a common database architecture makes it possible to demonstrate which features in the different available approaches are equivalent to each other; to establish efficient translation of data definition and data manipulation statements from one data model to another; and to support a single data structure in a system.

Past experience points to the wisdom of using a single structure for data within a system rather than separate file and database systems. This results in data models that are better suited to end users and simpler to implement and understand.

The choice of the proper retrieval scheme is the next basic requirement. In the past, large scale computer based text retrieval systems were inhibited by two factors:

> the cost of storing the billions of bytes needed for comprehensive storage and the cost of entering the data into the machine.

Starting with the data entry, this may be done as the event is taking place (through an online terminal) or in the form of daily, weekly or monthly data input. This will materialize at the settlement procedures level (money in, money out). But the database should not be organized to serve only that level. Indeed, the following two reporting layers should be of primary concern in a DB architecture:

> functional management for the stated allocation and optimization purposes, and
> top management for policy decisions.

Figure 5.2 illustrates the approach of a pyramidal construction. It describes a practical example from a manufacturing company we studied a few years ago. Two problems come to mind immediately: the first is that of needed storage. The second, and more vital, is the organizational prerequisite: from online data entry to the structure of the IE.

Advances in memory technology, particularly in the area of high density disc systems, answers the first challenge.

In 1970, the storage of 100 billion characters would have required 15.000 IBM 2311-type disc drives, at 7.25 million characters per discpack. Now, commercially available drives can store 1.1 gigabytes on a single disc drive, correspondingly reducing the number of drives required to about ninety. New

ORGANIZATIONAL LEVEL
FREQUENCY
LONG RANGE BUDGETARY PLANNING AND CONTROL
TOP MANAGEMENT
AS REQUESTED
ONLINE INTERACTIVE TERMINALS SUPPORTING COLOR AND GRAPHICS
RESOURCE MANAGEMENT EVALUATION
OVERALL PRODUCT PROFITABILITY
RISK ANALYSIS
CASH FLOW FORECASTS
SALES NETWORK DEVELOPMENT
DETAILED PROFITABILITY ANALYSIS
FUNCTIONAL MANAGEMENT
MONTHLY BIMONTHLY
SALES RESEARCH
SALES FORECASTS
PRODUCTION PLANNING AND OPTIMIZING
RESOURCE ALLOCATION
SERVICES AND DEPARTMENTS
DAILY WEEKLY MONTHLY
BILLING AND CUSTOMER ACCOUNTING
EXPEDITING TO CUSTOMERS
PAYROLL
COST CONTROL
SUBSYSTEMS
ORDER INPUT
INVENTORY CONTROL
PRODUCTION SCHEDULING
PRODUCTION CONTROL
MAIN DATA ENTRY

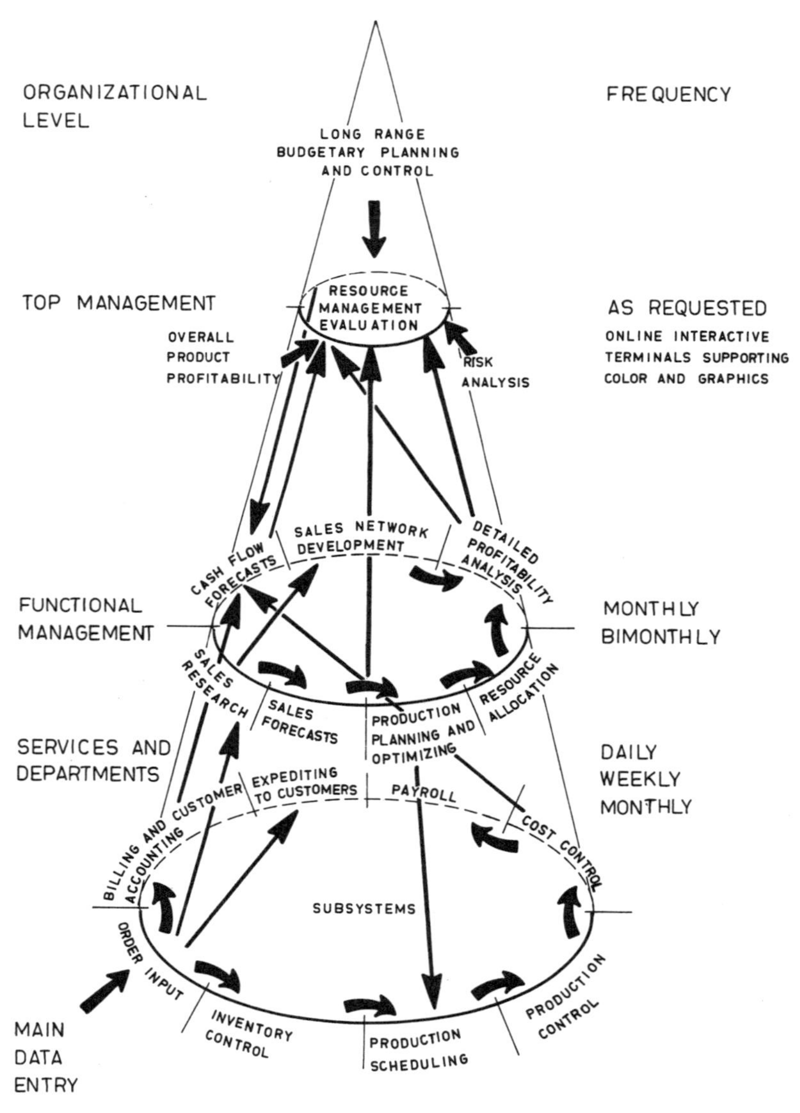

FIGURE 5.2

developments will reduce the number of required drives further. Technologies such as

> electron-beam,
> optical, and
> holographic memories

may provide greater capacities at reasonable costs.

While these "read-only" storage techniques are not suitable for constantly changing databases, they are a perfect match for archival document retrieval systems.

The data entry problem is also on the way to solution. Data transmission, word processing, computerized typesetting, and voice input alter the data collection perspectives. Thus, the development of a valid DB architecture poses a lot of challenges. The fundamentals are to:

> identify the data organization needs,
>
> review and revamp the data processing requirements, and
>
> integrate the data organization and processing operations into an architectural environment.

Data organization (like data load) requirements are best identified by conducting a series of interviews among the various users. The result is a list of all the issues of interest; the information elements needed to support these issues; and the relationships between these IE.

Finally, attention should be focused on evolving text handling opportunities. Shortly after the invention of the stored program digital computer, storage and retrieval of nonnumeric information became an important application. This problem has existed since 1946, but with only a few exceptions, the file access mechanisms—all of them logical—were mapped onto a conventional Von Neumann computer.

The first technical difficulties showed then and there. While the desirable way to access nonnumeric data is by value, the Von Neumann architecture precludes this solution.

As a result, artifice has been used to convert a value into an address. The methods include sequential, indexed, and other ways. But there has also been constant research into many aspects of file and database systems for improved functionality and performance.

(An exception to the Von Neumann architecture was the Univac File Computer. First delivered in 1954, this machine allowed data in mass storage to be addressed by value rather than by address. This was done by storing the value

*of the desired key in a search register, and then comparing this value sequenti-
ally to values on a drum.)*

DB ARCHITECTURE FOR TEXT PROCESSING

The R&D into file handling in the mid-50's led to file access; the mid-60's to
DBMS; and in the late 70's to the logic over data solutions. For the 80's, a
major challenge will be in text processing.

Three main classes exist for text retrieval systems:

1. A selective dissemination of information (SDI).

This takes an input stream consisting of new documents. Then, based on specifications, it attempts to route all documents of interest to a particular user.
The other two classes allow the user to retrieve information from an established and growing database.

2. Bibliographic systems contain index and abstract material.
3. Full text systems contain the entire original document and (possibly)
   additional indexing information.

These two classes share common difficulties. The retrieval of text is not
the same as the retrieval of formatted data. Limited or no formatting exists in
databases for text retrieval; though bibliography follows more formalisms
than full text.

Full text contains widely varying field lengths, such as individual words,
sentences, paragraphs, and documents. It is virtually impossible to find a consistent definition of the fields within a document.

These differences show up in the applications possibilities. For instance, a
user is generally limited to searching and displaying information within the
database.

Equally important is the need for a very good query language to locate
only the desired information in the relatively unstructured database. On the
other hand, highly decentralized solutions, made feasible through microprocessors, now provide the possibility of creating versatile rearend facilities, and
DB specializations, through logic over data approaches.

Yet, it cannot be too often repeated that the crucial test is that of the
organizational and procedural study. Even the gigabyte memories will prove
too limited unless all unnecessary or obsolete information, whether data or

ext, is pruned out of the system. (And let us not forget that text will impose requirements in storage needs easily surpassing those of data handling.)

A DB streamlining and unification is necessary to eliminate the high costs associated with redundant filing; to weed out the sources of mutations and errors; and to assure that information (whether data or text) is current. As the volumes of both text and data storage increase (Figure 5.3), periodic pruning of the DB will become a fundamental responsibility.

Text processing poses a particular requirement which, by and large, is taken care of in data processing by the fact that data are presented in structured fields. But:

1. Text must be formatted.

2. The fields must be defined.

3. The length of the fields established in advance.

4. Their position in a textual presentation must be subject to formalisms.

Banks, and to a lesser extent commercial companies, have experience in text formatting because of the difficulties they have steadily faced in input of documents coming from their clientele. Such documents (for instance, letters, customer orders) are renowned for their lack of format and for non-observance of formalisms.

This fact has led many financial institutions to establish a two tier system for document handling costs charged to their clients. A lower one when the client firm presents its orders—for instance, foreign exchange orders—in a standard format provided by the bank. A higher one if the client uses a free format. The same is true of telexes. The latter, if formatted, can be directly input into computer memory, eliminating manual handling.

Furthermore, with text processing,—and, sometimes, even with data processing—formatting formalisms should not be a preoccupation at only the local level. The issue is much broader. Indeed, it is network-wide. Communicating word processors pose the requirement of generally applicable standards, and any deviation would bring delays, errors and complications. These can be easily avoided through a unified approach.

A careful study will be helpful to logically unify the DB and the communications perspectives; streamline the IE; segment the storage (and the associated processing capacity) into standardized modules; link these modules together to create a network—physically unifying the database. (The entire network would act as a single database.)

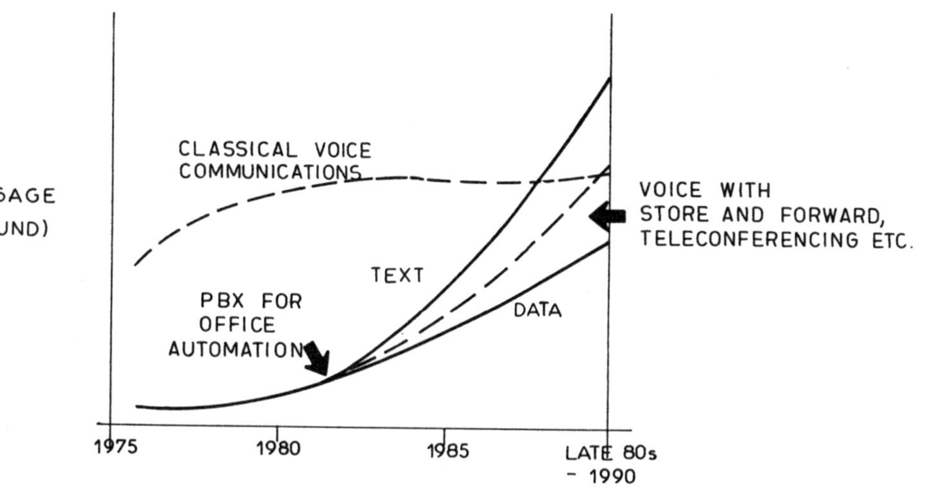

THE "TEXT USAGE" OF COMPUTERS MAY SWAMP
DATA USAGE.

FIGURE 5.3

DB RELIABILITY AND AVAILABILITY

Among the key issues relating to the study and redesign of the database are performance, reliability and availability. All three should be emphasized.

The performance characteristics of alternative DB designs must be examined in the light of user experience and methods of tuning the database to reflect accessing patterns. Here reference is made to grouping of fields and records into blocks; placing of records in a logical structure; selecting an access method; choosing record and block sizes; and proceeding with device assignment.

Some of these issues have been known for years, but they have been limited to certain cases or some devices. An example is block size. It has been traditionally used with magnetic tapes. But high capacity discs make this a requirement with disc systems in order to assure good performance.

Block sizes of 1K to 2K bytes are suggested as the optimal with 1.1 gigabyte discs, with 256 bytes as the minimum block size. Since these dimensions fit the packet switching needs, the time may not be far off when block sizes for storage or transmission will be standardized.

Providing for error protection is the next fundamental requirement. This calls for control over means used to connect external devices to the DB and, therefore, for checks which have not been traditionally available on memory-to-memory links.

Techniques for protecting the data for reliability purposes must be surveyed, including: integrity checks; audit trails; rollback; check pointing and restart. The problems of concurrent access synchronization, an area in which the traditional performance/reliability tradeoff is very evident, must also be studied. The same is true of privacy enforcement, change control, input validation, test database generation and the like.

Generalizing communications, file processing and networking functions are the ways of the future. They call for providing standards and a controlled redundancy to help increase reliability. Failsoft capabilities; data integrity features; and autoreconfiguration should come along with this, as necessary.

From the user's point of view, a lot of data checks must be provided. The file management supervisor will: build duplicate files; retrieve from the second file if the first is in error; and automatically rollback and restart, if necessary.

Shared mass storage solutions on a multiprocessing or network basis can ascertain that different computers share the same disc space, even if they do not work together as a dual processor (though each may work as dual with another). This might concern: system output files; catalog files; the data dictionary; and all permanent storage.

The DB architects must anticipate problems of database maintenance. Whatever keeps a database dynamic: updates, insertions, and deletions and the way they affect overall structure must be examined. In most organizations, the cost of accessing the database increases with time due to structural changes caused by such updates.

One might answer that this need has been known for many years. What is different today? This question can easily be answered by looking at Figure 5.4. In the past, the General Ledger routines had their own files to manage. Eventually, other processes closely related to the Ledger were run on these files. (For instance, the economic accounts of the firm.)

As new processes utilized the same files a common DB was created. On-line input placed some limitations of its own. But these requirements in no way resemble the prudence and standardization which has become necessary with the addition of a great variety of tasks ranging from responsibility report-

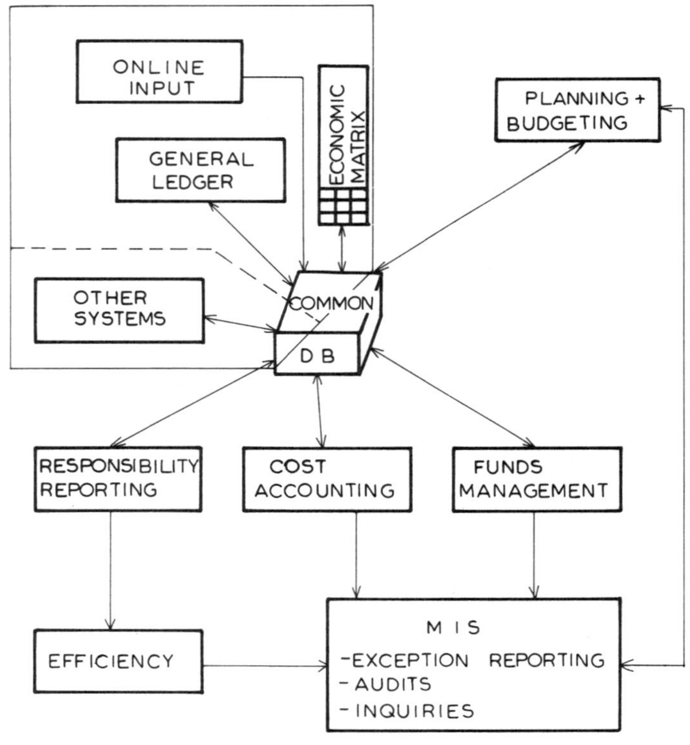

FIGURE 5.4

ing, to planning and budgeting, costs accounting and funds management. Finally, management information systems (MIS) prerequisites have been added, including:

> exception reporting,
> audits, and
> inquiries.

This led some organizations to the creation of dedicated DB segments like those supported by Citibank's IAMIS (Internal Accounting MIS). The objective is specialization which permits a more contained DB size and better, more efficient DB maintenance prodedures.

A reporting structure should be established for DB maintenance reasons along with a set of rules to guide such activity. Reports should be available in a special system maintenance DB (but not necessarily produced on hardcopy) when the DB is modified. The same is true of the need to verify additions and changes.

System structure, size and picture reports, are examples. Data structure reports will include

> data usage, and
> DB design.

Deviation reports should describe the data process. There should be user exit reports, if user exits are assured by the system.

Furthermore, implementation requirements and the training of the user must be integral parts of the work which we are outlining.

The need for an implementation assistance requires no particular explanation. Once a database system is developed, reliable information must be available in a structured and timely form. The system should be implemented so as to permit the extension to cater to a variety of user needs whose information requirements cannot be satisfied by the classifical batch interfaces.

The operators, too, must learn to work with the new DB structure in accordance with its capabilities. They should be instructed not to restart without putting the system in order; to insert personalized messages for guidance purposes; and when in doubt, to restart from the beginning. Since in a distributed environment operators and end users are often the same person, this is generally a valid reference.

6 Priorities in DB Design

INTRODUCTION

The first priority in designing a database is to assure that what is done is solid and efficient and that it can serve the user well during the foreseeable future. Database design must be a thoughtful action able to account for current needs and project into the coming implementation. It should in no way resemble some past DP practices where people used databases, computers and networks instead of brains.

In making a decision on how the database should be designed, the specialist should: establish the real needs; study what technology offers; project on the architectural issues; elaborate a budget; outline the timeplan; and always remember the importance of factors such as critical mass, knowhow, training and selling the idea to the end user.

The next priority is to assure easy transition. Systems, and most particularly databases, are not born overnight. Generally, new projects are a development of already existing equipment that will be incorporated into the new structure either as it stands or after a conversion. This leads the analyst to a decision matrix with the basic choices of: enhance, replace or proceed with a new development (Figure 6.1).

The end user must be happy. This end user will most likely be online and interactive. He will look for an immediate answer to the problem at hand; search for references, statistics, even solutions, by query; and will be gratified if he can get assistance by computers in the domain of human communications (verbal, written).

These perspectives will have a major impact on management decisions in terms of databases, including issues related to:

> investments,
> projects,
> implementations, and
> maintenance.

DECISION MATRIX

	PRODUCT	PROCESS	PROCEDURE
ENHANCE			
REPLACE			
NEW DEVELOPM.			

VALID FOR BOTH
- R + D PROJECTS
- IS STUDIES

FIGURE 6.1

Through imaginative design approaches, the system to be developed must assist in areas which go beyond the "classical needs." New areas of attention are: management decision; statistical support; and internal audits—improving coverage and augmenting vision without exceeding the time needed for a less sophisticated solution, such as manually searched paper files.

SETTING THE GOALS

What are some specific aims when designing a DB? The goals can be divided into two large classes. One is specific to the situation. As such, it is the less fundamental. The other is basically generic and has broad applicability. Situational considerations are preferably handled through parametric approaches, and database designers should concentrate on the factors which support the understructure. The groundwork is provided by the word "independence," which is applicable to three areas of reference:

devices,
location, and
applications.

Device independence means that the equipment must be transparent to the user and preferably support one level memory, probably served through VS. (We will consider this issue when we discuss ways and means to optimize the DB faculties.) Location independence implies transparency both to the user and to the programs, with the identification of the location accomplished through a computer-run directory. This also means no physical addressing associated with the processes, and leads to applications independence. The latter assumes recognition type memories.

Other generic issues include the formalisms; protocols; simultaneous update mechanism; protection, security, authorization; and generally the evolving DB handling perspectives.

The provision of these faculties is part and parcel of a modern, online, query-oriented DB design, so are algorithmic approaches for interactive solutions. We have already referred to such prerequisites as error control; pruning and revamping; journaling, recovery, and backup. And we have underlined flexibility, feasibility of steady evolution, and the need for performance criteria.

Many separate aspects of performance can be isolated and subject to evaluation:

1. Is the existing DB design capable of concurrent online and batch processing?
2. Are there any practical limits to the database size?
3. How easily can database relationships be changed?
4. To what extent do database changes affect the programs?
5. Is there a checkpoint-restart facility?

Many factors entering the design equation contradict rather than support one another. The questions are: Can we make knowledgeable tradeoffs between processing speed and main storage allocation? What level of application independence do we wish to obtain? Contrasted to this, what is the level we can afford? What about data independence, does the system maintain data integrity by type and by value limits?

Documented answers cannot be given without considering the applications environment and the resources we wish to put on this job. In turn, the interaction between resources, environment, and requirements, poses other questions. How many physical accesses are needed to retrieve a data item from storage? Do structural modifications require reconstitution of the physical files? What kind of hardware and software monitors are available?

Usage considerations bring into perspective the database management system (DBMS) and its capabilities: Does the DBMS to be chosen support the current software environment? Does it support anticipated additions? Is there a data dictionary system? What are the limitations of the query language? Does the query language allow the user his own "view" of the data?

Still other basic questions concern the applications software now available to do the DP job. What application programs are available? How do they fit with the particular DBMS under consideration? And since hardware resources change, it is legitimate to ask: How easily can the DBMS be moved to another computer?

A thoroughly thought-out list will include questions on the utilities which are available, and on whether the DBMS meets the user needs for protecting data against destruction. Because terminals will be around in tens, hundreds or thousands, we should ask what sort of terminal prompting is available. And how extensive (and useful) are the system defaults?

Documentation is always a sore point with software, and the DB designers will be well advised to ask: Is the system documentation updated regularly? Is documentation accessible to all user levels? What level of skill is required by the user? How many people will have to be trained in system use, and how long will the training take?

We will return to the issues concerning the able selection of a DBMS and its incorporation into DB design in the chapters on database management systems (which will constitute a separate volume). The few references made in this section were necessary to underline the key role of a DBMS in database design and establish beyond a doubt that this is one of the basic priorities. Other prerequisites, however, must also be satisfied.

PHYSICAL AND LOGICAL INDEPENDENCE

The efficient organization of a database calls for a logical independence between storage media and the data stored in these media. The problems presented for consideration concern both hardware and software. While current computers are well-suited to scientific applications, they are not projected for the demanding task of information storage and retrieval.

Information storage and retrieval applications require addressing by content, while conventional computers are designed for referencing by physical address. This introduces inefficiencies in both the processor and storage areas: data access tends to become computerbound; and tables required to locate data can (in some cases) consume more storage than the data itself.

What has just been said particularly concerns;

1. *The database* itself; the meaning and structure of the data without reference to its "physical" representations within files.

2. *The information element*—as a container of information.

An IE (whether byte, file or record) must be considered as a whole and cannot be identified as such. This can be done with or without referring to the meaning of the data it contains.

The pruning of current databases and the structuring of the new building blocks will be helped by the data dictionary, but procedural approaches can also be used. One solution is described in Figure 6.2. It calls for an outline of the retained information elements at the desired level of detail (byte, field, file, record); the definition of their functions; and an identification of the application programs they serve.

The goal of this scrutiny is to identify duplicates and inconsistencies; weed them out; and help streamline the DB content. Experience has often documented that programs written, for example, to handle suppliers have company file structures which are totally diverse from those of the client files—yet, the same party can be a client and a supplier. The same is true of item descriptions (spares, machines, supplies, other goods). They are differently structured in the supplier's files and in the inventory files (Figure 6.3). But with an integrated approach to databases, these items should be homogeneous even if addressed by diverse application programs.

3. *The data* (within an IE) represented according to local operating system conventions.

4. *The logical units* or the blocks of information of which a file is often structured.

These are the basic references that access information within the file.

5. *File management* providing two kinds of services: file access and file maintenance.

A file access method consists of a set of standard primitives to store data into files and retrieve it. The file maintenance program's usual function is to make a copy of a file; to delete a file; to reorganize a file and so on.

6. *DB media*, their organization and the logical solutions which are followed, such as virtual storage (VS).

7. *Interactive/dialogue* approaches for the user.

8. *Distributed databases* and their infrastructure, including the needed supports such as the simultaneous update mechanism.

9. Finally, *database management* (DBM) as a whole.

The DBM will provide access to the actual information, just as file management permits manipulation of the physical representation of this information. As previously stated, the database management faculties must be examined, and the necessary procedural steps properly outlined: check validity requests; check authorizations; locate data; lock data; order data; unlock data; and map data between schemas and subschemas. Along with the outlined procedures,

APPLICATION PROGRAMS
FUNCTONS
1 2 3 ... n ... 1 2 L
A
B
C
...
...
E
I.E., FIELDS, RECORDS

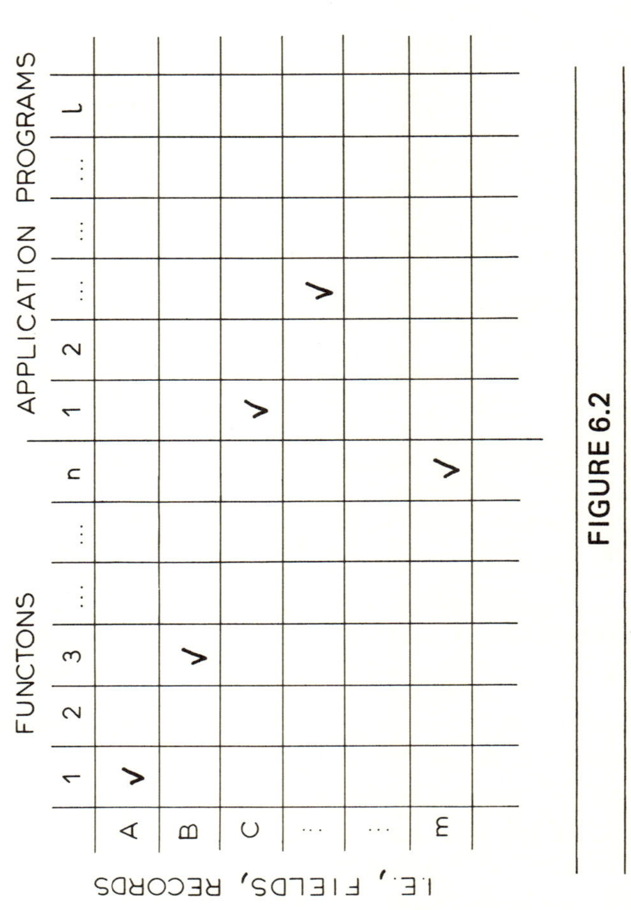

FIGURE 6.2

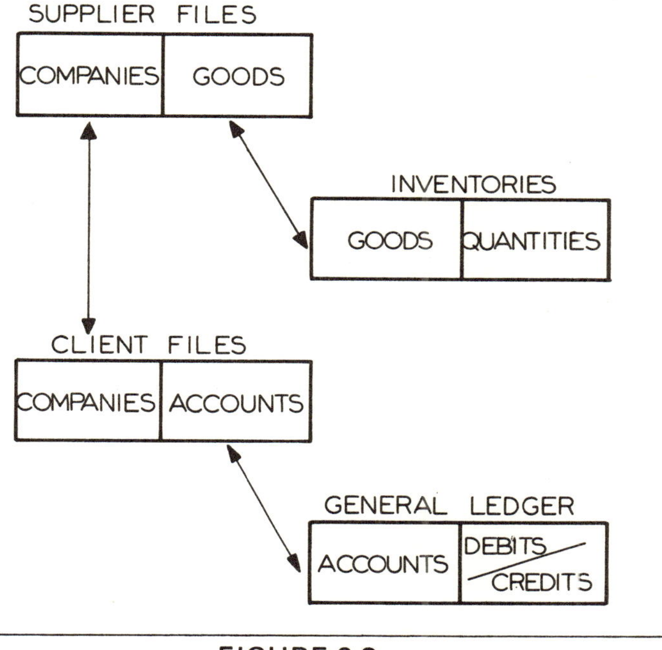

FIGURE 6.3

evaluation criteria must be announced from the early design stage. They should include:

> object modularity,
> fault tolerance, and
> control

A careful, detailed study must settle these issues in order to establish solid procedures for databases.

CONTENT ADDRESSABLE APPROACHES

This is a subject which will gain in importance in the 1980's and will concern mainframes rather than minis. Associative or recognition memory differs from conventional memory by eliminating serial searching.

The principle is simple. An item may be accessed simply by being named. If it is present, those locations which have it, recognize it and respond instantly, reducing search time (compared to conventional memories) and the amount of money and memory space invested in conventional software.

Generally, recognition memory (REM) can be written into and read from ordinary memory, but it also has parallel processing functions that include

recognize, and
multiwrite

Multiwrite is the ability to write data into multiple locations with a single instruction. For instance, the user can write data into recorders; into all responders to a preceding recognize operation or sequence of recognize operations; or, if such is the case, into all nonresponders.

Some complex operations that are made possible by the abilities of REM include:

1. Incrementing the count field of all records meeting specified recognition criteria.
2. Bit by bit comparison of an input pattern with stored patterns.
3. Locating the record having the maximum value for a specified byte position or field (e.g., the count field).
4. Similar to "3" for minimum value.
5. Various logical operations.

Furthermore, careful study will indicate the wisdom of using:

6. Various logical operations upon flags.

As the above examples illustrate, an associative or recognition memory is most useful if it has a very large word size—much larger than that of ordinary computers. This is, for example, the case with IBM's System 38, which presents potential capabilities for the implementation of REM.

Current technology sees to it that the present day associative memories have generally been built with their own tailor-made CPUs, capable of operating with very large word sizes. This will not necessarily be true tomorrow. As the costs of processing capacity and memory storage drop, we will see increasing use of REM approaches incorporated into computing equipment as a matter of course, and an impact, by this fact, on DB design.

OPTIMIZING THE DB FACULTIES

It is quite evident that a good deal of emphasis should be placed on database design. But some of the goals (and the criteria) are, we said, competitive with one another, and there are also contradictory assignments in terms of aims.

To sort these problems out the right way, let us review the most important issues, considering where each one may lead. The goals set must be reasonable, dividing into the following classes.

Goal 1: Device Independence.

All protocols used within the DB, and all the routines relating to memory devices should be transparent to the user. The now leading policy of a "one level memory" should eventually be adopted and served through virtual storage.

Goal 2: Location Independence.

As stated in the beinning of this chapter, this means that, within a distributed environment, DB handling will assure that the specific location of IE is transparent to the user, and the program or processes. This presupposes that no physical addressing is being used.

Goal 3: Regenerate rather than recall.

By storing a simple algorithm we can order the computer to regenerate data rather than storing all detail and searching into trillion bit memories to get the information we need.

We have underlined in a preceding chapter that it might be easier and better to reobserve something rather than to retrieve stored information. And the leading hypothesis today is that this is the way the mind works.

Goal 4: Simultaneous Update Mechanism.

This is one of the most challenging problems with distributed databases (we will return to it when we talk of DDB). It means that the system must provide for continued updating in the face of outside noise and with the probability that some of the component DB sections may be failing.

These four goals are realistic and point to a desire to obtain practical results. They account for the fact that the system, and its DB structure will be integrated into an application environment, and this environment will impose operating constraints. Many of them will be relative to transaction processing, online handling and communications requirements.

THE COMMUNICATIONS PERSPECTIVE

The implementation phase will require a good deal of software support—for DB not only database management but also communications routines. This has to be located and evaluated prior to final design commitments. The supporting software should be modular. The reference is valid for:

> *the communications software*—which is practically the transport mechanism.

The handling software should support one copy of data. This remains with the originating office; while a log of all activities can be obtained in one or multiple copies.

> *the transaction software,* needed to handle the transaction proper; the traffic issues; and the commands.

As far as the system is concerned, transactions traffic and commands are seen as data.

> *the command interpreter* includes the execution of commands, and operates on *one* local DB.

In other words, the command interpreter program receives the DB commands and is responsible for their execution with respect to the local database.

> *the command distributor* routes the commands to the place where data resides; and handles transaction recovery.

The end user (man or process) will communicate with the segments of the database via a DTE (data terminating equipment). The transaction he initiates may involve the examination and/or updating of various parts of the database (parts which may reside in different nodes).

The database command distributor will establish which node contains the relevant information; control the overall handling of a transaction; and assure that the data is brought in an error-free form from the residual node (host) to the location where it is needed.

> *the DB handler* administers a local, most likely, micro- or mini-computer run database.

Precisely, the mission of the database handler is to manage the access to the database. The following basic commands are used:

> start transaction,
> operating primitives,
> backout transaction,
> end transaction.

Start transaction gives an indication that a new transaction is started. The database software responds with a (unique) identification for that transaction. The start transaction may be followed by any number of commands.

After all commands have been executed, a transaction may be ended in one of two ways: through *backout*, the transaction is revoked. The changes, which should be brought about in the integrated database because of the various commands issued, are not executed.

The *end transaction* is the counterpart to the start transaction, when everything is completed. The transaction is made final; that is, all changes in the database because of the commands issued are incorporated definitely in the IE. We will return to these functions when we discuss transport protocols.

DECIDING ON DATA VOLUMES

The amount of data to be distributed may be large or small. The frequency of updates high or low. Different specific cases must be considered (Figure 6.4). There are no precise rules for adopting one solution over the other. The tendency in distributing small amounts of data is simply to replicate them if the realtime update frequency is low. The additional storage cost is low and this specific case presents no severe simultaneous update problems.

For a small amount of data and a high update frequency, replication becomes unattractive because of the heavy communications burden. Even though the update rate is high, most action is to the local partition. However, if the amount of data is large, the best approach is to partition, unless both a high rate of exceptions and update frequency mandate centralization. In either case, the challenging factor in partitioning data is the requirement to change the *home location* of a particular IE because of changing patterns of access.

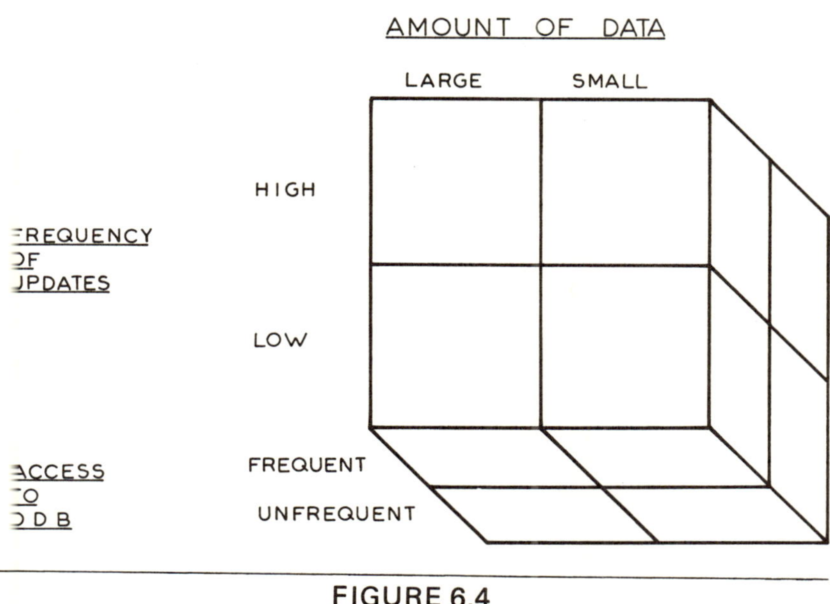

FIGURE 6.4

Another challenge is deadlock. Deadlock problems that can arise in centralized multiprogramming systems also arise in a distributed environment. The solution can be more flexible because of the distribution of physical and data resources.

One way to prevent deadlocks is to request all required resources at the beginning of the transaction. This is a demanding task because the resource requirements are often data dependent and not known at the beginning of the transaction.

Yet efficient deadlock avoidance calls for advance knowledge of the resources used by the transactions. This permits one to determine, at each point in time, whether the sequence of transactions that have been initiated but not completed is sufficiently valid, and if the transactions can run to completion.

Furthermore, for recovery purposes, audit trails and checkpoint dumps must be used. When a failure occurs, all transactions are suspended while the system tries to recover, using the before-and-after maps. Failing this, the audit trail is backed up to the last checkpoint dump, and the dump is copied into the database and processed forward, using the audit trail, to the point of suspended operation.

Of course, it is prudent to maintain an up-to-date duplicate copy of the data to speed recovery of storage failures.

Problems encountered with DDB revolve, to a large extent, around the subject of *internal consistency*. To assure it, we need a set of predicates. Say that there is a transaction, and a given algorithm manages the update mechanism. This must provide for

locking prerequisites.

A local controller asks the regional or central controller for the right to handle the transaction. The transaction must wait until permission is given by the central controller. The problem here is that, if the central controller crashes, the system is down.

backup policy.

To avoid time out, somewhere a backup facility must exist to assure that, if the central controller crashes, system update can go on.

decentralized locking algorithm.

When a transaction wants to update, it asks the local (not central) controller. The local controller asks the other local controllers for permission to update. We will return to this issue when we speak of voting algorithms in connection with the simultaneous updating mechanism.

DATABASE MIGRATION

Quite often, within a distributed database system, the data are used only once, or they may not even be used at all. Therefore, databases need pruning and vigilance. DDB optimization can be assisted through simulation studies, but tuning requires elaborate database processing statistics for performance purposes.

The basic structure of a performing database should be stable, but the contents of a DB record may change as a function of use requirements. This is a prerequisite, as databases operate within dynamic environments.

In many cases, the type of change is the addition of new data items. The collected data usually have a hierarchical structure that may be as evident in the physical layout of the data as it is in the logical relationships among the information elements.

The types of reports needed by performance analysts contain many common features. One of the most valuable is *data migration*. A DDB must provide a data set migration facility. Migration mechanisms call for address tables that are accessible at all times to authorized users (and processes).

Such a facility must be supported by use statistics, characterized by the following attributes:

1. IE marked with the date last referred to.

2. IE not referred to for more than a specified number of days should be compressed and migrated from a local to a central site, or from the online disc volume to demountable disc volumes, stored offline.

3. The number estimated to maintain a safe level of online space available should be calculated in function of use needs.

4. If a user refers to a migrated IE, the system should inform him that it had been migrated, telling him how to obtain it.

5. Users should list the names of all migrated IE; voluntarily migrate IE not needed in the near future; and erase unneeded IE.

A more sophisticated mechanism should see to it that, if a user repeatedly specifies migrated IE, this is restored automatically without additional action. Alternatively, the user should have the faculty to initiate the restoration process, waiting until the restoration is completed.

IE migration routines should be designed with the objective of increasing the productivity and effectiveness of online users; allowing them to spend more time on their work and less time on defining or manipulating IE.

This greatly improves the speed of problem analysis. Similarly, IE handling routines should free the user from dealing with the details of input and output formatting, also automatically performing many useful forms of error control.

Other improvements may result from a lowering of the time that users wait on the "eligible list" for storage and the time they wait for pages while in storage. Reducing storage contention through proper migration indirectly increases the CPU time available to users by lowering the CPU time used for IE handling. Having more dispatchable users in storage increases the CPU utilization.

The relationship between IE transfer rate and page-in time should also be studied:

> at lower page transfer rates, the page-in time is relatively insensitive to the paging rate;

> at higher page transfer rates, the page-in time rises rapidly as the paging rate goes up;

> the specifics of interactivity depend on the particular system configuration;

> channel contention, speed of paging devices, control unit contention, disc access speed, and so on, influence the time distribution.

If there is insufficient main memory available for IE storage, the users are in a wait state longer than they should be. The system can react to the shortage by placing users in the eligible state. The need to do more remote IE transfers might also cause a high paging rate, and that would overload the paging system, thereby causing further delays in interactive communications. Finally, dynamic studies on storage access—particularly within a distributed information environment—should consider both:

> query type traffic, generated through man/information communications, and

> communications processes in the DIS.

Special attention should be given to interlocks due to processes operating in a synchronous mode within the network.

7 Database Protocols

INTRODUCTION

Access to the elements contained by one program (mainly batch) in a given database which contains custom-made records and fields, poses no particular challenges. The problems start when the DB and its information elements are accessible to many users: from processes to interactive terminals. We need a system of traffic lights to regulate the operations, and this we do through protocols.

As stated in Chapter 1, a protocol is a rule of conduct. It is a formal set of conventions governing the format and control of data—whether for communications purposes or for transfers effected inside the machine and its database. The protocols comprise well defined procedures which are clearly understood by all parties. They constitute logical levels of connections between the database segments, local or remote.

Batch procedures do not require elaborate rules of conduct. The use of protocols has come to the foreground with the time sharing engine; a machine that both performs calculations and moves data from one location to another under the control of explicit instructions. Protocols serve a purpose similar to traffic light systems. They can handle many processes (or people) using the computer simultaneously.

Since the early to mid-1960's, time sharing has enabled many users to maintain, write, and change programs; cause programs to be executed; and interact with programs during execution—all within a reasonable response time and in a systematic manner. The last two points are what really makes a computer system a time shared service. To interact with a program with fast response time during execution means either a time sharing system or a dedicated computer. The advantage of an orderly systematic procedure has, on the other hand, been assured through protocols.

LAYERED SOLUTIONS

Protocols can exist at different levels: from physical, such as the terminal and the modem, to the establishment of the communications link and the database access. Figure 7.1 illustrates the division of relevant protocols into thirteen layers that comprise a full communication. This division is necessary to specialize each layer to the work to be performed and also for reasons of modularity.

When the technological characteristics, conventions or standards describing one layer change, all that is needed is to rewrite the software for that layer rather than having to revamp the whole system from end to end.

Protocols reflect the network architecture. ISO has, for instance, established the line access protocol "A" (LAP "A") for vertical, hierarchical solutions, and LAP "B" for horizontal. Today, however, direction is mainly toward horizontal (symmetric) solutions in network structure and organization. This implies that every nodal database is on the same level as all other nodal databases in the network. Though each nodal DB is an entity within itself, such DB taken together compose one integrated database (IDB).

A *transport protocol*, able to provide an interface between the communications software in different nodes, is a good example of handling the work of three layers: routing, virtual circuit and flow control. If we have communicating databases (or even terminals addressing a DB), these are fundamental functions in establishing the end-to-end circuit.

The transport protocol handles aspects of the communication not covered by the underlying physical network. (An example from packet switching is the division of messages into packets.) Assuming an X.25 discipline, the user packets (from man, machine, or process) should be segmented at the level permissible by the network.

Message segmentation can be actuated from the user terminal (if qualified) or from the proper interface: packet assembly and disassembly (PAD) facility, this may be a concentrator or a network interface message processor (NIM). The latter assures that not only packet segmentation but also terminal characteristics (buffers, code) will be observed.

(For circuit switching connection the international standards are: X.20 bis for asynchronous DTE; X.21 bis for synchronous DTE. For packet switching: X.28 for S/S via PAD; X.25 for intelligent DTE; X.29 for intelligent DTE via PAD.)

A relatively universal observance is assured by international standards. But the key mission of protocols concerns getting information to the other node in a reliable way. Though it may be aware of the format of the information, the protocol is completely unaware of its meaning. In other words, the contents of the information passed are known only to the DB handlers involved in the transaction. This is true for all the layers described that are served through formal rules of conduct.

LEVEL 12	FILE ACCESS	LOGICAL	IN DEVELOPMENT
LEVEL 11	D B M	LOGICAL	
LEVEL 10	PROCESSES (A P)	LOGICAL	
LEVEL 9	TERMINAL MANAGEMENT	LOGICAL	
LEVEL 8	PRESENTATION	LOGICAL	
LEVEL 7	SESSION	LOGICAL (ON TWO USERS)	
LEVEL 6	WINDOWS	LOGICAL	
LEVEL 5	FLOW CONTROL	LOGICAL	NOT EXACTLY STANDARDIZED
LEVEL 4	VC / D	LOGICAL	STANDARD X. 25 (FOR V C)
LEVEL 3	ROUTING	LOGICAL	STANDARD X.25
LEVEL 2	DATA LINK	LOGICAL	NON—STANDARD. BUT TRANSPARENT
LEVEL 1	D C E	PHYSICAL	STANDARDIZED
LEVEL 0	D T E	PHYSICAL	NON—STANDARD. NON—TRANSPARENT

(LEVELS 3–5 are bracketed as TRANSPORT.)

FIGURE 7.1

USER LEVEL PROTOCOLS

The best operational example on data access protocol capabilities can be made at the user level. Several examples illustrate the role of user level messages in providing database access. Briefly, the procedure could be described as a three-phase operation, first:

> set-up, *then*
> data transfer, *and concluding with*
> termination.

As previously discussed, the set-up phase involves the establishment of the connection. This includes the exchange of information necessary to authenticate the user and the access to the files.

Figure 7.2 gives an idea of the primitives involved with the user layer: open, read, write, control and close. The first three may be involved in the open operation. The functions are:

> get, *and*
> execute.

The primitives just described are pertinent to the user layer. This is, however, higher up in a sequence of seven layers which include: a user interface supporting man/machine (M/M) links including query and library services; a transport layer concerned with remote file access and job networking; a logical system monitor to make virtual circuit or datagram facilities available; network routing capabilities; a data link driver to establish the communications; and two hardware layers, respectively data communications terminating equipment (modem) and DTE.

Each lower layer in the hierarchy makes its services available to the higher one up. This way, the user protocol layers profit from the services provided by the other six. Notice that most layers, particularly numbers three, four and seven, use very similar primitives such as open, read, write; but they do not use the same routines. This is a function both of the lack of standardization and differences in the finer programmatic interfaces due to the nature of the environment within which they operate.

The characteristics described did not appear overnight to serve networks and databases. They are a technological development of the three "multi-nodes," multiaccess, multiprogramming and multiprocessing, in use since the mid-1960's.

Multiaccess has been initiated from the time we attached online terminals to the machine, even slow, nonintelligent teletypewriters. It is characterized by access to the CPU at all times from a variety of external media—such as consoles, interactive units, measuring devices, and other computers.

90

The discipline of *multiprogramming* has been developed in an effort to use the internal capacity of the computer system more efficiently. Its application demands that different programs can be called into main storage and handled simultaneously. This capability leads to a multifunctional system and poses a number of prerequisites.

Multiprocessing requires that two or more processors be interconnected into a system. Each processor is able to share main memory with the others. The system can operate its component computers in a master-slave mode; but

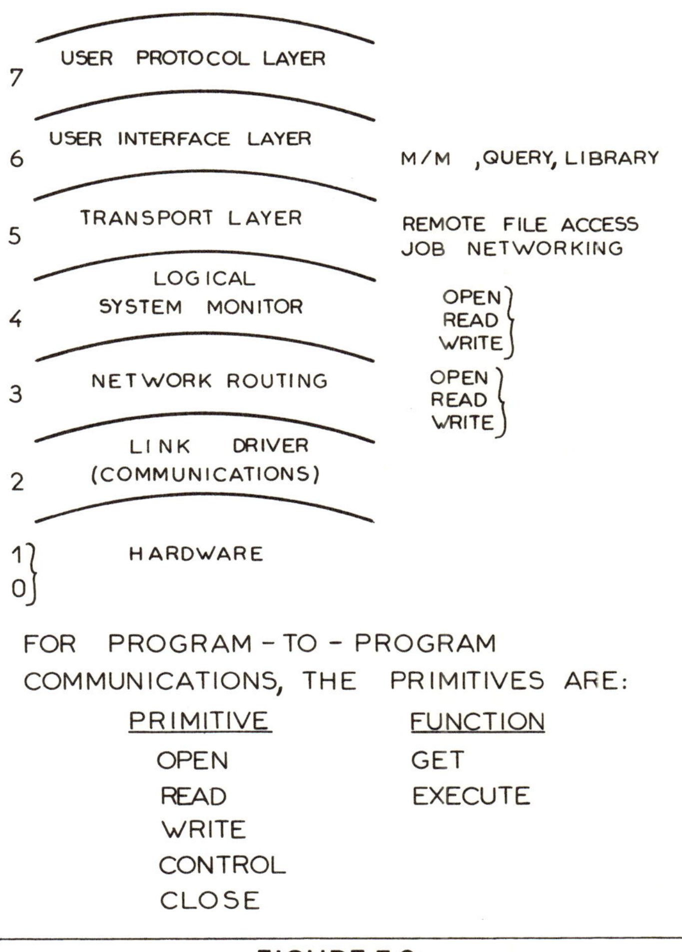

FIGURE 7.2

these functions must be performed by the OS in multimode operation. The point is that multimode operations call for the services not only of supervisory and monitor routines, but also of specialized control programs which must: host a communications network of mixed devices; manage a wide mixture of transactions which are serviced by a variety of AP; and assure effective, controlled access to the DB—including privacy and integrity.

The supervisory routines must manage resources and keep the system in operation (including restart and recovery requirements). They must maintain priority for use of the processing facility, and also provide rapid response to terminal demands.

The services should include at least a multitask controller (scheduling and support of concurrency); terminal management; data transfer between application programs; file management (scheduling and institution of all file item requests by the AP); storage management (allocation and controlling of storage for programs, including I/O areas and timing); and finally perform error handling (for hardware, software, communications, and databases).

To be assured, these functions require many routines, and the routines need status and other information. Such information is given to a substantial degree through the header and the trailer contained in a message. (Remember that a message is a file in the database.) The exact nature and structure of this information is described through the formalisms of the protocol characterizing each layer.

That is why, in the future, manufacturers will protect their customer base through network architecture in general, and protocols in particular. The differences in internal computer instruction sets will disappear as horizontal microcoders are used increasingly to emulate the instruction sets through hardware solutions of existing equipment. This way program portability will be assured, but not database portability.

A FILE TRANSFER DISCIPLINE

The transfer of the actual file data occurs after the set-up phase is completed. Software-wise, there is a need to optimize retrieval so that there is a minimal overhead for control messages (the file transfer operation itself being regulated by a flow control mechanism). Here, supervisory programs economically pool resources; provide easy file access with minimum hardware cost and software overhead; and assure a monitoring action which is transparent to most programs but able to give full access to all authorized database resources.

A key point is authorization. Following the exchange of messages to set-up a communications link, the engine requesting access sends a set-up sequence including a user identification message; attributes data; and provides specific access information. The receiver responds with an attributes message and an acknowledgement. Messages are then transmitted for each file until the end-of-file is reached on the accessed DB; the accessing engine decides it has completed the access; or an error occurs on the accessed system. In the latter case, an error message will be sent. Then, the accessing system may send an "access complete" command and wait for a response which terminates access or try to recover, using the appropriate message.

To terminate access prior to end-of-file, the accessive system sends an 'access complete" command and waits for the same response. This disconnects or accesses another file. For retrieval, error messages are sent synchronously over the logical link.

For record retrieval purposes, transfer is, in principle, similar to the aforementioned case except that a control file message must be sent by the accessing process for each record to be accessed. When end-of-file (EOF) is reached while accessing a file, the accessed process sends the message "end of file detected." If a file request specifies a nonexistent record, or an error is detected during access, the accessed process will return an appropriate error signal.

Furthermore, distributed databases have special requirements for data flow management along the communication paths leading to the databases. As communications systems extend from a simple point-to-point path to multi-point networks, the need for a "machine-to-machine grammar" so machines can converse with each other in an orderly manner becomes apparent. Thus, we return to the references made concerning the functions of protocol. At each layer, they must allow a volume of information to be transmitted in a given time period, effectively reducing cost per unit volume of data transmission. In addition to transmission of standard text, other functions performed by the protocol include acknowledgement of rejection, error detection, retransmission after error, and other sequences. Protocol analysis and design is a complex and challenging procedure. It represents the highest level of a complete data communications and database handling procedure. In a way, this is the DB/DC equivalent to the software troubleshooter. The difference is that with protocols practice is still thin.

FILE TRANSFER PROTOCOLS

The service needed to transfer files between different hosts, minis and terminals can easily involve more than access to a file and its transfer by a transport medium. It may be necessary to provide for added services, such as code conversion; create a file copy in another physical or logical resource; and assure security/protection.

Online transfer is the preferred solution (for evident reasons), as offline transfer (for instance, through cassette or floppy) takes time and is prone to errors. Both the online and the offline transfer share common problems, such as incompatibility of peripheral devices, storage media and data codes. These problems, some resulting from historical reasons, add to overhead and more errors.

Both online and offline file transfers have prerequisites. Among the requirements with data communications are; control languages, OS, DBMS, and file management capabilities. The operation on file transfer must be organized under the system control of the destination host. But, if the preparatory work is well done, the user will benefit from a fast, reliable, controlled activity.

A protocol based file transfer service presents one standard interface to the user. Additional operations on the copied file can be managed during the transfer of the data, such as: conversion of file structure; add-on functions; recovery procedures; the handling of data structures; copy of data files from and to mainframes and/or minicomputers; transfer of program modules, tables and so on; and, if need be, remote spool services.

Two basic components constitute the file transfer architecture. One concerns the communications function and the other that of databasing. The functions of a communication protocol can be divided into:

> framing,
> link management, *and*
> data transfer.

Framing is basically executed at the receiving end of the link. It consists of locating the beginning and the end of the bit stream sent over the link.

The process of *link management* is precisely controlling transmission and reception, over links where two or more sources and two or more destinations are active—that is, connected to the channel in a given direction.

Data transfer is the process of transmitting sequentially and with EDC (error detection and correction faculties) user data over the link. Among data transfer features are:

> pipelining,
> piggy backing, *and*
> acking/nacking.

We have only mentioned the last one. Data transfer mechanisms or (when they exist) the higher layers must assure that outgoing data from a link are the same as incoming data to the link. To perform this at the node level (assuming nonintelligent lines) it is necessary to use identification numbers (per packet) and routines able to detect missing and duplicated (packets), always maintaining information on (and for) senders and receivers.

The functions revolving around a server providing access to files in the involved DBMS are required at the database level. A control activity supervising and synchronizing the operations of the server is also needed.

One control activity and two servers are needed in the general file transfer process. The one on the host where the source file resides is called the "producer." The other on the destination host where the file is to be transferred is called the "consumer."

The control activity on a host represents the interface to the user. It supervises the two users. The flow of commands for the synchronization and controlling of the server take place between the user site and the DBMS. (If these DBMS participate in a network, then the data transfer between producer and consumer can be performed through a direct link.)

Synchronization leads to the need to establish a file transfer protocol. Most files have a structure that is ignored by a conventional file transfer protocol, but could be exploited by identifying elements that are invariant under normal operations. For instance, classes of files could be identified according to their content, and the file transfer protocol be specific; or another kind of transaction involving a file transfer protocol may be required in which a mapping is necessary to reduce the quantity of information transported from one system to another. This requirement is likely to grow in importance when using public networks which charge for the quantity of data handled.

DATA COMPRESSION

Techniques exist to compress data prior to transmitting, expanding it back to its original state after reception. One possibility is strings of blanks compressed to two characters. The first is a count of deleted blanks; the second a special sign designating blank compression.

The other possibility, strings of numerics plus six extra special characters (such as $) being compressed from eight bits per character to four bits per character plus two extra characters (count and numeric designator). Furthermore, strings of alphas plus six extra special characters (such as ?,") can be compressed from eight bits to five bits plus two extra characters (count and alpha designator). Finally, redundancy in headers is also compressed.

The start of the record "n" is compared to the start of record "$n-1$" for matching characters. Matched characters are replaced by two characters-count of matched characters, followed by a header compression designator. Formatted records receive special consideration. Formatted records have a fixed header format:

        origin,
        date,
        message type,
        message number,
        destination.

Formatted fields, except the message number, are often identical from record to record. To eliminate termination of header compression at the "message number" position due to different message numbers, header strings are compressed.

In this process, the character represents the absolute difference between the message number; the second character, the count of matched characters; a third special character is representing "special" header compression. Furthermore, data is compressed and expanded in the same buffer where it originally resided.

However, the data must not contain any of the above mentioned "control" (special) characters designating compression, to guarantee that the expansion does not erroneously try to expand noncompressed data.

Control compression identifiers are chosen to be unassigned ASCII, or EBCDIC values and can be reassigned at will. An error indicator is set during compression if any of these characters is found as the data is compressed. The routines are table driven. The programmer can choose which characters he wants included in each compression type by merely changing table entries.

A typical result of such a compression procedure is two to one. Three to one is also frequent. Compression/expansion should be done in a double buffer environment to avoid losing line time.

In order to optimize communications costs pay attention not only to data compression possibilities but also to the size of the record to be transmitted. Figure 7.3 illustrates this point by relating record size (in bytes) to transfer rates in KBPS. With current technologies an optimum seems to exist at about four Kilobytes.

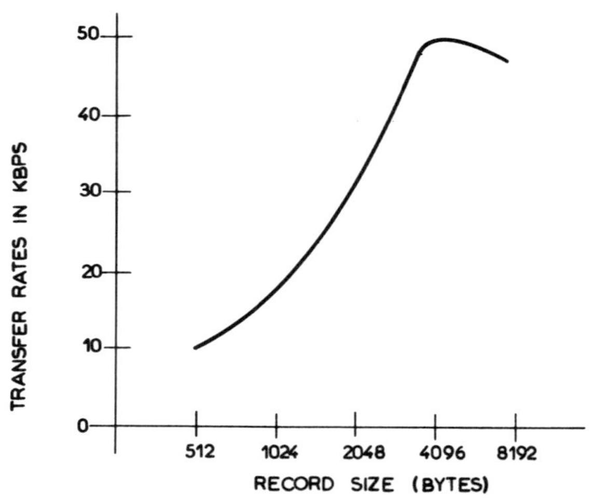

PERFORMANCE INCREASES WITH RECORD SIZE

FIGURE 7.3

8 Communicating Processes

INTRODUCTION

Protocols are an integral and valuable part of data communications, and they might not have fit in the context of this book except for two basic reasons. First, the 1980's will be characterized by an increasing interest in formal ways of data exchange between the end user and computer run DB and information elements. Second, the decade of the 1980's will highlight database organization along distributed lines.

Distributed DB imply interdatabase communication. This is not limited to the level of downline or upline file transmission. The most challenging part is that of *communicating processes*. Application programs run in a given host will require data stored in another host or in a specialized database. This brings into perspective the need for logical solutions involving multihandling communicating processes which are running on interconnected computers through a network. The reasons for logical solutions are fourfold:

1. Structuring the processing of functions.
2. Assuring modularity (extendability) in a network—both in a physical and in a logical sense (add functions, increase capability).
3. Studying the transparency capability.
4. Opening a window on the new facilities to be developed through VLSI both in communications (intelligent lines) and in databasing (logic over data).

Reliability and availability are equally important reasons. Interconnected processes running on multiconnected processors increase the overall availability of the system.

ESTABLISHING A CONFIGURATION

A configuration of communicating processes makes it possible to operate the network in a gracefully degraded mode. However, this has a number of requirements. With distributed information systems one of the most difficult requirements is to say which function (process) is running on which processor (resource).

With distributed systems, the effect of an error is not necessarily an indication that the resource is at fault. To answer the identification requirements the following layers have been included in one of the architectures under development:

1. AP,

2. support system,

3. architectural design,

4. transport facilities.

5. components (microprocessors).

Layers two, three and four have implications both on AP and on components. The model AP has been projected as a set of cooperating processes—explicitly communicating among themselves.

Usually, processes are local and involve local variables. If supports and communications are distributed, then architecture (not the processes themselves) must look after the requirements and capabilities implied by the distributed environment, considering both local needs and their integration in a total system perspective. The system has specific requirements to function in a dependable manner.

Let us look at the situation realistically. Say that a given application program is to:

> send messages,
> receive and store messages, *and*
> synchronize communications.

This is based on operations defined as part of the software machine (Figure 8.1). *Send* is a remote operation; *receive* and *store* are local operations. Remote operations have priority over local operations. Local operations can be independent of the remote, *if* the software machine has work to do (i.e. it is not blocked by missing information).

Global management (I/O control; job management; resource handling, program management, and processor handling) are three main activities of the support system layer. If one hundred programs are running and all are equipped with time out, then management of time out is a program management responsibility.

Like global management, processors too have requirements. They must handle tasks. Processor handling includes primitives dedicated to: CPU implementation (the most basic); send and receive messages; load activities. (At the architectural level, the system is considered as a network with a number of processors connected to it.) These processors must be able to communicate *asynchronously* to avoid central control (implied by *synchronous* operations which impose a nonflexible discipline). Let us study this idea in greater detail. Notice that the terms synchronous and asynchronous relate to the *processes* and not to the particular line discipline which is used (start/stop or BSC).

DESIGN PARAMETERS IN DB/DC

Some basic parameters have been used to describe the nature of communications to nodes in the network. The first of these parameters is the form of the

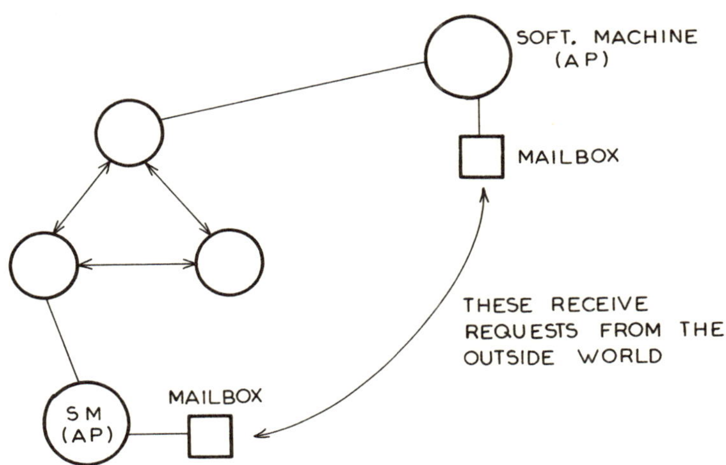

SYSTEMS CAN BE PROGRAMMED IN TERMS OF
COMMUNICATING PROCESSES

FIGURE 8.1

communication. The second is the request/response content of the communication. The third is the needed authorization.

When we refer to the form of the communication, we mean the mode in which this is carried out:

> batch (asynchronous), or
> interactive (synchronous).

In other words, the communications required for sharing or passing data between programs can be accomplished synchronously or asynchronously.

Synchronous communication implies that both programs are in execution simultaneously and that messages pass in both directions, with one program waiting for the other to respond to its last message.

In an *asynchronous communication* the sending program does not wait for a response and the two programs may not be in execution at the same time. Often, in the asynchronous mode of operation, the messages that comprise the communications are queued and processed in a batched mode.

The request/response content of the communications impacts on three issues:

> input messages/output messages
> data request/data records
> application/defined messages.

The latter denotes any communication not in the pure forms of the first two types. All classes presuppose that the means of communication may be a shared direct-access storage device or a telecommunications link.

The nature of, and the requirements imposed by, input messages/output messages lead to an investigation of this form of the communication. Implementing this data distribution service typically involves three types of remote batch:

> *one originator, one addressee.*

The storage/retrieval function acts as a mailbox service. A subscriber just selects a suitable moment for checking if there is anything in his mailbox.

> *one originator/many addressees* (current or potential)

For instance, in a typical banking application a batch of the day's rates of exchange of currencies, available to all offices (broadcasting, narrowcasting).

> *many originators/one addressee.*

Data entry applications fall in this class. In the network the batches are queued. The addressee may retrieve portions of the queue (LIFO, FIFO, batches from a specified sender or other criteria).

Finally, we must briefly return to an issue already discussed, that of *authorization*. The implementation of a mechanism for authorization/authentication calls for the presence of good protective capabilities. Typically:

1. Each user identity is covered by a password and logical function key.

2. Each console has a unique logical console key.

3. Each command function is allocated a function lock and a console lock.

A function will be carried out only if "a function key and lock match" signifying that the user is authorized coincides with a console key and lock match. This is an indication that inputting the command from a particular position is allowed.

The network control database should hold information on all relevant network entities: data links; users and their identification; internal/external names of subscribers, and so on—including their attributes and their interrelations. For instance, which user—in which subsystem. Also, which data link connects network node to end node.

INTERACTIVE APPROACHES

The design parameters we are outlining clearly indicate the type of prerequisites demanded by a network-wide database supported by minicomputers. These parameters suggest a new way of looking at databases. Storing vital company information in a distributed manner, properly classified and identified, supported by data dictionaries, and interactively available to the end user, opens up all kinds of possibilities for utilizing computers and communications in management's decision-making processes and routine company activities.

But, we must repeat, there are prerequisites to be met: organizational studies; software packages; a database administrator function; online query facilities. Meeting these prerequisites would give us a capability we did not have before. A distributed environment would maximize accessibility to data resources and also provide a means of sharing costly equipment. It is becoming increasingly apparent that good business organization includes meeting data requirements, performance, and availability needs. These are vital tools in the competitive marketplace.

The concept of a network able to support a distributed database is not necessarily the prerequisite to DDB. Databases can be distributed on minicomputers (and mainframes) *with* and *without* interconnection via network. However, "without" ends up by losing the overall picture of the DB. Also, it does not allow mass storage and array processors.

"With" a network solution involves many prerequisites and brings job networking into perspective. These prerequisites include:

1. the whole range of applications,
2. memory to memory communications (which are part and parcel of communicating DB),
3. file access algorithms,
4. I/O service of all types,
5. I/O accesses—particularly those of an interactive nature,
6. priorities,
7. interfaces,
8. protocols, and
9. functional definitions.

The queuing functions necessary for process to process type communications are a vital part of the supporting software. Programs may enqueue messages; then dequeue them. When a message becomes available, the machine must have the ability to continue handling the process which has requested it.

Furthermore, there are: delays in communications; prolonged blocking of IE; different levels of blocking probability; and an increased chance for deadlocks.

Because of the need for gateways to translate between different models' and codes' interfaces, heterogeneous networks and/or DB create additional problems. Present day solutions are of a sequential type and this is not the best solution for distributed DB operations.

Prerequisites for job networking are best initiated during the design phase:

> starting with database integration,
>
> then, segmentation,
>
> the establishment of a hierarchy of IE, (primary and secondary indexes), and
>
> the building of a DB prototype.

Thus, the structure defined by the database administrator (DBA) can be tuned prior to implementation.

The prerequisites for interactive approaches concern primarily the mini- and microcomputer levels. Those of networking range in scope from micro to mainframes. But there is another area of interest in DB design which concerns, in the first place, the mainframes and, in the second, the mini supported databases. Not the micro. This area is bulk transfer.

Communicating databases lead to the capability of a bulk transfer of data, and pose specific requirements. It would be redundant to underline the need for a computers and communications network and for DB planning. Just the same, the requirement for support media of bulk capacity, high reliability and fast access is self-evident.

Perhaps less evident, but just as real, is the need for a well defined "DB engine" (Figure 8.2) which will support both:

> the physical management of the storage media, and

> the communications discipline necessary to use the network.

The communications discipline involves a data link; routing; virtual circuit (provided X.25 is adopted); and flow control facilities. The latter mechanism should also assure the capability of making up for possible architectural differences.

(Let us add that layered approaches are the modern way of handling DB, DC and OS (operating system) problems at large. See also D.N. Chorafas: "Data Communications for DIS" Petrocelli/McGraw-Hill, NYC 1980.)

Communicating databases will come into action in order to support concurrent batch, interactive processes and program development activities. Solutions must face-up to the fact that both priorities and workloads are dynamically changing, and the functions to support these activities must be present.

To run the physical devices in an intelligent way, the DB engine requires "logic over data" approaches which can handle both its own housekeeping (Figure 8.3) and buffering solutions (Cache) designed to accelerate data access.

The decision "where to locate the data files" is an integral part of communicating databases. The following criteria can be used as a guideline:

1. read activities,
2. updating,
3. response time,
4. data load on network,
5. splitting of access files,
6. DBMS availability,
7. independence of DB sectors vs. dependence,
8. synchronous vs. asynchronous update.

Operating statistics are of vital importance in establishing how far these criteria should be used. Supervisory programs should be in a position to monitor synchronous and asynchronous occurrences that take place during execution. And this is true of other machine-defined events such as message enqueue/dequeue, I/O requesting completion, errors in data transmission and the like.

DB ENGINE
FLOW CONTROL
VC
LINK
PHYSICAL
VC
LINK
PHYSICAL
FILE ACCESS
VIRTUAL STORAGE
DBMS
FA
VS
DBMS
AP
PRESENT. CONTROL
SESSION CONTROL
FLOW CONTROL
VIRTUAL CIRCUIT
ROUTING
LINK
AP
PC
SC
FC
VC
ROUTING
LINK
* FOR INSTANCE, A PERMANENT VIRTUAL CIRCUIT

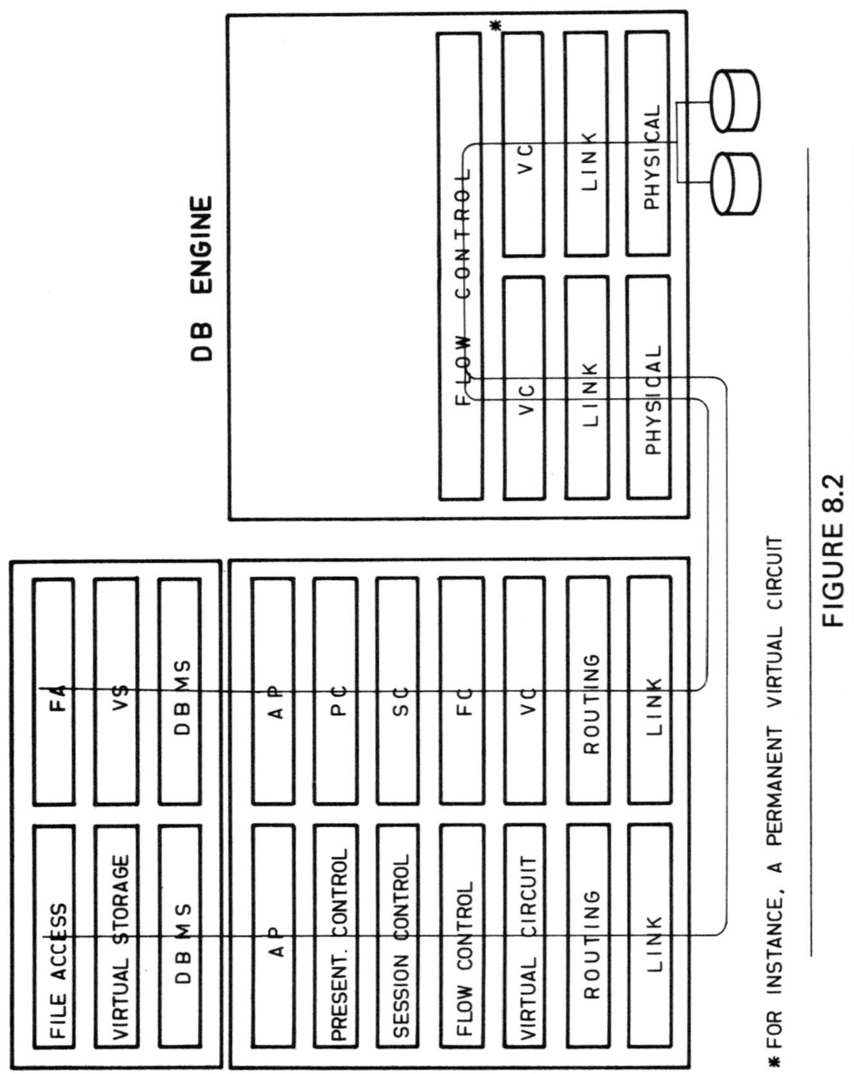

FIGURE 8.2

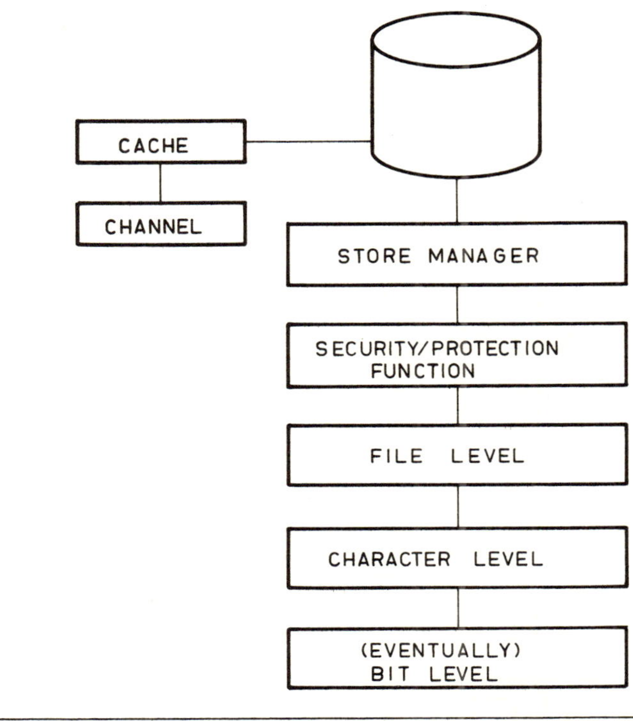

FIGURE 8.3

DB/DC RELEASES

As with any DB architecture, the objective of the early releases is to project a roadmap on system provisions. With this as a basis, users can configure their current and projected equipment to meet requirements; assure a transition path from current file access solutions to networking; and project the possibility to internetwork microfiles with the developing VAN (public value added networks).

DB/DC software, written to support communicating processes, should offer users the choice of employing both private high speed lines for their distributed mainframes and VAN for the distributed DTE (data terminating equipment). The software should also make it possible to implement a layered functionality:

> file access prerequisites
> network characteristics
> the DTE, and their
> topological distribution.

It should assure consistent "user" interfaces: at the terminal level; the processes (AP); the addressable information elements; and the different administrative languages in use to facilitate the duties involved in running the network. Furthermore, through a network control center facility it should be possible to distribute the status, and error information at the level of the DB component itself.

For internetworking reasons, it is advisable for the system architecture to follow the ISO approach of "Open Systems" characteristics—including the definition of the activity boundaries of the DTE and of the host(s). This involves the support of:

> *port(s)* which are hardware bound.
>
> *sockets* (or End Points; Entities, E) with both software and hardware boundaries. (Sockets act in a way similar to a telephone number: a software convention, conditioned by hardware characteristics.) and
>
> *logical communications paths* which connect socket to socket (Figure 8.4).

The software/hardware boundaries assure that the transfer of data will follow formatting rules. Entities (E) and virtual terminals (VT) are two layers within the broader terminal management (TM) layer. The goal of the virtual terminal service is to establish the formatting rules common to all communicating DTE on the network—and their databases.

The VT layer defines how terminal management looks to the inside of the system. This may include several references: Editing (CRT), Graphics, and so on. Towards the higher-up layers, the TM action can be Schema-based. In facing the lower level layers (communications), TM includes the drivers that worry about the exact specifications of each DTE type.

In different terms, a major reason for having TM is to provide a generally supported Virtual Terminal Capability. Within the framework of the *Logical DTE*, the TM layer(s) fit between session and presentation control in the one side and AP-DB in the other. The latter are higher-up layers to TM (Figure 8.5).

To support the online communications characteristics of the system a number of routines are necessary, for example, the common exchange interface, able to handle the communications between the Flow Control layer (which belongs to the networking side) and the Session Control layer (point of entry to the DTE). Typically, Session Control will define

> authentication, and
> privacy.

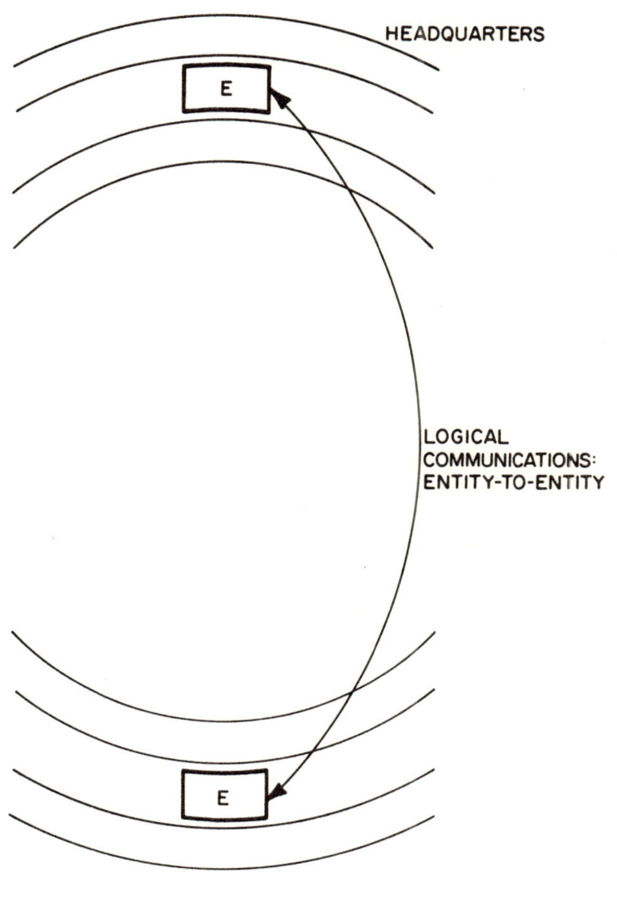

FIGURE 8.4

PHYSICAL DEVICE
F A
D B M S
A P
STANDARD
DEVICE
PROTOCOL
INTERFACE
VT
(VIRTUAL TERMINAL)
TM
E
(ENTITY; END POINT; SOCKET;
IT IS ADDRESSED BY ALL)
TERMINAL
MANAGEMENT
PRESENTATION CONTROL
LOGICAL
DTE
SESSION CONTROL
VISIBLE TO ALL AP;
(THE LOWER LAYERS
ARE TRANSPARENT)
WINDOW
FLOW CONTROL
COMMON
EXCHANGE
INTERFACE
VIRTUAL CIRCUIT
NETWORKING
THE MAIN REASON FOR TM IS TO PROVIDE A
VIRTUAL TERMINAL CAPABILITY

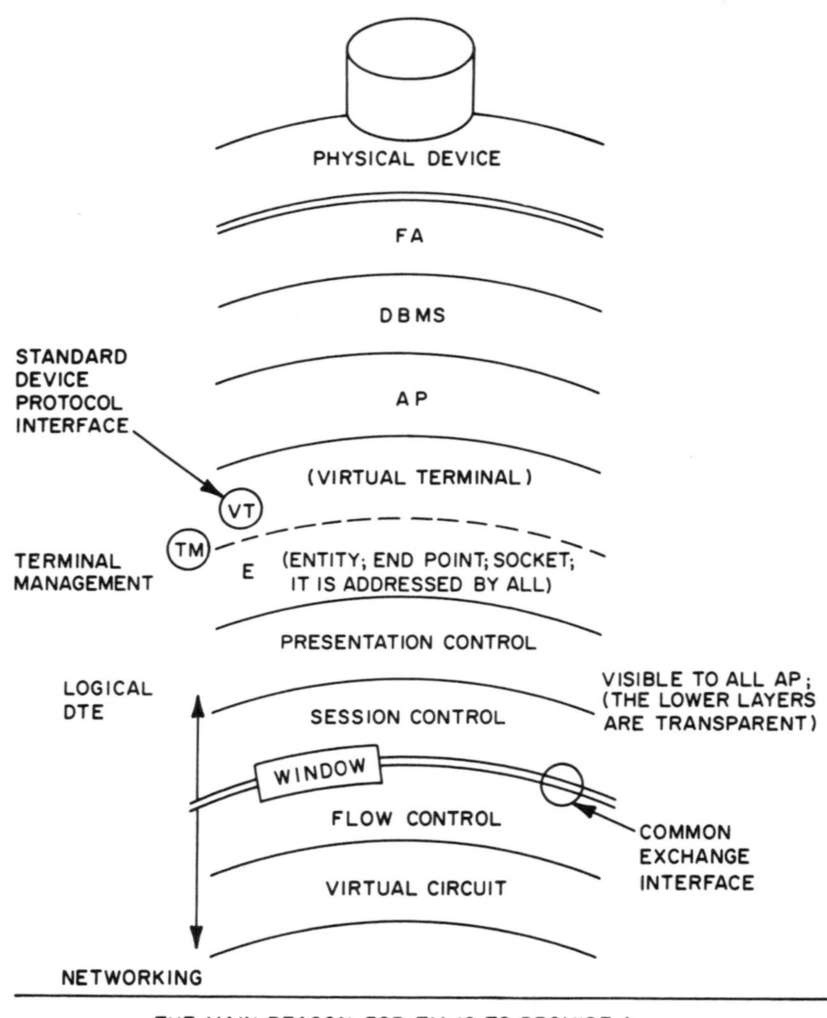

FIGURE 8.5

for all exchanges. Next to it, Presentation Control will take care of the finer programmatic interfaces, among them encryption. A standard device protocol interface will look after the formatted form of data transfer supporting the way Presentation talks to the AP (applications programs, programmed products, procedures). There can also be a nonformatted form.

Figure 8.6 demonstrates this point. If two different DTE: one at headquarters, the other at the factory level, run three procedures:

> personnel (AP 1),
> general accounting (AP 2), and
> billing (AP 3),

then AP 1 at the factory DTE needs to communicate with the host DTE. A *logical* connection will be established to assure this communication. Everything else (in terms of subordinate layers) is transparent to this logical connection.

CRITICAL FACTORS

Two features characterize a layered architecture: a dedicated software routine exists for every function; and the dialogue (between two programmers, programs, users) is not casual but structured. When we have the opportunity to implement a layered structure in databasing and datacomm, we can dedicate one mini per layer (Figure 8.7) and obtain better, more timely and dependable service.

The support of interactivity by a given process (or equipment) will provide freedom of interaction between man and information. This is one reason why (as we will see in the following chapter) the concept of interactivity is far reaching and influences not only development and usage but also software testing and maintenance.

The following six basic commands are needed to support an interactive system:

1. submission,

2. display,

3. cancellation,

4. priority handling,

5. reentry programs (multiusers),

6. conditioned commands.

Procedural requirements call for support of data independence; data structures at multiple indexes; automatic back-out; the ability to restructure text and data; access control (including authorization, authentication, and passwords); recovery and restart.

PAYROLL CALCULATION
AP
1
2
3
VT
ENTITY
PRESENTATION
SESSION
HEADQUARTERS
LOGICAL CONNECTION
(EVERYTHING ELSE IS
TRANSPARENT)
S
P
E
VT
FACTORY
AP
1
2
3
PERSONNEL
(DATA COLLECTION)
GENERAL ACCOUNTING
BILLING

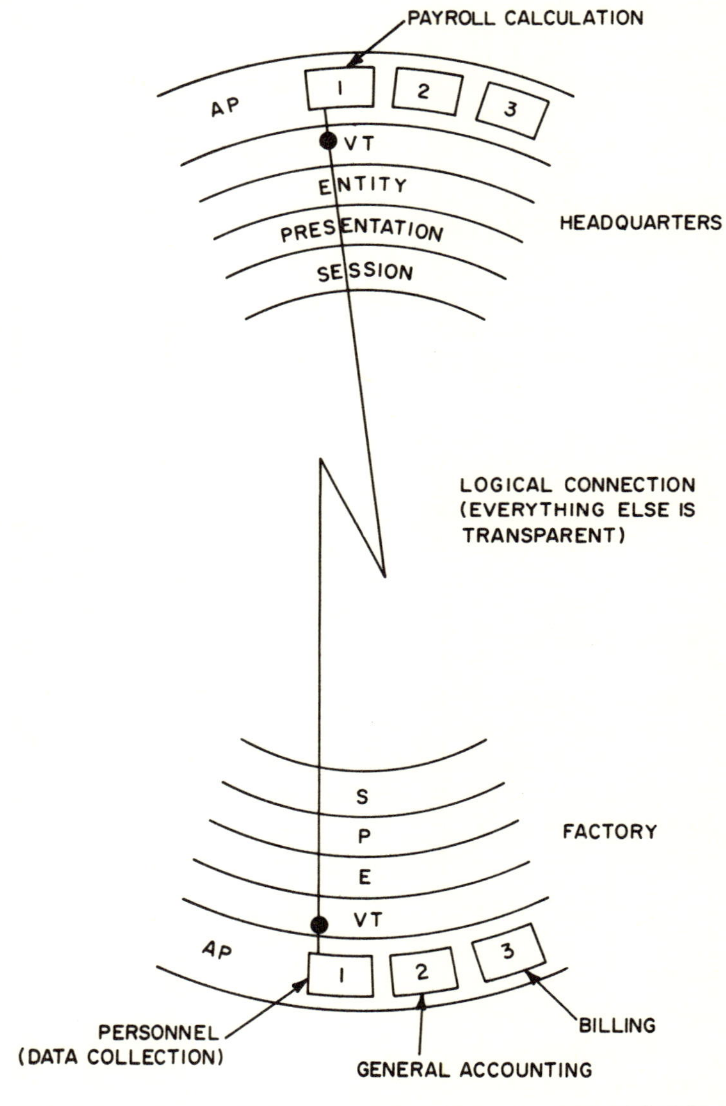

FIGURE 8.6

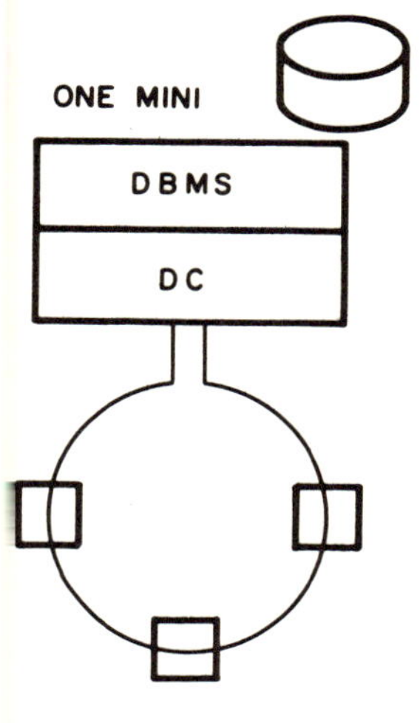

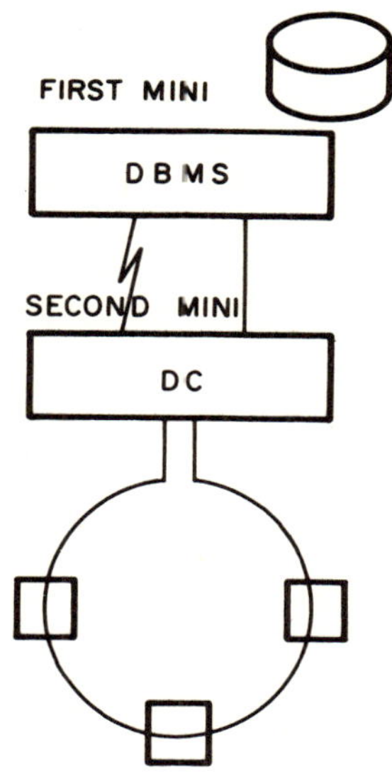

A DATACOMM ENGINE

FIGURE 8.7

Projecting, designing and implementing databasing and networking capabilities will be much more successful if the key requirements listed below are included:

1. Standardized Applications

2. A Common Data Dictionary for:

   A. Development Assistance

   B. Self Teaching

   C. Standards Capability

3. An Online Development Facility

4. Applications Modeling

   A. Test

   B. Documentation

   C. Maintenance

Chapter 11 will discuss some features the computer-based data dictionary should perform such as: processes, tables, data, text, videograms, and cross-references. Within a distributed information systems environment, organization and structure should be able to support central control, local autonomy and the end faculty of usage (Figure 8.8). In the design and implementation of any DIS, compromises among these three axes of reference must be made.

The development language chosen should be self-standing; facilitate the creation of information elements; and be supported by a number of utilities: select; copy; dump; restore; debug; map; data-definitions; and cross-reference.

A structured discipline should avoid the usual spoilage of resources. For over thirty years of practice, each program repeats: definitions; controls; data descriptions and edits. The result is that about sixty percent of programming effort is redundant.

For the proper design of a distributed information environment, choices should be based on:

1. Type of Application(s)

2. Use within the Network

3. Text and Data Load

    A. Networking

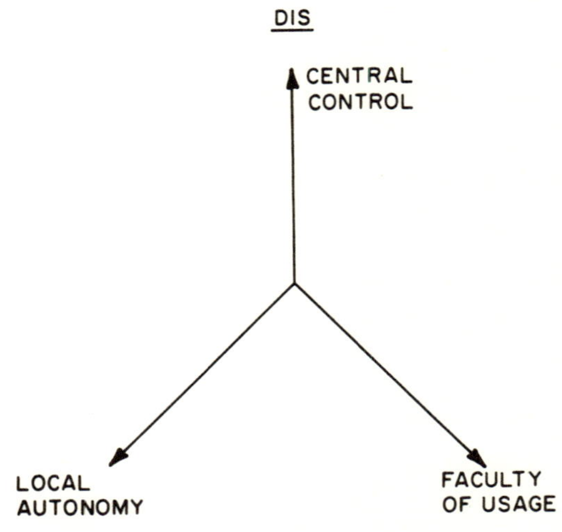

FIGURE 8.8

  B. Size of Storage

  C. Processing

4. Ability to integrate with other hardware/software, and

5. Sharing of:

  A. Applications,

  B. Database Segments,

  C. Terminals, and

  D. Lines.

Applications modeling should follow a valid methodology when projecting new user-oriented interfaces and processing routines. The designer should consider elements found in the company's storehouse of system knowledge; classifying the applications requests into:

  As is,
  Similar to, *and*
  To do.

This activity should consider all the components of the system. Figure 8.9 classifies them into four main categories; processes; information elements; videograms (for interactive applications) and print formats; tables. The common elements of a good design will be:

  1. Networking capability,

  2. Reliable data communications,

  3. Interactivity,

  4. Response time,

  5. Text and data management,

  6. DB security,

  7. Availability,

  8. Controlability,

  9. Migration capability,

 10. Flexibility and growth.

These elements can be organized into a comprehensive group of logical and physical resources required to serve a computer and communications network (Figure 8.10).

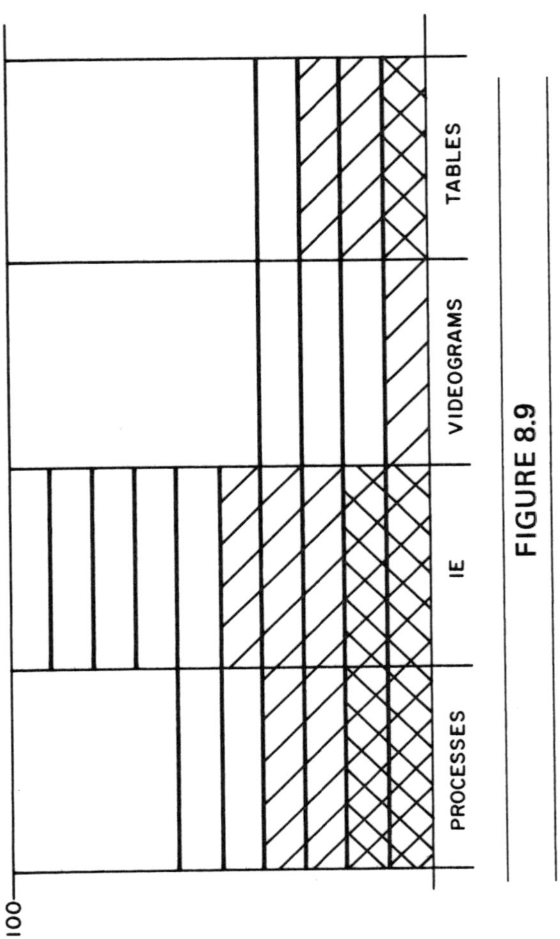

114

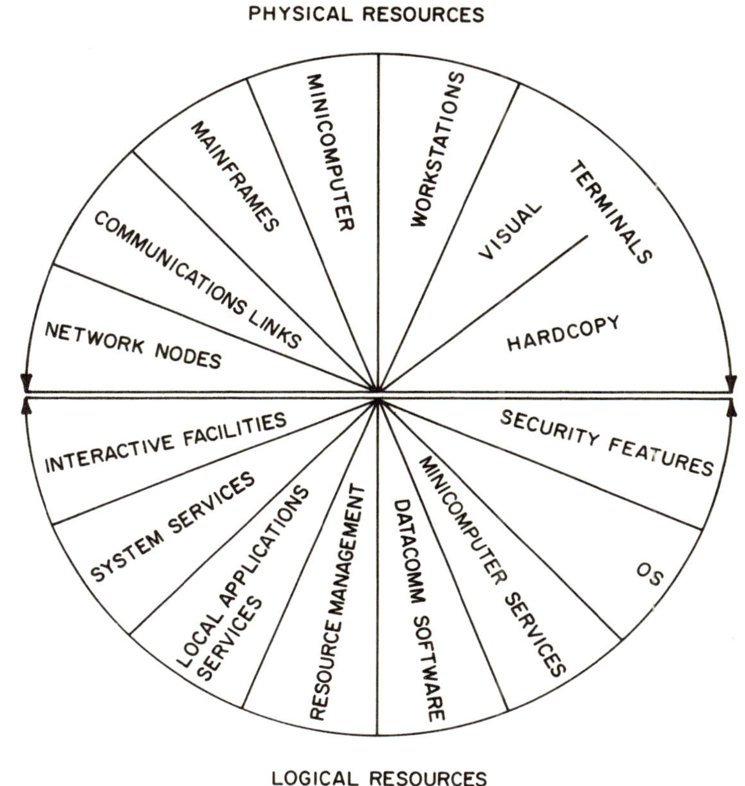

FIGURE 8.10

Design experimentation can play a key role in the development of a successful system. Typically, such a process must account for five concrete phases as Figure 8.11 documents:

1. Conceptual modeling,
2. Information element definition,
3. Program development,
4. Program and system text,
5. Steady maintenance.

Projecting a new application involves the first four phases, and there is an interplay among them and what exists in the library. The rising cost of systems development not only necessitates good methodology but also requires avoiding redundant effort.

115

DISTINCT ENVIRONMENTS
EMULATOR
DB
APPLICATION IMAGE
1. CONCEPTUAL MODELING
DD
I. E.
EXISTING
I.E
NEW
2. I.E. DEFINIT ON
"n" TIMES
DB
DOCUMENT
LIBRARY OF ROUTINES
GENERATOR
3. PROGRAM DEVELOPMENT
DB
TEST
DOCUMENT
4. PROGRAM AND SYSTEM TEST
DB
DOCUMENTATION
LIBRARY
GENERATOR
5. STEADY MAINTENANCE

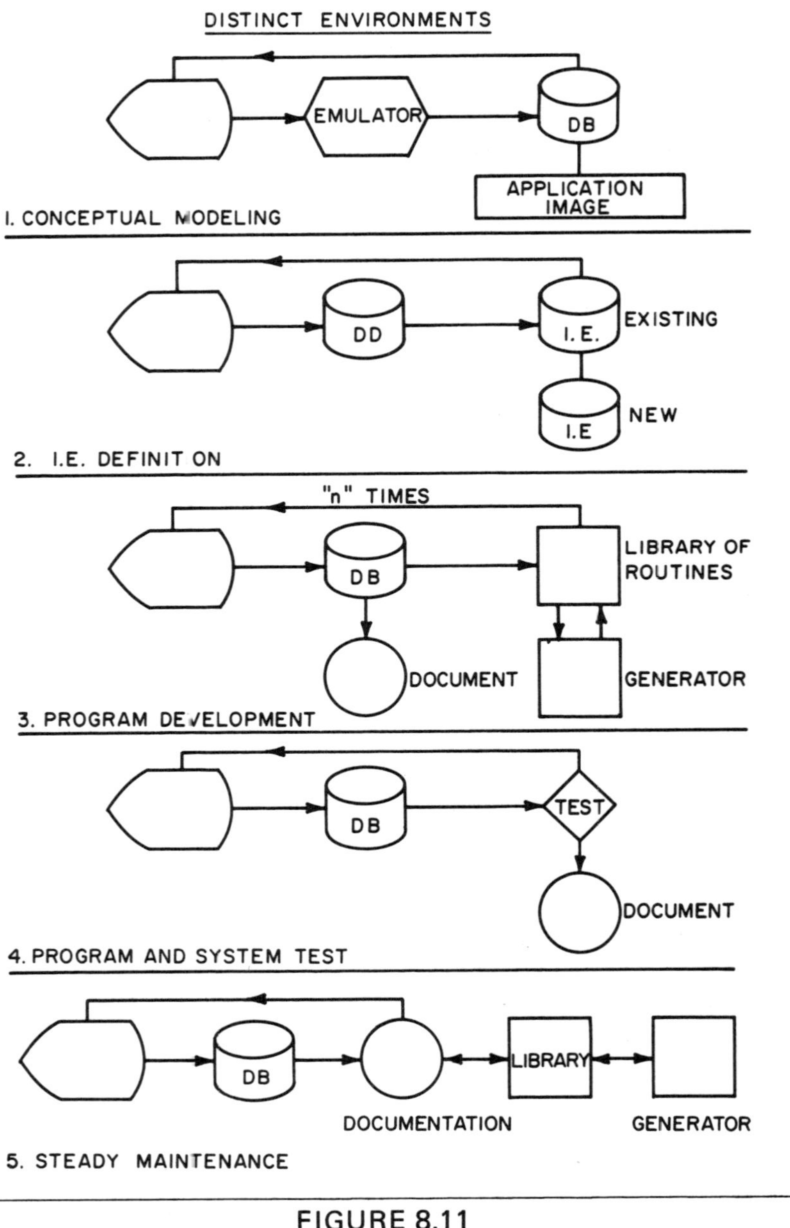

FIGURE 8.11

9 Interactivity

INTRODUCTION

Create the information elements; integrate them into a database; store them in proper form; display, modify, and/or delete the IE or whole files; create a directory and data description—these are prerequisite activities for working with databases. But when prerequisities have been completed, other problems must be solved.

Form access procedures mean establishing a methodology for opening a file; locating any IE in that file; making the data available to the program requesting it by moving the IE into a buffer, and closing the file. Other processes necessary in man/information communication are the terminal access procedures that provide read/write access to a terminal. These include:

> opening a terminal as a file,
> writing output from the program buffer to the terminal,
> reading input from the terminal to this or another buffer, and
> accessing remote databases.

Fundamentally, these procedures represent an evolution of manual solutions. Manual approaches have been practiced for many years: They may be stand-alone; not necessarily related to a detailed IE; or they may contain data in addition to the search item; and the user must explicitly add or delete all entries. But with an integrated, computer run solution, the IE should be related to one or more detail data sets and must contain a search item.

Routines must be provided to record information about related events and allow retrieval of all entries pertaining to a uniquely identifiable entity. Batch processing and classical realtime applications emulated the manual approach. Interactivity and distributed environment applications require different solutions.

DATA ENTRY

Interactive environments call for sophisticated data entry approaches. An indispensable routine to any interactive application, the *data entry manager* must contain an interactive form maintenance program to enable the user to

> create the IE,
> store them in proper form,
> display, modify, or delete specific data sets,
> list all IE in a special file, *and*
> delete IE on entire files.

Form access procedures such as open a file, locate any IE in that file, make the form available to the program by moving it into a buffer, and close the file must be assured by the data entry system.

Terminal access procedures will typically provide read/write access to a terminal: open a terminal as a file; write output from the program buffer to the terminal; read input from the terminal to this or another buffer; access remote databases; request status information about the terminal, and invariably close the terminal file.

Data entry processes require editing procedures that validate the general content of user input to alphabetic, alphanumeric, and numeric fields and assure that form and content are correct. The same is true of high level interfaces that combine some of the IE access and terminal access operations. This interactivity between user and terminal is demonstrated in Figure 9.1. The process brings together

> the man with the problem,
> the server (OS), *and*
> the task stream.

Though this reference has been specically made for the data entry facility, it is nevertheless valid throughout the field of interactive applications. In fact, several minicomputer manufacturers developed data entry software in an experiment used to identify potential problems for supporting interactive systems. These programs were designed and implemented in an evolutionary manner to study the feasibility of a system with given attributes.

This approach introduced two main topics: the study model itself and its implementation. Results have provided insights into distributed information systems design, control, recovery, and intercomponent communications. At the same time, this data entry software answered the needs of data collection at point of origin, one of the first areas of minicomputer application.

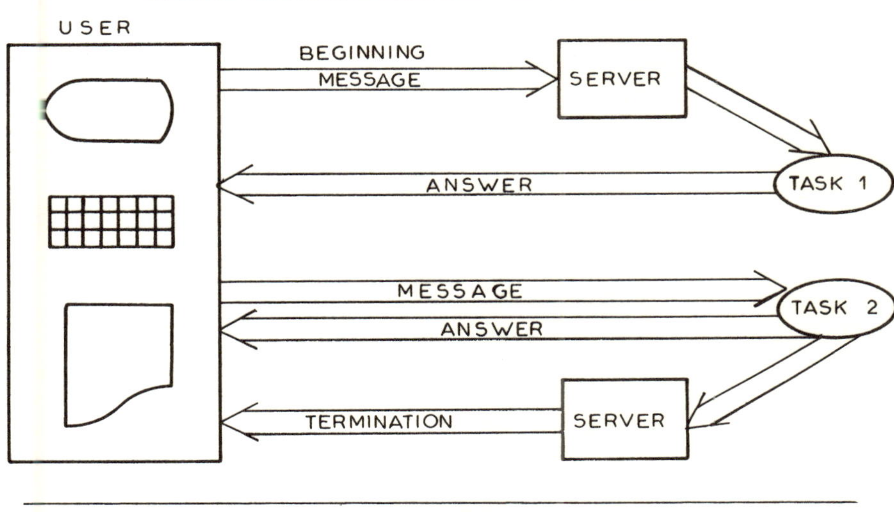

FIGURE 9.1

TRANSACTION HANDLING

Transaction handling coinvolves many elements of the information system. At least three distinct levels come into play: physical; logical; and user. Each is composed of several layers of detail (Figure 9.2). The object of the user is the single task. This coinvolves a number of functions.

All of these layers of detail need routines to run them, must be actuated to start operating and appeal to memory. Given the differences which exist between the distinct levels and their layers, the computer memory and its data is *de facto* segmented. For that reason, we have underlined that DB segmentation is a way of life (with modern IS)—whether we speak of centralized or distributed systems.

Implementing the concept of segmentation allows better utilization of time, physical and logical computer resources, and of computer memory capability. Furthermore, the proper physical segmentation to distributed systems has been preceded by the logical segmentation required for multiprogramming.

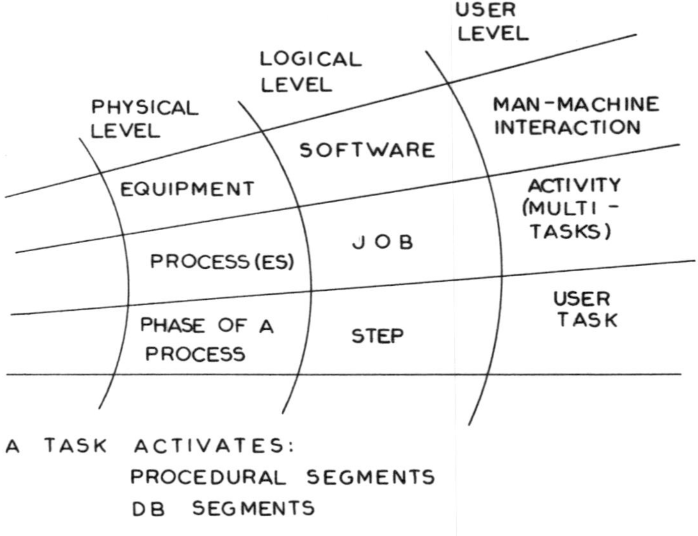

FIGURE 9.2

Figure 9.3 gives an example of three different programs using the same server element (1 E); totally different procedural segments; and some common data segments. This image of memory allocation in a centralized maxicomputer will be replicated to a large extent with dedicated, distributed machines linked through a network and sharing the same special software.

Let us repeat, distributed systems are a geographical (topological), functional, or task extension of centralized systems. But the concept of physical and logical segmentation has not been invented with DIS. It came about through multiaccess, multiprogramming and multiprocessing. Interactive solutions, implemented with distributed environments, have been a logical extension of our search for ways to reduce the complexity associated with new computer functions and ways of taking advantage of technology.

Because interactive approaches open broad and new perspectives to test the feasibility of system design, experiments and walkthroughs are advisable (particularly for the company that starts working with DDB) to identify problem areas before they are encountered in actual operations. We must identify areas that require further work, provide structure for environmental characteristics, analyze implementation alternatives, and assure ways to reduce the operational dependence on a single resource, as characterized by centralized solutions.

In this work, special attention should be given to the routines employed for transactional and DB management purposes, and to the way the database

DE FACTO DB SEGMENTATION
(3 SUBSCHEMAS)
USER AREA 1
PROCEDURAL
1 A
1 B
DB
1 C
DB
1 D
SERVER
1 E
DB
1 F
PROCEDURAL
3 A
DB
3 B
DB
3 C
DB
3 D
PROCEDURAL
2 A
USER
AREA 2
USER
AREA 3

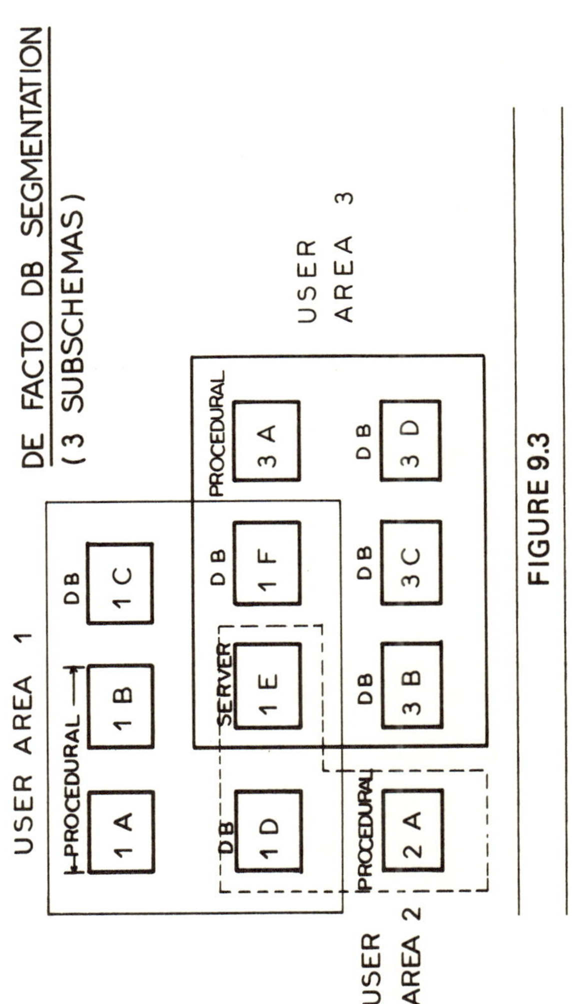

FIGURE 9.3

is used. Buffering for DDB is an example of an issue that calls for special attention. Three subjects must be carefully examined:

1. *Message buffers:* message size; message rate; transmission rate; calculation of message buffer size; and form of buffer allocation.

2. *File buffers:* including rate of file requests; block size(s); physical record(s); transmission rate; and transmission time (hold buffer). We must decide on the probability of a file *not* available when requested (the user requests are usually random).

3. *Program segment areas:* number of instructions to be executed; time to process instructions; and time to handle data: fetch, sort, store.

Distributed databases are not limited to networks of computers. It is quite reasonable to distribute data over the storage hierarchy of a single processor, with the storage devices (ordered in terms of access speed) having direct access between each level and the next higher or lower level. The most significant feature of this arrangement is the buffering of data. If data is found at any particular level, it is also present at all higher levels (more remote from the processor). Finally, journaling is an integral part of transaction handling. Preferably, it should be made on more than one media, and supported by the proper software. This function is detailed in Chapter 19.

ACCESS PATTERNS

To outline the main features of an efficient database organization projected for interactive handling, we must assure: reliability; adaptability; modularity; ease in end user training; the capability to evolute and accommodate new technologies; and expandability for experimental purposes. The whole approach will best utilize:

1. common, easily modified display and report structure,

2. a homogeneous IE design,

3. a common hardware configuration,

4. a standard command language,

5. a means for pruning data incompatibilities.

Data incompatibilities are a major problem that face the designer of a distributed DB composed of multiple software systems on a heterogeneous network. The subject is complicated by different logical structures in database systems. Since these differences are a fact of life in data processing, a method of database translation is necessary for the most general distributed network.

The art of generalized data translation is currently at the prototype stage. One of the limiting factors in the development of heterogeneous distributed database systems is the progress (or lack of it) in data translation. Two major problems currently faced concern structural and query translation.

Structural translation can involve a "brute force" machine-by-machine approach to fairly sophisticated techniques involving intermediate languages. Another crucial issue present in the study and implementation of access patterns is that of DB deadlocks.

A good file allocation scheme results in efficient utilization of a distributed database management system. However, if a distributed DBMS designer ignores file allocation, the system will probably still operate, although perhaps very inefficiently. This will not be the case if the designer fails to consider the possibility of deadlocks, which occur when two or more tasks have blocked each other from execution by locking shared portions of the database.

Deadlock in a DBMS is an unfortunate side effect of the need to establish temporary exclusive control over a portion of the database. If a record is to be updated by a task, no other task can be allowed to the record during the updating:

> failure to provide a blocking mechanism can permit incorrect information to appear in the database;

> if portions of the database may be addressed simultaneously by several tasks, then a deadlock condition may occur.

For example, two tasks that ordinarily are executed independently may both require the same two records at one time, but in reverse order.

The underlying cause of deadlock in database systems is the organization of conventional secondary storage media. In order to optimize the utilization of secondary storage, several requests must be processed simultaneously. This organization tends to reduce disc head movement and latency, which is often the limiting factor in the performance of database access.

In principle, the deadlock problem can be avoided in systems which do not use conventional secondary storage. Associative machines, for instance, batch all data requests and provide the task issuing the request exclusive control of the database, thus avoiding deadlock.

The DBMS deadlock problem is compounded by the need to ensure that uniformly correct data is maintained throughout the system. These technical problems make the management of large databases with many users a complex undertaking. Partitioning is a good solution.

In order to study at the drafting board how different access patterns can be optimized, assumptions need to be made about the behavior of interactive processing, and about the program each processor runs. Within a multiprocessing environment, and in networks addressing distributed databases, each processor must make consistent decisions regarding the rest of the system. Any decisions a processor makes that might affect its neighbor's decisions must eventually be communicated to the neighboring processors to assure a good synchronization.

In fact, each processor encounters the problem of synchronization when it executes a phase of the programs which it runs. Information about the rest of the network is usually incomplete at each node, and algorithms must be designed so that each processor can make its own decisions based on such information. Delays in data transport compound this problem, when messages between databases and processors, or among DDB segments, may take some time to arrive. This is the case not so much because of transport delays but of deadlocks and interlocks.

The message here is that distributed systems provide a good degree of integrity, extensibility, and performance which is needed in an interactive environment. However, the end result is not necessarily positive just because a computer system is distributed. We must study the use environment, the DDB structure, the resulting data flow rates between the processes; the execution process; and the overall memory requirements which are imposed.

These factors are critical to the design of a distributed system. For every specific applications environment a number of restrictions must be added to the design equations. Such restrictions will, to a substantial measure, be concerned with data traffic and with access patterns. Furthermore, it is advisable to experiment with modes able to tune a particular application in order to assure that delays, incompatibilities, errors and possible system failures have been established beforehand—and therefore corrected.

THE SEMANTIC INTEGRITY OF THE DB

The discussion on database access patterns leads us to the issue of semantic integrity. With reference to databases, this issue deals with correctness (consistency) of the DB with respect to specifications, and relates the DB data values in different data structures.

Protective rules must be established which assure that the professional users (the SA and the programmers) are not committing themselves to things they consider inappropriate. At the same time these rules must protect the DB from the occasional user who does not master the system trade. This is a necessity as, more and more, the end user accesses the DB from a variety of terminals. In a sense, the semantic integrity complements the I/O procedures and involves three levels of specifications included within the DDB architecture:

> applications driven,
> data model level, *and*
> operations.

Not only must design prerequisites be established, but also to satisfy these three levels it is necessary to outline beforehand: enforcement methods; performance analysis; system evaluation; proof of correctness, and implementation methodology. It is also important to clearly distinguish the semantic integrity mechanism from that of the operational integrity. The latter deals with an *integrity assertion* dictated solely by system operating considerations. As an example, take a network with only three sites. Terminal one executes transaction one. However, between the *subject* and the *object* is interimposed a *reference* monitor and a *semantic integrity* monitor. (These may be hardware or software implemented.)

Transaction one to be executed at site one is subject to the SI specification of terminal one. This requires answers to the following questions: Where have the needed data been stored: locally only or distributed? How will the data needs of DTE one be best implemented? Should we send transaction one to site two and site three, or send data from sites two and three to site one?

To answer these questions knowledgeably, we must know:

1. Size of messages,
2. Frequency of messages,
3. Software availability,
4. Network delays,
5. Supported network facilities,
6. Network costs, and
7. Operational deadlines.

Potential violation may result because of: the user transaction itself; operational failures; concurrent processing of transactions; redundancy of data; errors in the data directory; and system crashes.

Violations due to user query must be evaluated in regard to: proof of correctness; dynamic validation; possible drift; data dependence and data redundancy. The application of validation models must be done carefully, as this process could cost more than the original query. The validation overhead includes:

> the construction of the needed models
> the search of directories
> DB accesses *and*
> data processing.

To help reduce the overhead, we can transform the validation of queries from data dependent to data independent. This can be done by asking the crucial question: Does this query violate semantic integrity rules? This calls for copies of the DB data; critical constants and functional descriptions identifying *if* and *how* the different IE can be validated—and the rules governing them enforced.

Operational characteristics still dictate the solution, within the limits designated by hardware and software technology. Quite often, it is advisable in terms of costs and effectiveness—to leave the data where it is. Another issue is complexity; a fourth data security. Comparisons among competing goals are inevitable. A software complete and complex enough to handle all aspects of the job simply does not exist.

Furthermore, the currently available database management systems (DBMS) have not been designed to handle the complex requirements of a modern interactive environment extended to a whole range of operations, for instance, a bank, an airline, an industrial or a commercial concern. And there is a decreasing function of the value of information as system expenses increase.

We also know from experience of the last few years that DDB can give *much* more if we know how to partition the database; how to access the IE, and how to optimize the access results. This requires a whole new approach in man/information communications, where the "old way" of doing business plays no role whatsoever. (The old method still followed today is exemplified in Table 9.1.)

TABLE 9.1

The Old Method and the New Method in Data Processing

Levels of Human Interfaces	Old Procedures	Levels of Machine Interfaces	New Procedure
1	User	1	User
2	Expression of user's needs	2	Interactive description of videoforms (output needs)
3	SA	3	IE structure (in collaboration with SA)
4	Programmer	4	Minicomputer checks data dictionary
5	Production of Files	5	Minicomputer provides linkages between output videoform and SA

TABLE 9.1 (continued)			
Levels of Human Interfaces	*Old Procedures*	*Levels of Machine Interfaces*	*New Procedure*
6	Production of programs	6	Interactive description of videoform (input; data entry)
7	Real Data		
8	Extracts (Sort, Merge)	7	Minicomputer provides linkages between IE and data entry element
9	Reports	8	Minicomputer compiles documentation document
10	Distribution of Reports (it takes time to move files)		
11	Miscomprehensions		
12	Errors, Corrections, New Reports		

All 12 steps involve errors, delays, costs, misunderstandings.

The new approach is a direct "user-video-mini" relationship. It can be very effective, but to implement it properly it must be studied in depth, all ramifications must be considered: assurance, protection, and semantic integrity of the database elements. It must be implemented in a user friendly manner—eventually in an English language interface for the user.

THE COMING INTERACTIVE ENVIRONMENT

We have emphasized the understructure needed for interactive applications, as this is the way to the future. Distributed information systems are a subject of the 1970's, not of this decade. Distributed information systems evolved mainly because of economic considerations relative to potential savings in communications costs, a greater responsiveness to new applications, the sharing of costly resources, and in some way a higher user productivity.

The key subject of the 1980's is interactivity. Indeed, we now realize that the most important subject with computers and communications is not computing proper or communication between man and the machine. It is communication between man and information—both the data and the algorithm—stored in the computer system.

Like every new subject, interactivity presents a multitude of technical considerations. Many of them stem from the aim to

> reduce the response time for specific applications,
>
> improve availability to the end user, *and*
>
> assure system simplicity within the range of tradeoffs required for a functioning system.

We must assure the capability to relate computer power to organizational structures and information flows. By separating and distributing databases and applications, we can provide controlled access and sharing of data within an organization. As dependency on these data grows, more formalized techniques to manage the access and flow are required. Add to this the impact of interactive approaches and the need for coordination, integrity, synchronization, timeliness, consistency and so on will become clear.

Issues of security, of acceptable response time, application requirements, and organizational matters impact on the way the system will be designed. The need for preparation and experimentation cannot be overemphasized. In the 1980's there will be extensive reliance on software (and databases) for simulation and evaluation techniques. To be generally accessible by management, the resulting interactive system should be:

> user oriented,
> portable, *and*
> simple to operate.

It must assure reliable, integrated, easy-to-reach facilities. With local computers installed by the hundreds and DDB availability, the resulting system will require new criteria for evaluation. This is also true of investment decisions, management appreciation, and data auditing. Furthermore, new types of usage call for new standards.

The usage of interactive systems will be more extensive if the content of the database, and software implementation, provides the basis for cost control and productivity improvements. This must be created from the bottom up and proved through operational, financial and management audits.

A distributed information environment or an interactive application will not automatically allow reduction of the implementation constraints of traditional centralized information systems. The physical distribution of data over several computing facilities will remain a transitional fact without further impact if, from an organizational standpoint, this capability is not put to use, permitting better operations and allowing management control.

As we have so often emphasized, the key to success is in the right preparation. The interactive access to a distributed information system should emphasize both technical and managerial considerations, including the assessment of the communications system, the data dictionary, the data management system and, above all, the database structure.

The following list outlines the proposed, thorough reorganization of a medium size bank to provide the needed structure for a developing distributed, interactive environment. Ten systems are identified, each employing more than one minicomputer at the functional level—according to requirements. All applications are open to realtime and DIS. They are best run on dedicated systems with online executive terminals.

10. Foreign Operations

11. Foreign trading (import/export; including the production of legal documents)
12. Foreign exchange (retail and wholesale)
13. Swift
14. Management of balances at corresponding banks (foreign and domestic)
15. Arbitrage/spot
16. Arbitrage/forward
17. Foreign operations management
18. Client claims.

20. National and International

21. Corresponding banks
22. Money transfers
23. Corporate banking
24. Public financing (governments, cities, utilities)
25. Management control on legal requirements

30. Securities Handling

31. Securities/inventory management
32. Securities/investment management
33. Stock exchange/spot
34. Stock exchange/options
35. Stock transfer/securities
36. Dividend reinvestment
37. Transactions in foreign stock exchanges
38. Management of bank's own assets

40. Current Accounts

41. Demand deposit (DDA)
42. Check processing
43. Credit cards
44. Debit cards
45. Savings
46. Time deposit plans
47. Account reconcilement
48. Client mirror (management reporting)
49. Trust management

50. Loans

51. Small loans (integrated with credit card)
52. Major loans/retail banking
53. Corporate loans
54. Personal loan plans
55. Loans database
56. Mathematical programs for loan management
57. Mathematical programs for liquidity research
58. Other quantitative aids to decision

60. Client Services

61. Data clearance for commercial paper
62. Commercial paper management
63. Discount on commercial paper
64. Bill payment
65. Letters of credit
66. Collections
67. Lock-box

70. Personnel

71. Payroll
72. Personnel management
73. Loans to personnel
74. Educational programs

80. Computer Center Utilities

81. Program library management
82. Security/recovery file management
83. COM programs

90. Management Reporting

91. Authorized queries to database
92. Quality control charts
93. Risk calculation
94. Economic accounts
95. Cost accounting
96. General accounting
97. Accounts payable
98. Reports for government authorities
99. Tax calculation

100. New Information Services to the Clientele

101. General accounting
102. Accounts payable
103. Accounts receivable
104. Payroll
105. Inventory control
106. Other programmed applications
107. Online access to database, by business
108. Online access to database, by households

Finally, to be able to use the faculties of computers, communications and databases to their full potential, the five percent of the time of the "communicators" (employees, managers, auditors, etc.) must be spent on training. Training must assure the human capability to use the faculties of efficient, accurate, and timely information resources made available at rates and levels of increasing sophistication.

10 Virtual Memory

INTRODUCTION

The original intention of developing a virtual memory (VM; or virtual storage, VS) capability was to central memory extension. In the mid-60's, when the virtual memory effort started giving some concrete results, the high speed memory then available was very expensive. Hence, extending CM capabilities into disc storage was an exciting possibility.

Even in the early 70's, when virtual memory was implemented at client sites, the high speed memory was still expensive. Most importantly, the user requirements had outgrown the then available CM sizes. If nothing else, the OS consumed a good deal of central memory capacity and multiprogramming requirements added their weight.

Today, memory size is no longer a problem. For the coming large scale systems, we easily talk of six, eight and ten MBytes of central memory. Furthermore, for disc based auxiliary storage, the trillion byte capability is considered to be within the operating and financial perspectives of the Fortune 500.

Yet, virtual memory is the future. Virtual memory has become the interface between:

> the physical resource, and the use of the memory, *and*
>
> the applications library and the changing configuration of the supports.

This parallels the role of the microcode as an interface between the structure of the computer system and the instruction set—consequently, the AP investments. Today, the basic role of virtual memory is to enhance portability. The opportunities for the years ahead lie in the broad role of the interface (Figure 10.1).

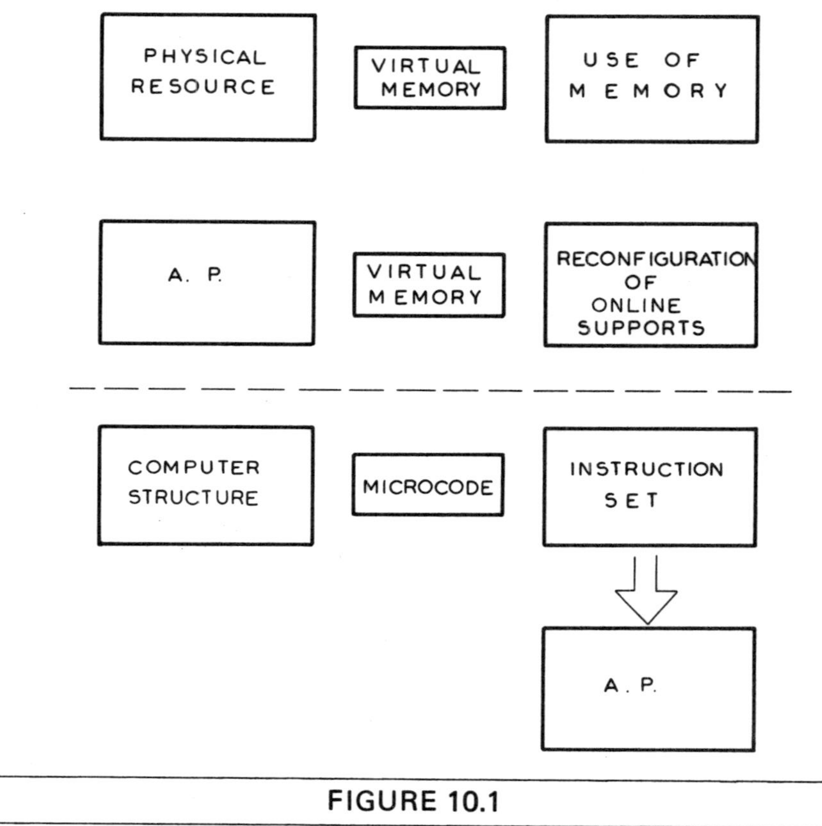

FIGURE 10.1

APPRECIATING VIRTUAL MEMORY

To appreciate the impact of virtual memory over the coming years, we should take a quick look into the present and coming use of microcode, particularly from the standpoint of program execution. Programs are converted into a finite set of instructions. These can be executed by a microcode (machine language, ML). Yet it is well known that language constructs are lost in the translation to ML. Hence, there is a trend toward adding sequences of micro-instructions to speed up execution of some language dependent operations (for example, floating point representation). With semiconductors we can bring this practice a step further: building language dependent microinstruction sequences in separate processors.

A more unique point with language processors is that several of them can be available on any one computer. To emulate an existing machine or to acquire a new language capability, the user will simply buy a language capability and virtual memory. High speed memory space will need to increase.

This reference to much greater central memory capability also applies to external storage where we will experience trillion byte memories. In turn, the need for very large memories (considered as such under current standards) will favor the manufacturers who have used a 32- and 36-bit architecture.

The task of implementing new memory technologies (and of migrating to the 1980's architectures) will be much easier if the word format does not change in the process. This is a new goal for virtual memory developments which originally started as an attempt to answer the problem of programs and databases too large to be contained in the real addressable space. We will return to this issue when we discuss pages.

The second basic role of virtual memory is programming simplification. At a time when hardware costs are dipping and labor costs are mounting, simplification of the programming task is a key requirement. Through virtual memory, the user does not need to be particularly concerned with

> the length of the program, *or*
> the size of the data files.

VM makes feasible the use of new database management (DB) technologies such as relational solutions (as we will see in a subsequent section). The physical location of the database is not a user consideration and relocation becomes a machine responsibility in case of:

> configuration changes, *or*
> migration to new systems.

In other words, virtual memory emerges as one of the key software techniques which, if well-used, makes virtual systems possible. We can expect, over the coming year, a host of virtual machine monitors, variable microcode capabilities and the stated direct execution of high level languages.

CHANGING CONCEPTS OF PROGRAMMING THROUGH VM

As the preceding section has suggested, the basic concept of VS has changed over time. In the mid-60's memory was expensive and VS was seen as a means of knocking down memory barriers. One benefit was using large programs without segmenting.

But memory costs dropped dramatically and this changed not only the whole DP structure but also the aims of the different software tools. The goals of virtual memory can now be expressed in these terms:

1. Reduce complexity,

2. Provide for extension of CM into external storage (discs),

3. Increase portability,

4. Cancel the need for overlays,

5. Ease programming skills and better productivity,

6. Enhance interactive capability,

7. Design for device independence,

8. Integrate DBMS,

9. Move towards rearend solutions, and

10. Use associative memory approaches.

A good deal of the ease of programming skills and productivity improvement comes from allowing construction of AP (applied programming work) and other software without considering long term operation of the machine (and its resources). Yet, the greatest benefit is that of bettering the ease-to-use of a given system by creating a one level storage.

With VM facilities the programmer is not concerned with where he puts the data. The system does it for him. This is of help to both the professional and the nonprofessional programmer. Furthermore, personal computer facilities will rest on one level storage.

Program-wise, another basic benefit comes from enhancing software portability between machine systems. Machine *independence* and *portability* have thus become main goals. A virtual memory can serve as an interface between:

> physical media, and their logical supports, *and the*
> user needs, including the AP libraries.

In a whole range of activities, VM provides the bridge between the past and the future. Furthermore, the use of VM concepts in writing basic software have brought in new possibilities. For instance, for scheduling purposes, IBM's MVS employs a "systems resource manager" (SRM)[1] which accepts job profile parameters (such as CPU time, number of pages, and so on), confronting these demands with the current job stream in the computer.

Taking into account what happens inside the machine, the SRM reacts by rescheduling resources, and reallocating priorities. (Notice that a system

---

[1] Announced in 1972, released in 1973/74.

136

resource manager does not need to operate every ns. Every twenty sec. or every minute is enough for optimization purposes.)

Scheduling and rescheduling capabilities become more feasible and more effective when the system can deal with one level storage situations. The latter are enhanced by VM. We should always remember that both ease-of-use and system optimization are served well through virtual memory approaches.

In conclusion, there is a tremendous programming advantage with one level memories. The same is true of the end usage. VM helps avoid transferring data around; it leaves it where it is; and makes use of homogeneous memory structures. But there are also cost issues to deal with.

We must strike a balance beween the cost of the software and that of the computer resources employed. The benefit and impact a homogeneous memory structure can have on applications is the direction to take toward an evaluation. This direction is enhanced through the partition of programs and data into pages.

THE PAGE

Pages are abstract storage units. They have a fixed home location on secondary (external) storage, this is not deallocated when the page is swapped into central memory. Since the mid to late 1960's, there are two major techniques used—paging and swapping—to allow a computer to share its resources among users. They are similar in purpose; both allow the programmer to better employ the computer and give the impression that the machine belongs entirely to each user. System design and supporting software dictate the maximum size of programs that can be executed, as well as the response time of a system to commands from a terminal.

Memory swapping is the older of the two methods. Paging machines differ from swapping engines in the way internal memory is allocated to the user. Let us look at them as though a program was written on the pages of a book.

Paging would have several books present in the system simultaneously but only a few of the pages would be present in central memory at any one time for a given user. Swapping would have the entire book in memory during the given user's share of CPU time. With both, a mass storage medium is used to handle inactive pages or books.

Take timesharing as an example. With the paging concept, *active program portions* are present in the central memory while idle portions are kept in the external memory. With swapping techniques, user's programs are transferred from the external to the internal memories in their *entirety*.

The concept of active and less active program portions is a development of an older practice of overlays. One of the first approaches was to partition the program into overlays, taking into consideration the dependence or interdependence of certain parts of the program. The operating system responded to explicit commands and swapped those program parts in or out according to instructions.

The segments we are referring to are the pages. The first VM pages were of modest size: fifty words, then one hundred. Now we have reasonably long pages (one thousand to two thousand words are not uncommon) and in the future, with emphasis on data communications, the ideal page size will be that which the transport protocol can handle without further segmenting. (Let us always remember that a message is a file in the database.)

The internal processing requirement must also be observed. This calls for increasing the page size so that a high percentage of programs will not need more than a single page. Moreover, there is the requirement of *telesoftware*, which brings together internal processing and telecommunicatons perspectives.

Present day telesoftware concerns reasonably small programs which can be squeezed into one Viewdata page: 24 x 40 = 960 bytes. Typically, such programs are loaded downline to the user's microcomputer, or intelligent TV set, by a central resource. Experience will increase the size and complexity of the programs of the future.

PAGES, DATABASES AND DATACOMM

Future paging capabilities must respond to DB/DC needs, this should definitely include the performance of all the housekeeping functions in the page, the activities generally associated with the access method software.

Pages must be designed for intelligent devices. Both frontend and rearend machines must be intelligent for managing the system hierarchy. We must be prepared for more powerful frontend processors performing packet switching, a trend which will probably evolve further.

Another reason for a rational page design is to give processors centered around a storage control capability that permits multiple computers, I/O units, and other devices simultaneous access to a common memory. The functions of the individual channels will be increasingly determined by microcode or stored logic.

If the page is regarded as a brick to build the edifice of databases and data communications, the realities of the equipment on which these processes will be run should help shape the size of that brick. This interplay between programs, data and physical capabilities is not new. A concrete example from the 1960's is the concept of memory partitions.

Swapping systems can have a fixed or variable partition delimiting each program. With fixed approaches, this partition automatically limits the size of the executed program unless techniques are employed such as overlays, chains of linking which share a given portion of central memory with various segments of a single large program. As stated in the preceding section, paging systems, since the beginning, delineated that maximum program size could be much larger than what could support the actual central memory of the machine. Having done that, paging schemes opened another perspective. This perspective, *pipelining*, was originally introduced on large arithmetic units, and slowly generalized to include the segmentation of any large transaction into serial substractions which could be processed on separate devices. Each device accepts as input the output of the previous one in a series.

By creating the concept of assembling data and programs into bricks cut to be handled by a dedicated device, processes become functionally specialized. This was feasible as long as a centralized overall control was retained.

This approach is most important. By using the capabilities microprocessors present, the present large scale monolithic processors will be replaced by new modules which, as stated, will feature direct execution of high level languages in microcode. (This provides more speed and up to thirty to forty percent more throughput.) Furthermore, microcode control will be used throughout the system, not just at the language processor level.

A distribution of operations can be very effective in the area of I/O functions: They are well defined, and the interface with the CPU is not ambiguous. The same is true of almost all other application dependent processes that can use intelligent approaches handled through microprocessor based facilities. Typically such facilities will be:

> error checking,
> retries, buffering, queuing,
> scheduling,
> interrupt handling,
> channel diagnostics, *and*
> data formatting

and the broad area of using Cache (Figure 10.2) whether at the CPU level or at the peripheral memory device level.

Pages and the paging concept will be needed in session control—as the page is related to the basic data unit which constitutes the fundamental:

> mapping reference, and
> calling reference

between memory levels and among the different computer systems in the network. Furthermore, as page use increases, larger groupings will become necessary, such as *scrolls* or VSP concept (virtual sheets of paper) which permit the handling of much larger data units, each divided in a number of pages.

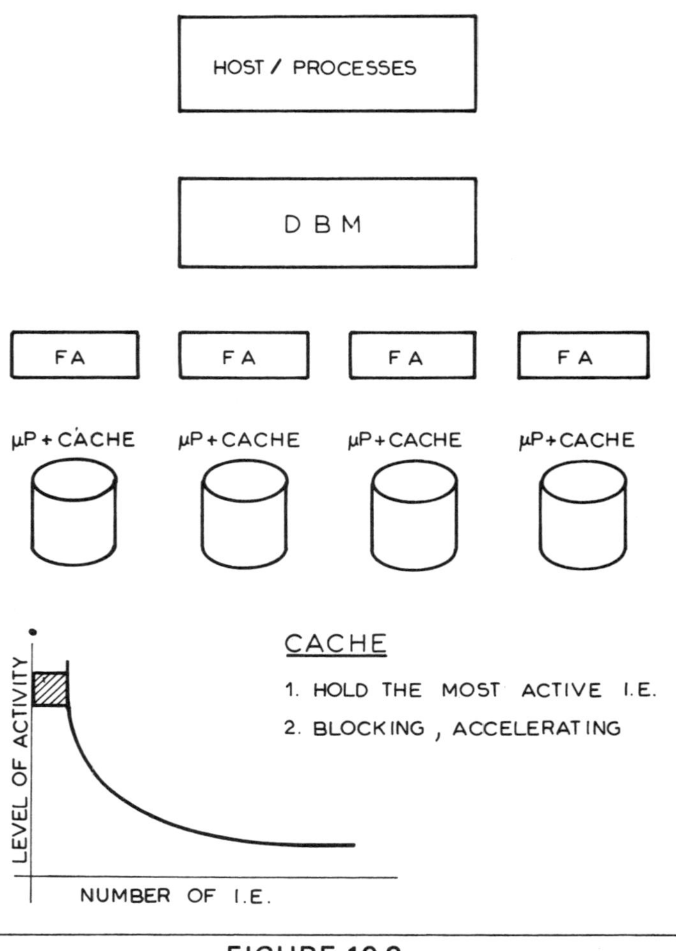

FIGURE 10.2

Processes run by computers in a network will address themselves directly to the page structure. To access a page, a process must first obtain a capability for that page; then, indicate where in its virtual address space the page (specified by the capability) is to appear; and attempt to refer to the page.

Since each page is a separate object, controlled sharing of individual pages is easily done. The basic operations on pages are:

> swap-in,
> reflect, *and*
> free.

Swap-in copies the page in secondary storage into main memory. The secondary storage copy is preserved. *Reflect* updates the secondary storage version to match main memory. *Free* deletes a page from control memory. This operation is permitted if the secondary storage version is current.

REAREND AND VIRTUAL MEMORY

It is not the objective of this chapter to enter into a discussion of rearend solutions. However, it should be noted that evolving rearend approaches present the user with potential benefits—which parallel those of virtual memory.

First, a program can be changed without affecting the others. Second, the logical database structure can be improved or added to, with minor or no effect on previously existing programs. Third, the aftermaths of changes in the physical layout and structure of data can be contained.

We could look at the rearend approach as that of a *virtual machine* designed to support a given function (the management of the database) and implemented at different systems levels: For instance, adjacent to the main processor, shared by different processors as an independent entity, or a concentrator of disc units—or as a *logic over data* solution attached to a single disc drive. Multilevel DB management capabilities could provide an alternative to paging. Table 10.1 briefly lists some advantages and disadvantages of virtual memories and virtual machines.

Among the advantages of the virtual machine concept is that storage hardware can be changed, without a great impact on the logical database—or the

TABLE 10.1

	Virtual Memory	*Virtual Machines*
Advantages	*programming productivity	*ease of migration
Disadvantages	*limitations due to pages, but *possible performance increase in a multijob environment *cost	*equipment performance *partitioning of resources

programs. Also databases can be merged, without reviewing all application programs; and data can be used or searched through different access paths.

By employing logical solutions at the storage level, it is simpler for users to gain access to data. Users can also easily know and understand what data is available to them. New application needs can be met with existing data rather than by creating new files; while security, privacy, accuracy, and reliability can be improved. Finally, programmers do not need to be unduly concerned with memory size—and data location. Synchronization of DB accesses can be obtained through optimization (in-storage algorithms) without hardship at the programmer's level.

11 The Data Dictionary

INTRODUCTION

The data dictionary (DD) is a rallying point for databases, data communications, interactive approaches, and the new generation of computer applications at large. It contains the directory of all IE in the database, and also the data description. It is the indispensable component of the DB and of the computing resources.

The data dictionary is becoming a basic information systems (IS) instrument which allows the user to answer such questions as:

1. How does a modification influence existing structures?
2. Which data exist in a DB?
3. What is their format? their security level?
4. Are the human resources organized and trained to handle the database elements?
5. What is the level of authorization for access purposes?
6. What is the descriptive model of the IE and other computing resources: fields; records; terminals, etc.?
7. What is the degree of interaction among these resources?

The data dictionary identifies and localizes data distributed throughout the system. To accomplish this function properly the data dictionary must be in every host. As this solution may lead to unwanted duplications, the usual policy is to keep subsets of the DD at each host and the complete dictionary at a central location to be consulted whenever the local subsets do not include the needed item (Figure 11.1).

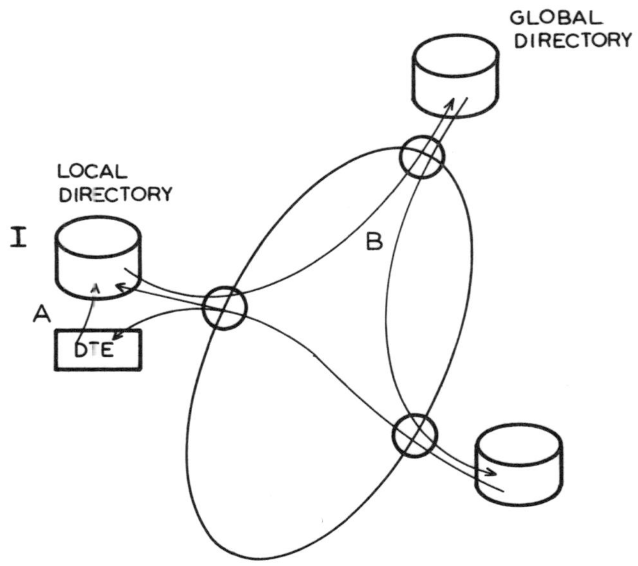

SIMULTANEOUS ACCESS MECHANISM

FIGURE 11.1

THE DATA DICTIONARY AS AN INFORMATION SYSTEM

The data dictionary is an information system in its own right, containing information about an organization's database—more precisely about the elements in the DB:

> their attributes,
> the usage, and
> standard definitions.

A data dictionary will not incorporate the values of the data objects (information elements), though it will include information about the objects. The nature of this information is pointed up by the two areas a good data dictionary should include:

> conceptual, and
> implementation.

The organization can be: alphabetic; by general, homogeneous type; at user's choice, according to defined object. This organization is presented to the reader in either of two forms: linear (or matrix); and hierarchical (tree structure.)

As an information system, the data dictionary can be a valuable work tool to the system analyst, the database administrator and the DBMS (Figure 11.2). What the analyst needs in a data dictionary can be classified into six main categories:

1. *Data structure terminology:* name; organization; description; component data elements; information on volume (where the data structure has an independent existence).

2. *Data element definitions:* name; description; aliases (other names by which the same data element is also known); allowable ranges of values; and meanings of different values by code.

As the analyst proceeds and the physical structure of the system becomes clearer, the length of each data element and its physical encoding will be added.

3. *Precision on data flow,* identifying: source (external entity or process or data store from which the flow starts); destination; description; data structures that flow down that data flow; and volume information (where not carried at the data structure level).

4. *Process definitions:* name; description; inputs; outputs; logical details.

5. *Description of external entities:* name; associated data flows; descriptions.

External entities may be: other systems (e.g. payroll/personnel); departments (such as accounts); functional entities; logical classes of people; and things (for instance, customers, temperature sensors).

6. *Glossary terms.* It is very useful to be able to store and retrieve user jargon terms.

Both the end user and the analysts on a project can save time by defining each item once. Each can use the data dictionary as a central store of definitions, where the information is held in machine readable form. Through the same process, the analyst will be supplying programmers with data definitions directly from the data dictionary. That is, without the labor of coding and re-entering definitions each time they are needed.

But also the analyst should be left with some local freedom to define articles (including keywords and attributes) with text description (see also the following discussion). Such articles can be fed into the DB incrementally. In short, through the facilities supported by a data dictionary, the analyst should

QUERY
LANGUAGES
FOR MAN-INFORMATION
COMMUNICATION
DATA
DICTIONARY
ON-LINE
ANALYSIS AND
PROGRAMMING
FOR BETTER DOCUMENTATION
AND HIGHER PRODUCTIVITY
DBMS
DBA
FOR AVOIDANCE OF
REDUNDANT EFFORT
AND FOR
COORDINATION

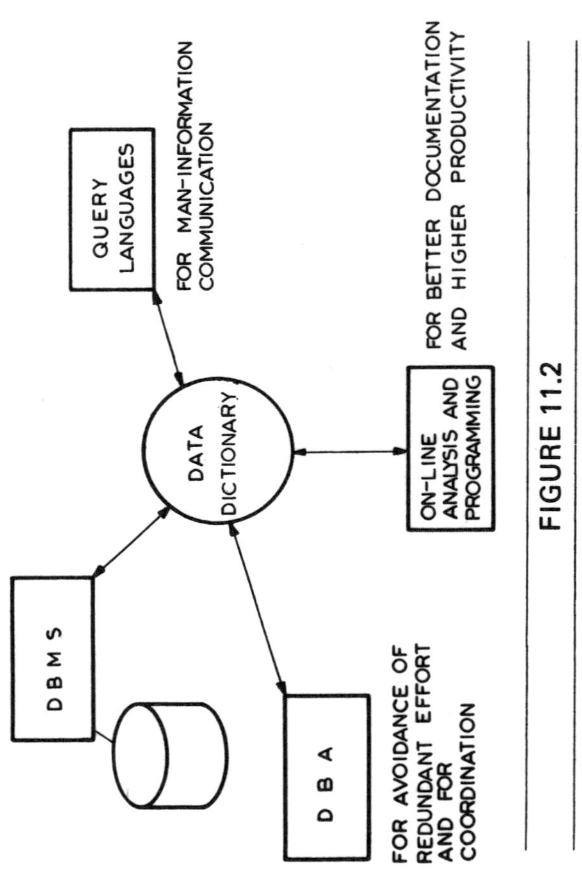

FIGURE 11.2

be in a position to observe DB design prerequisites which require the defini-tion of:

1. The information content of each IE,
2. The size of the projected DB,
3. The support media,
4. The internal organization and structure (IS, S, R, direct addressing),
5. The access capabilities,
6. The code to be used,
7. Policies, such as device independence, and
8. Security issues.

ATTRIBUTES OF A DATA DICTIONARY

A good data dictionary must have several attributes. It must permit sort/ select. Specifically, the sort faculty must allow order by different attributes and by subset. The function of select is the partition into subsets:

> a look for similarities, and
> the pruning of dissimilarities.

Like a good reader, the data dictionary logically groups the "words" from the defined logical groups, extracts the meaning, and makes the information available to a query. The reader (query) who has a rich vocabulary can decode a text more quickly and easily because he knows the majority of the words.

Query resembles a good reader in the sense that the latter evaluates what he is reading: he asks himself questions all the time and he needs a dictionary to find some of the answers. If the system analyst or the programmer wants to define a new information element, he must access the data dictionary on-line. Is this information element defined? *If yes*, he *must* use the name which exists in the DD.

In other words, a data dictionary helps the specialist to find an *element* if he does not know its name. However, the exact issue of what IE can be des-cribed differs from one data dictionary to another. One reason for this is that early data dictionaries were made to serve the database management system. Whichever structural approach the DBMS chose to follow imposed require-ments on the data dictionary largely oriented to the function of file access.

This brings into perspective another key issue—thorough preparatory work prior to using a DD. We need, for example, a preparatory job to define the most common keywords and attributes. We must work to classify all IE; identify which one is used by which process; look into structural requirements; plan for homogeneity; develop common terms; and integrate all this into the data dictionary.

This task is similar to what an Ansi report calls "building the conceptual schema of the enterprise." In a way, it is more extensive, since it also includes identifying all the processes that interact with the entities in a conceptual schema. The complexity of the work is clearly substantial, and a data dictionary system can be used as the basic tool of the project—though the project itself must develop the needed understructure for implementing a DD.

Let us add that in the process analysts and users alike have an interest in clarifying the concept of data storage within the operating environment they are studying and establishing the form in which data will be kept. This reference goes back to the ideas advanced in Chapter 1: that information storage costs money, keeping unnecessary intermediate layers of manipulated data makes a system inefficient and prone to errors (Figure 11.3).

To recapitulate, a data dictionary can be assimilated to a computer run DBA function. It tells the DBA/user what has been validated. All validated IE (also schemas and subschemas) can be accessed through the data dictionary.

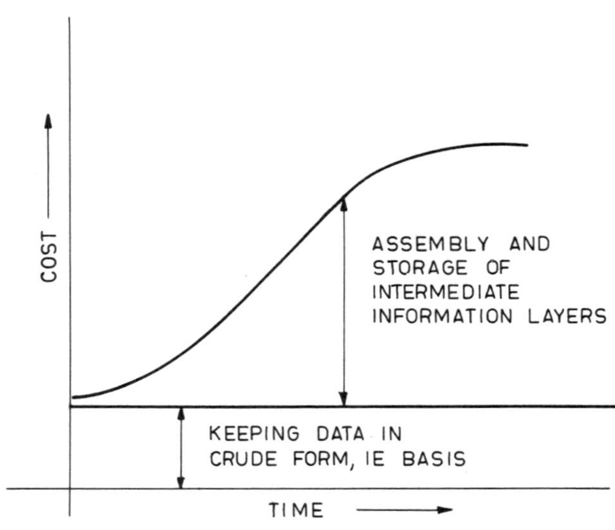

FIGURE 11.3

The same is true about programs, as a DD defines what programs have been validated. Data dictionaries can also answer questions such as which fields have, for instance, "A 22" in them.

Data dictionaries formalize the function of "How you access the database"—but *not* the physical/logical access into the DB; this is the function of the DBMS. To do so, well defined component parts such as

1. *A directory* able to hold the name of the IE in different order and to say where they are.

2. *Data definitions* able to contain text type information (not necessarily formal statements) pertaining to the IE in the database.

3. *Quick index* able to help identify redundant names; overlaps; discrepancies.

4. *Storehouse for database controls* ranging from library references to the keys necessary for authentication.

are needed.

In an effort to standardize, even inverted words are an unwanted attribute in the DB. For instance, "Manufacturing Payroll" and "Payroll for Manufacturing." One of the terms must be weeded out. The data dictionary must be developed as a unique and complete source of documentation pertaining to information on actual and potential issues, able to determine all processes related to IS whose structure has been established so that the processes themselves may be referred to in a standardized manner.

In the following sections we will examine these issues in greater detail, starting with the reference to directories. Though the needed facilities will vary from one organization to another, it is inadvisable to start developing one's own DD system. Good dictionaries are available to purchase as a package, and any DBMS will come equipped with its own dictionary.

CHOOSING A VITAL COMPONENT

The information systems of the 1980's will not only use the database concept extensively, but will also need an online, multifunctional Data Dictionary. It is, therefore, not surprising that the question of a DD comes up during the studies industrial companies and financial institutions undertake to revamp, modernize and streamline their IS operations.

The basic need is for an active dictionary to support the end users, the DBA, and the software investments made over the years. Systems management is, therefore, well advised to look for a data dictionary/directory solution to service existing users. The goal should be to get an adequate product able to keep impact on current systems minimal and on future enhancements incremental.

How should we choose a DD product? First we should see that it incorporates:

> a directory of IE, and
> data definitions functions.

As soon as experience is gained with these two subjects, we should stress:

> links to applications programs.

The applications environment determines the direction. By and large, it is a wise policy to begin by implementing the links and associated controls via the Batch interfaces, then to proceed to the RT programs. These steps will involve:

> all Text and Data in the Database, particularly

> update and retrieval (for reports, queries) via batch or online TP system, while assuring

> input via freeform format or forms mode terminals.

A good data dictionary should place no restriction on number of entity entries or on maximum number of entity relationships. It should feature predefined entity types and relationships—which might be changeable at any time; assure that the entities have version and status; guarantee an access and deletion protection; handle multiple aliases; and provide for cross reference and entity attribute reports.

To avoid upsetting current data structures, the dictionary should be populated from existing schemas, subschemas, and Cobol data descriptions. Restart/ recovery must be done through batch or TP. As Figure 11.4 documents, the basic approach should focus on eliminating the Cobol data division by providing as-you-go online data definition capability. Starting with basic functions, implementation can be extended to support a broader range of faculties.

Companies eager to implement the facilities supported by a Data Dictionary have found out that they can eliminate about half the currently written Cobol statements (though these, by being data definition-oriented represent only ten percent of the programming effort) and also handle

> cross-references and
> directory capabilities.

The benefit is greater if the DD works parametrically (as new designs do) with the parameters controlled by the DBA (Figure 11.5). This is a needed faculty as the DBA function grows rapidly in an effort to keep corporate data under control.

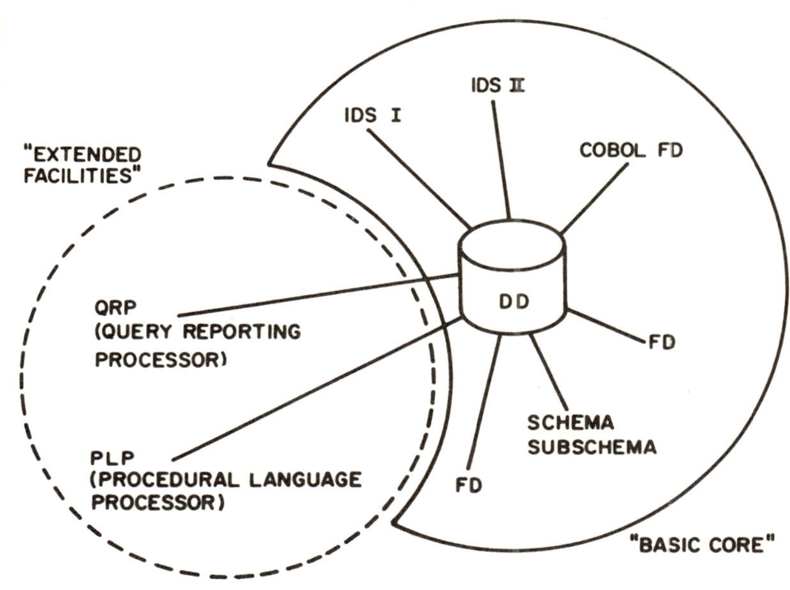

FIGURE 11.4

Table 11.1 identifies entities and relationships which must be supported in the general case. The control verbs should be simple to record and manipulate: store, modify, delete, copy, link, unlink. The same is true of access mode: read, delete, modify, null. Highlighted among the needed reports are the data dictionary master catalog; entity and cross reference reports; summary reports; keywords; in context reports; access control; user profile; and schema/record analysis.

These are the basic requirements. Enhancements will typically involve: user defined entities; query support; no restrictions on relationships; a full interactive system; and terminal/forms support. A good DD should point toward a fast access to the database; a directory generation capability; language data definitions; data security and access control; presentation control; enhancements of data independence features; device independence; location of data capabilities; multi-system data models; and a cataloged query support.

The functions we are outlining will allow a single administrative view of a distributed system, its data and functions. Table 11.2 provides a comprehensive approach towards basic design features, through the identification of a Data Dictionary's contents.

FILES DB
NETWORKS TERMINALS
DATA DICTIONARY
PRESENTATION CONTROL
NETWORKING
EDBCS
DBMS
E U F

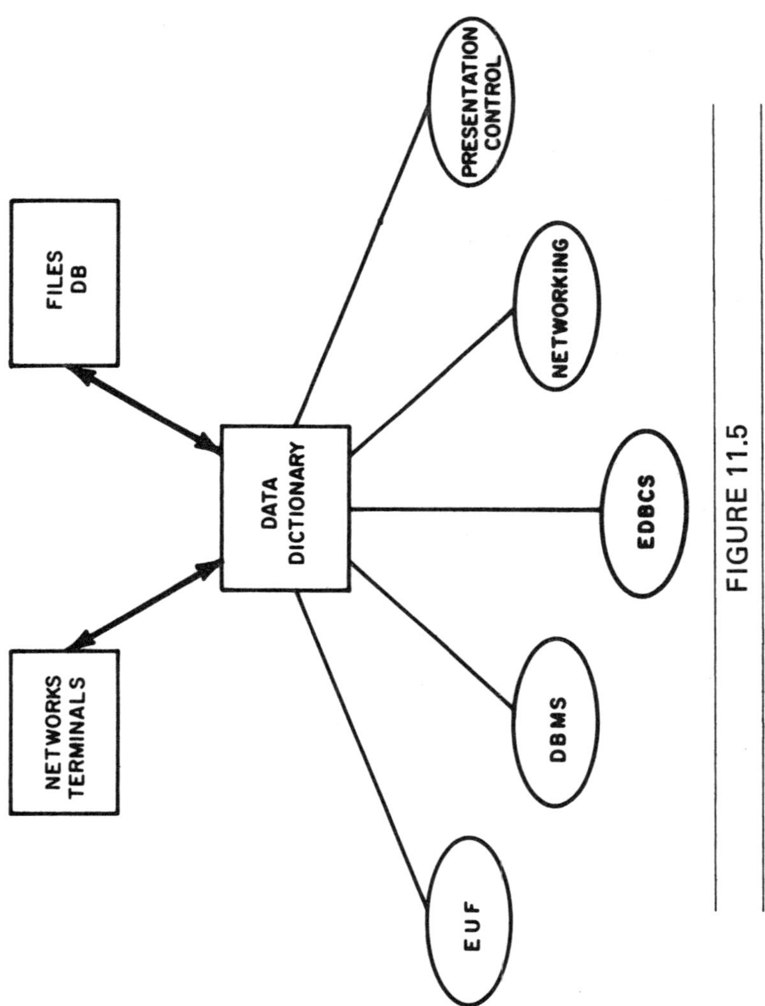

FIGURE 11.5

TABLE 11.1

Entities and Relationships to be Supported

From ↓ / To →	1.	2.	3.	4.	5.	6.	7.	8.	9.	10.	11.	12.	13.*
1. Area							x		x	x	x		
2. File						x	x						
3. Item					x	x	x	x			x		
4. Job						x						x	
5. Procedure			x			x							
6. Program		x	x	x	x	x	x	x			x		x
7. Record	x	x	x			x				x	x		
8. Report			x			x							
9. Schema	x										x		
10. Set	x						x						
11. Subschema	x		x			x	x		x				
12. System				x									
13. Transaction						x							

*Numbered Line and Column Headings are the same.

TABLE 11.2

Data Dictionary Contents

DP and DB World	Description of DP/DB World	Description of Real World (Conceptual Schema)	Real World
*Database Data	*Data Descriptions (Mappings to Information)	*Information Description	Entities
*Message Data		—Domains	Attributes
*Process Local Data	—Internal	—Entity Types	Values
	—External	—Attributes	Relationships
	*File Elements	—Relationships	
*Processes	*Workstation Descriptions	*Process Descriptions	Processes
*Process Groups	*Systems		
*Commitment Units			
*Sessions	*Message Descriptions	*Event Descriptions	Events

SUPPORTED FACILITIES

A directory depends on the applications to be supported and the related files. Because both grow as a function of time, the directory may become too large, leading to a need for segmentation. Segmentation brings up a hierarchical approach to consolidation, meaning that the search mechanism may have to move to the "next directory" (Figure 11.6). This creates a hierarchy of directories which can be either centralized or distributed. With either option, directories have the advantage of data independence in terms of updating; we can manage the directory without having to shuffle around the data.

Within a DIS, distributed directories have the edge over the centralized approach. They simplify access through terminals (query language) and are within easy reach of the user.

As stated in the preceding section, the next most important component is that of data definition. A data dictionary facility which reorganizes synonym record names is essential to effective use of the DBMS. But there are also other uses, the most notable relating to the work of the database administrator.

Keeping control over the database structure and the location of data without a dictionary will require extensive supporting software. It is likely that the software would cost more to develop than the cost of the dictionary package. Furthermore, planned redundancy can be a powerful tool in the design of any integrated database and may make dramatic differences in its ultimate goal.

Both the DBA and the programmers need to access an efficient, updated reference to file organization which will allow conflict prevention; the identification of group files; the identification of file classification; program linkages; header/trailer labels; system inquiries; system logging; passwords; authorizations; a security table and so on.

The data dictionary can be a valuable tool for the DBA in taking inventory of the existing system: files, file definitions and processes—including modifications. But facility of use is highly related to such supported features as provisions for: the entry of data to the dictionary; ease of access and query; the ongoing maintenance of the data the DD contains; and the effective development of procedures for its general applicability.

Careful planning prior to making a choice is essential. The same is true about the possible implementation of service which may lead to an online access to operating procedures (for instance, a formal library system that indicates the disposition of all application system data files, discs, tapes, and documentation).

Keeping up with the need for an active count of available software resources, DD can help as an online library reference, including the regular production load and reference to program modules during the testing phases of system development.

HIERARCHIES OF DIRECTORIES

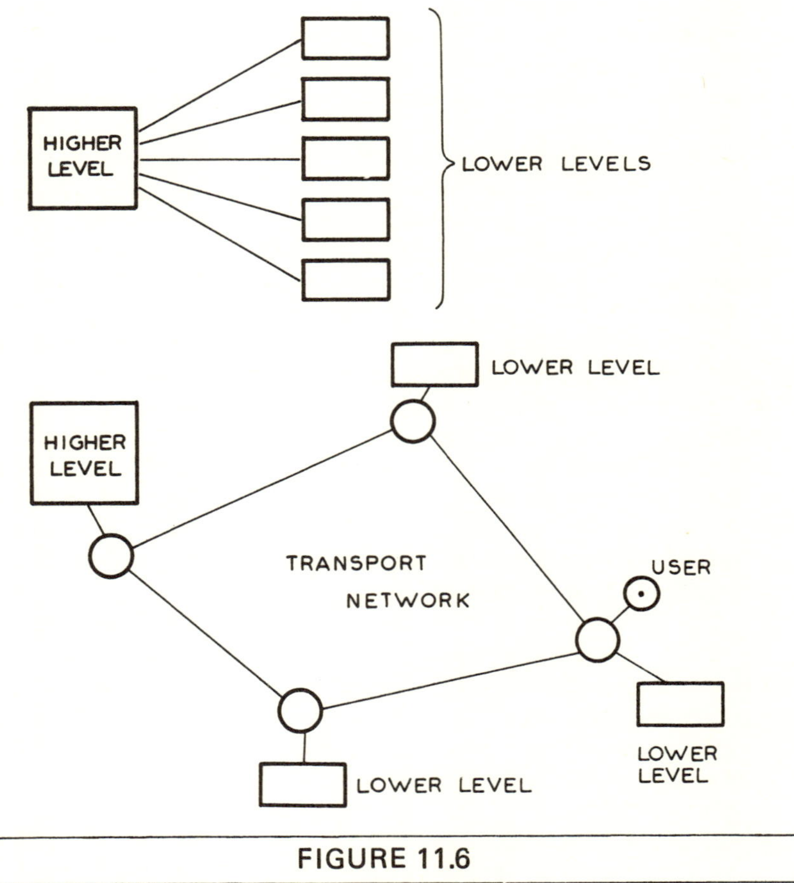

FIGURE 11.6

A DICTIONARY'S FUNCTIONAL AREAS

Such functional areas are likely to be addressed by a data dictionary system. The first is concerned with the design of a database. A DD can serve as a design aid. It is a depository of information collected during the analysis that leads to the creation of the databases. The information contained in a DB design aid will typically include:

1. The definition of data elements,

2. Estimates of usage frequencies,

3. The identification of ranges,

4. Delineation of security requirements.

Subsequent to implementation of the database, such references remain active. They serve as documentation for the system and as a base line for monitoring changes in data requirements and usage patterns. Furthermore, if usage indicates that changes are extensive, the data dictionary may help as a redesign tool.

A second functional area is in the actual implementation of database systems. A data dictionary will help provide a number of services. Collectively, these services improve the productivity of database administration and programming. Such services might typically include:

1. Database description,

2. The generation of database images,

3. The identification of logical grouping of IE,

4. Needed data description for application programs.

The need for these services is not limited to the DB construction phase. The functions we refer to must be supported not only during the design and implementation of a database system but in operations as well. Furthermore, being a storehouse for database controls and functional definitions, with practice, the data dictionary will become a fundamental component of system development, more precisely, a tool in facilitating the maintenance of both files and of AP.

Another functional area of the DD is that of online operational aids—particularly addressed to the end user. In this sense, the data dictionary becomes part of the understructure assuring that the interactive system is user friendly. The application is a straight extension of the DBA's usage assisting him in scheduling jobs; verifying security; validating transactions and so on.

Keeping track of use operations leads to another logical step: statistics which may be gathered on actual DD and database usage. This type of information can help determine the need for reorganization; for an extension in DD capabilities; for redesign of the database or even for user education.

These examples clearly suggest that there is no reason why the use of a data dictionary system should be restricted to the environment of a DBMS. The applicability is far more general and the more diverse, disorganized, or obsolete the files and their structure, the greater the need for a DD.

In other words, for data grouped in conventional files, the use of a dictionary can be more important than in a modern, well organized, streamlined environment. Obsolete file organization dates back to the time when data, and its management, was the sole responsibility of the programmer. Now with the use of a data dictionary an inventory of all files, records, and IE at large can be established creating a bridge of association between data and its usage. This enables an assessment of the current state of the data and of the existing degree of redundancy. The net effect reduces the costs associated with the management of the data; betters the quality of the data; and improves processing capabilities.

Data represent an important and valuable asset to a firm. It is therefore expected that steps should be taken to have this asset managed and controlled as carefully as other resources. This does not need to be restricted to data that exists in a computer based form. The full concept of resource management is concerned with all data regardless of the medium on which it resides—both to provide a basis for unification and to prepare the time when the conversion to an online DB will take place.

THE DATA DICTIONARY PRACTICE

Data dictionaries can be either manual or automated. Both approaches can be used for the storing and handling of an organization's data definitions, but given a complex job to be done, only the computer based solutions are of value.

In other words, a data dictionary could be a paperbased system concentrating all of the data definitions used by the units of an organization. Even in manual form, it can help reduce undesired redundancy and remove inconsistencies. If a manual form is adopted, by identifying the different definitions of the same IE, through the use of data dictionaries an organization can standardize one definition for that IE.

But the serious user should evidently look for machine processable approaches. A number of data dictionaries are currently available. They can be classified into two main groups:

1. *Independent of a DBMS*, such as Lexicon; UCC 10; data manager.

2. *DBMS imbedded*. Examples abound: IMS/DBDC; total; System 2000; Adabas; and so on.

Computer run solutions become a necessity when we consider reorganizing the database. In modernizing the corporate information system, building a new structure for APs, pruning the files, and rationalizing, the data dictionary should become integral to the definition of all system resources. This can encompass:

> hardware,
> software, and
> applications.

Once the dictionary has evolved to this level, it becomes a total system inventory manager. In addition, the data dictionary can be used as an enforcement tool—and it can serve for audit purposes.

Some prerequisites to this broadening approach are: a data subject extensibility, and a program interface. With data subject extensibility, a user may place any type of data declarative in the system inventory manager. With a program interface capability

> compilers,
> report writers,
> the database system, and
> database aid programs

can interface with the inventory manager providing a degree of data independence between stored data, user devices, and application programs.

12 The Database Administrator

INTRODUCTION

The database administrator's function is still evolving. A broad view of the responsibilities include eliminating undesired definitions, redundancies, and inconsistencies concerning the DB and its IE and to have (or at least share) responsibility for DB design. This requires the definition of:

1. The information content of the IE,
2. The size of the projected DB,
3. The support media,
4. The internal organization and structure (IS, S, R, direct addressing),
5. The access capabilities,
6. The code to be used,
7. Policies, such as device independence,
8. Security/protection issues.

Responsibility for information content (to name one of the functions) involves in itself a fairly substantial number of tasks, each with its own requirements.

The DBA should not allow two or more names to exist for the same data item, nor should he permit the same name to be used for two or more different data items. The database administrator should be able to control the acceptance and perform the updating of all "corporate" data definitions and data structures.

By and large, the DBA must be able to see things from a user's perspective. In fact, he himself is the first user of the database.

> If the payroll is erroneous because of the program, the analyst is responsible.
>
> If the payroll suffers a ten day delay because the data do not arrive in time, the responsibility rests with the DBA.

Evidently, the DBA's functions will impact on software. Programs will need revamping, and to proceed in an orderly way all programs that would have to be changed must be identified before approval to make the change is given.

THE DBA'S JOB

In order to examine corporate information requirements properly, establish data dictionary principles, and define the data flow

> from where information comes, and
> where/how it flows,

DB organization and the men entrusted with it must prove capable of:

> standardizing terminology,
> defining how the data should look, and
> setting the rules to be observed through decentralization.

The database administration task will invariably include all activities related to the creation, accessing and maintenance of a large collection of data containing complex interrelationships. Typically, a database:

1. Resides in a computer's secondary storage,

2. Is used by a number of different applications.

The data size complexity upon which an application is based has reached the point where a sizable portion of the resources allocation to the application are tied up in

> accessing, and
> changing.

The database is not to be confused with file management. The latter provides access to simple files with simple structures: sequential, index sequential and so on.

The DBA's task should not be confused with that of the project manager, whose particular objective is to create a "product," "service," or "process."

The two functions have certain faculties in common. For instance:

1. Their primary goal is the brainpower of men, professional specialists in their fields.

2. The next most important tool is the authority to cut red tape.

3. Essential to both the DBA and project management is a clear delineation of authority and of responsibility.

The basic responsibility of the project manager is to deliver his end product:

> in accordance with performance requirements,
> within agreed upon time schedules, and
> within budgetary limits.

Success or failure may hinge on the manager's ability to follow through on performance, time and budget. Skillful project managers aim at:

> balanced emphasis, and
> staying flexible and ready to adapt.

Projects have a timetable to observe. They must follow deadlines and be subjected to regular design reviews and walkthroughs. The following six points highlight the experience acquired over the years for successful project management.

1. The successful completion of a project in time, within budget and in conformance to specifications can best be achieved on a project management basis.

2. Projects must be dismantled upon completion of the mission.

3. Project staff should be a "mix" of brainpower appropriate to the mission.

4. Projects should be organized by task (diagonal structure) rather than staff or line.

5. In a diagonal structure, performance control rests on "autonomous" management capabilities.

6. A project manager has a higher proportion of professionals than any other manager in the organization—with the possible exception of the DBA.

This suggests that DBA and project management are divided by fundamental differences. A project is an organizational unit dedicated to attaining a short- to medium-term goal. It is "ad hoc"; not permanent. DBA is a permanent job.

The database administrator is concerned with design but also (if not mainly) policing responsibilities. Project managers and system analysts come to him for authorization to use data, to give names, to address databases. He must stand firm on the principles—otherwise, the database mission will fail.

HANDLING THE DBA FUNCTION

How is the DBA function to be handled? Ideally (and to a large measure regardless of organization size) the DBA faculties should be assured by two or three of the top men in the organization. The man to assure the DBA responsibility should:

1. Report directly to the director of Information Systems.
2. Get a data dictionary (with both directory and program/file management capabilities).
3. Use computer support (online, interactive) in performing his functions—and, after having done so,
4. Catalog all IS resources in the organization: not only the files but down to the byte level; not only software but all that has to do with databases, data communications, and data processing.
5. Put all this information on computer memory and manage it online.

The task is broad and complex. To do it well, the DBA and his associates must collaborate with management, project managers and the rank and file in IS. The DBA function is not a one-man job. It is one of collective genius—and it requires good organization.

The people assuring it must be knowledgeable of the computer business. They must understand many of its esoteric aspects. They must be strong in human relations. They must be able to express themselves and to explain why they favored one solution over another.

But even the best people facing a new job, are bound to ask themselves the critical question: How to start? The answer is: "with the easiest things possible":

1. An inventory of programs,
2. Identifying where the source program is,
3. An inventory of files—with
4. A file-program correspondence.

They should look up the files:

1. How many?
2. How many copies?
3. When last needed?
4. How old?
5. What is the releasing procedure, for instance, for a file on tape?

They should examine the standard DP jobs and make an inventory of instructions:

1. Who authorizes running the programs?
2. Where are the data descriptions buried?
3. Who uses the "copy file"?

164

And they should bring the descriptions under control. The DBA and his assistants must also look on processing specifications:

1. Which program accesses which file?
2. Which programmer wrote each program?
3. Who has authority to update?
4. What about schemas, subschemas?
5. Is a job control language being used?

They should be checking different records with the same information. And they should determine that the semantic definition of the enterprise is upheld.

Another crucial task is equivalences: entities vs. records. And the same is true of the descriptive structure of:

1. The organization,
2. The entities,
3. The files,
4. The data structures,
5. The file vs. description correlation.

These are the prerequisites. When these are satisfactorily completed, the DBA function in the organization will be approaching maturity. It will also have momentum. The results will clearly indicate the need for continuing its existence.

PROFILE OF THE DB ADMINISTRATOR

What sort of prerequisites should be observed by a man whose functions are as broad as those we have described and whose activities must reach every corporate operation concerning computers? Here is a profile of a DBA:

1. Five years in the systems area; particularly design,
2. One to two years in DIS design,
3. Experience in data communications,
4. Able to make independent decisions,
5. Knowledge of the industry: banking, merchandising, manufacturing, etc.,
6. Knowledge of internal policies.

His responsibilities will be:

1. Staff type,
2. Serve many groups,

3. Depend on IS boss—but not under the systems architect,

4. Have a veto on file design (but going into file design to control, not to project),

5. Have a staff of about two men,

6. Be one of the main contributors to system specifications,

7. Be one of the men to clear policies on equipment and software.

Given the importance and the novelty (for most organizations) of the DB task, let us recapitulate. In approximate chronological order, the DB administrator:

1. Takes inventory of existing data collection, storage, maintenance, and utilization.

2. Builds a model of the relationships between the information elements which exist.

3. Analyzes data/information requirements of the organization as a whole.

4. Builds a model of the relationships between IE which would reflect:

   A. actual requirements
   B. projected systems.

5. Collaborates with the SA and the programmers in assuring the separation between processing and DB access.

6. Develops a plan to evolve from the existing DB to the implementation of the evolving system.

7. Works on the concepts, normalization and administration of the database.

8. Manages a data dictionary.

9. Coordinates the decentralized operations concerning the DB.

10. Assures that the DB security/protection rules are observed.

The DB administrator must be able to assign security levels and "need to know" clearances for the use of both the data dictionary and the databases. And it is evident that within each and every organization, different security levels may be desirable.

AN APPLICATIONS EXAMPLE

Some years ago, a study requested by management at a leading New York bank proved that files used over the years in data processing operations were totally nonintegrated with only one or two cases that were integrated by application. These were functional databases.

As a result, a DB administration function was set up with its basic activities to be the identification of data elements required for specific projects and the separating of this data from data that had a corporate role. This seemed to be an easy role within the data processing organization, but in less than two years, it involved activities which were never thought of in the beginning:

1. Identifying all data points of entry and cataloging the media by which the data is recorded.

2. Tracking the data through the organization, noting where it is copied, where data/information is extracted, where changes can be made, where deletions can occur, and so on.

3. Observing and recording the creation of new media which carry information such as management reports.

4. Documenting each data form with frequency of recording and use, errors at origin, storage locations, privacy/security criteria, etc.

5. Following up on a number of subjects which developed as side issues but eventually took on a major importance.

Particular attention was paid to data integrity. As a senior executive was to comment: "When we receive information from two different places (particularly overseas) it is in different forms and difficult to consolidate. Also the timing is out of phase." This pointed up the need for classifying things and weeding out deviations, eliminating the incompatibilities which existed for years in the system—and with them the MIS interpretations.

Within a year data standards were established (including what the analysts and users should observe). Standards involved the determination of:

> characters,
> validations,
> errors,
> usage/writing, and
> interpretation.

The study considered all facets, even the detail of defining the information elements, putting particular emphasis on classification and identification. Roughly twenty-five standards were developed as a result of this work—to be applied throughout the organization.

These standards were submitted to the "systems review committee" (composed by senior management) and given to *all* departments for approval. Said an executive: "The concept was that of the benevolent dictator, but we did *not* have the dictator. So, we took the democratic approach."

Here is how management related the story: "After discussions, we started reinventing the information systems. This brought good will and collaboration. The direct result involved all user departments." The data dictionary was given priority in this effort, and along with the dictionary, the bank developed:

> a glossary for terminology, and
> a data catalog.

The aim of the latter was to identify which attributes could be associated with each information element. The IE were regrouped into three major classes:

> strategic,
> tactical, and
> day-to-day.

The next priority was to establish a "corporate DB activities management"— which the bank considered essential. In parallel to this, a study was conducted on the technology side to locate a good DBMS package. (The packages examined were IMS, IDMS, Total, Adabas.)

"In conclusion," management stated, "the key part of the work is to identify, classify, select and organize. But the top challenge of the DBA mission is getting people to agree on what needs to be done to streamline operations and which standards should be adopted applicable to every facet of IS work— and to every end user."

RECOMMENDING A SET OF PROCEDURES

The following is a recommended set of procedures based on the experiences of four different financial institutions, of three industrial concerns and two merchandising firms—all heavy IS users, with a quarter century of practice sharing among themselves a library of ten million Cobol statements.

Let us start with a study of the data dictionary, sorting out all our programs, files, forms, reports, and data assets at large.

Entry forms are a good place to begin, unless they are not well documented. The main things we will want to document for a data entry form are: origin, name, number, format, IE, information element names, computer usage and flow history. Do the same for the outputs.

A lot of "data about data" is generated by this study. It is an inventory in need of organization and documentation. The sooner we get a tool to store and analyze the data the better it is. Hence:

Let us look in a well documented manner into the available data dictionaries—and choose one.

We have spoken of the characteristics of the data dictionary and the assistance which it can offer. The criteria for choice have also been outlined. But to be realistic, their usage must rest on the information environment of the enterprise. Hence, the wisdom of starting with a first study to identify what the problem is. Now, after the DD has been chosen, here is the way to continue.

Draw the "flow history" both inside (Figure 12.1) and outside computer handling. A crucial issue is the interaction with other subsystems. We should draw a flow chart with nodes to represent every place something significant can happen to the document, such as data extraction, updating of master files, data changes and so on (Figure 12.2). This will point up the problem of interfaces. It will be necessary to look at priorities, formats, algorithms, files names, and the way updates should be implemented.

In this work, the DBA should be interested in providing comprehensive capabilities for file management while streamlining the IE required by the applications. He must stress the control of data redundancy:

> shared IE format,
> structured data,
> comprehensive data access,
> data growth, and
> evolutions in applications demands.

This activity will reasonably lead to the creation of utility programs for the construction and maintenance of the IE and to the development of system routines that interface with the data management facilities. Throughout the effort, records should be regarded as logical data units that are structured and accessed in accordance with application requirements, but within a total, integrated (and most likely distributed) DB perspective.

This prerequisite study must stress storage and retrieval capabilities and also the physical and logical supports which will be used. Data can be retrieved from a file without having to know the exact format and internal structure maintained by operating system routines. The file system interface should be transparent to the user, with software handling much of the data buffering and shared access capabilities.

The study should note that the system under development will be applied primarily within an interactive environment. Specific requests will result from this. For instance: multilevel privacy controls providing protection against unauthorized access; an applications capability requiring record access by one or more keys; efficient space utilization through support of fixed and variable length records; easy-to-use, interactive routines minimizing the time needed to learn and execute the primitives.

In this situation, particular emphasis is placed on the data dictionary. When the user calls for a certain IE, the system should first look in its diction-

HANDLING OF A TRANSACTION
INVOICE NO.
NAME
ADDRESS
PRODUCT
Q
PRICE
DISC.
TOTAL
TOTAL
INPUT STUDY
PROGRAMS
1.1
1.2
2.1
2.2
3.1
3.2
4.1
4.2
5.1
5.2
DATA ENTRY
INVENTORY UPDATE
CLIENT ACCOUNT UPDATE
BILLING
DATABASE
DB STUDY
INVOICE
OUTPUT STUDY

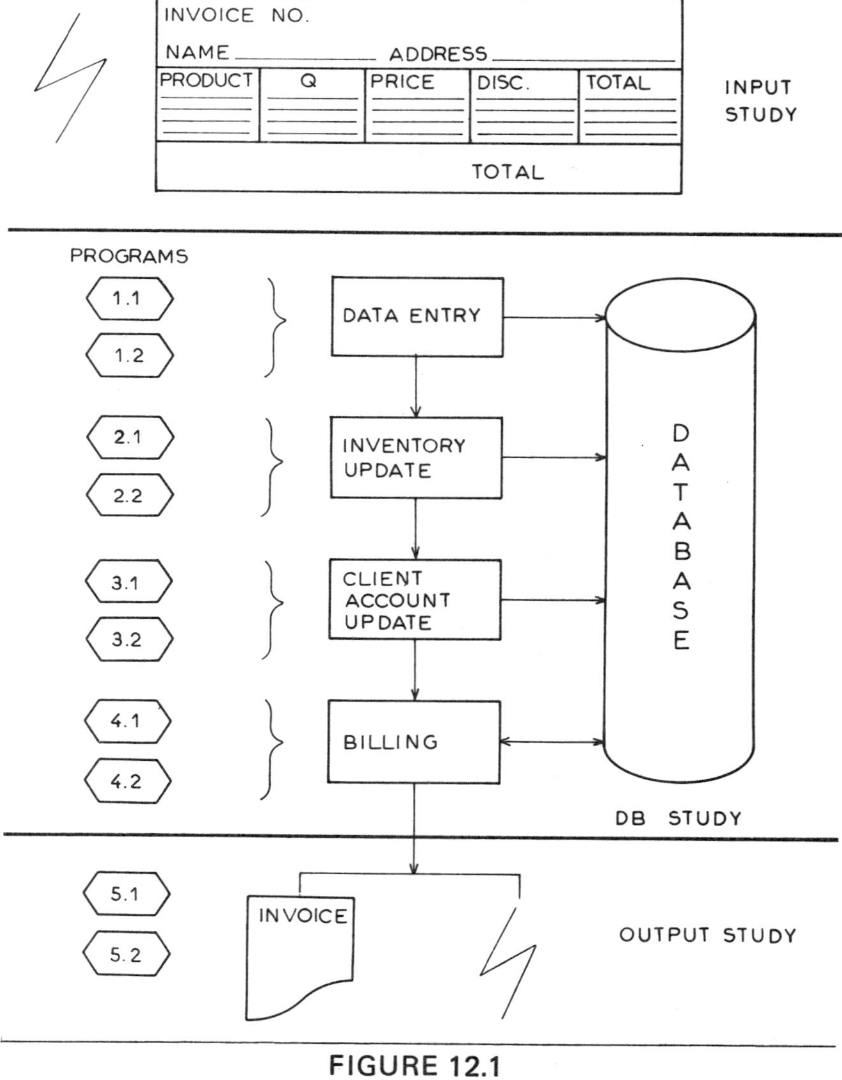

FIGURE 12.1

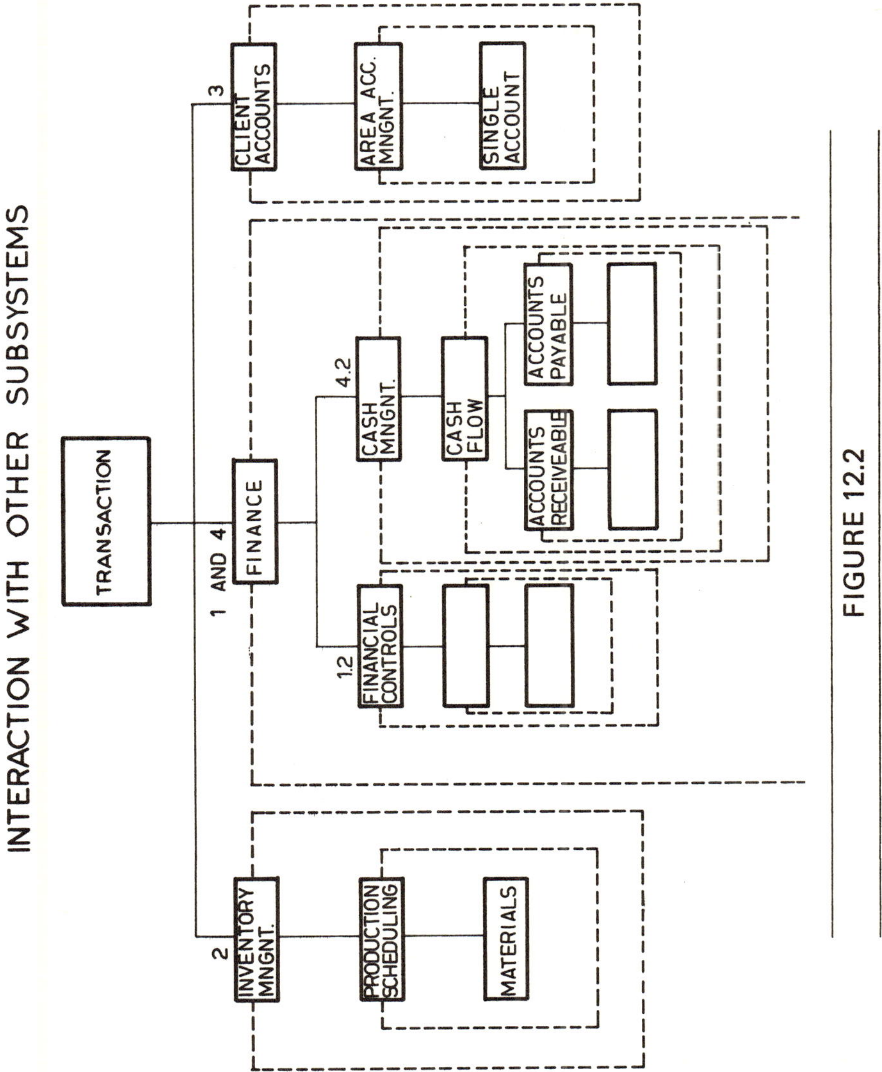

INTERACTION WITH OTHER SUBSYSTEMS
TRANSACTION
CLIENT ACCOUNTS
3
AREA ACC. MNGNT.
SINGLE ACCOUNT
1 AND 4
FINANCE
4.2
CASH MNGNT.
CASH FLOW
ACCOUNTS PAYABLE
ACCOUNTS RECEIVEABLE
1.2
FINANCIAL CONTROLS
2
INVENTORY MNGNT.
PRODUCTION SCHEDULING
MATERIALS
FIGURE 12.2

ary to see which files make up the database. Then each file should be loaded in its turn and processed according to the data management command chosen by the user. This involves a good deal of preparatory work; each database element must be entered in the DD and include at the minimum a form file, definition file and data file.

The form file determines the variable names, the order of the variables and how they will be displayed on video. The definition file stresses each variable according to size, type and data entry edit criteria. The data file contains the data records. (Other files may also be used to increase the flexibility of the interaction with the elements in the database. For instance, a coded value could be used to allow the user to substitute extended labels for abbreviated data values. And also an index to point to data that meet some user-selected criteria.)

As the application environment evolves and more end users are given authority to access the database, dynamic access capabilities will be advisable combining different access methods. (Dynamic access provides the means for changing the mode of file access within a program: the user can specify a starting point within a file and then access a portion of it sequentially.) However, over a transition period which may take several years, the DBA should assure that the record management service supports different file accesses: sequential, random, and dynamic. The first alternative is a legacy of batch processing used for those files in which all or most of the records in the file are processed each time the file is opened; while random access permits the user to reach a record in a file without passing through its predecessors (without regard to the last record read or written).

Finally, the DB Administrator should be the safekeeper of the videoforms made for interactive processing (videograms) as Figure 12.3 exemplifies. He must manage this inventory like all other data resources in his custody, assuring homogeneity, authorization, avoidance of duplications, and upkeep.

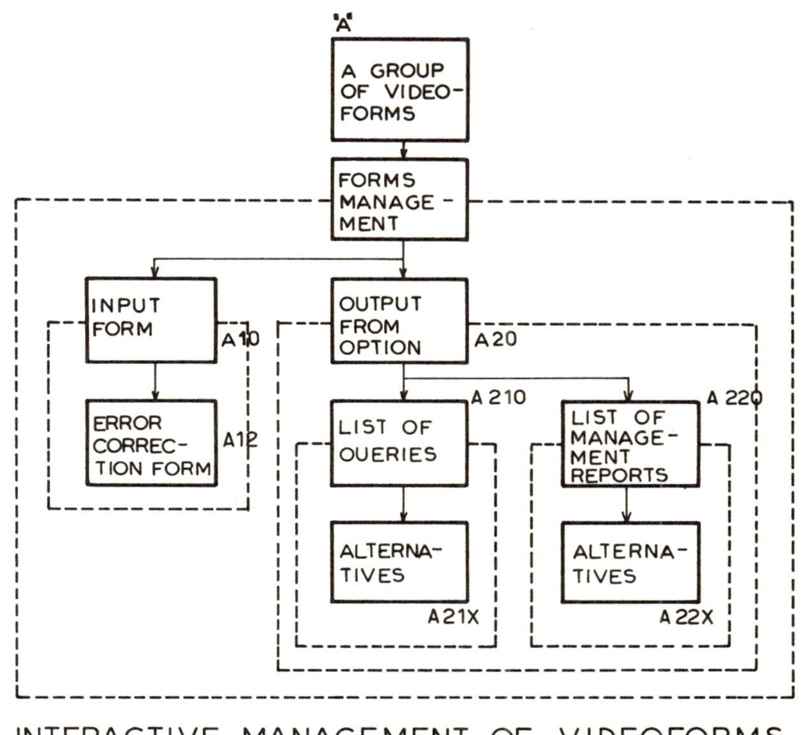

INTERACTIVE MANAGEMENT OF VIDEOFORMS

FIGURE 12.3

13 The DBA and the User

INTRODUCTION

One of the first lessons learned from DBA experiences is; do not underestimate the personnel problems involved in establishing a database.

It is understandable that users think of the data associated with their application as "their data." This is more pronounced as we distribute the database on minicomputers, place them near the user, and give the latter direct
access to information elements. These feelings are not eliminated just by
appointing a database administrator.

The DBA will be heavily involved with the user. His problems will be both
psychological and technical. He should not get so immersed in the technical
details associated with setting up the database that he ignores other pertinent issues. He must establish rules and enforce these rules. However, if he
does not explain to the users the "how," "when," and "why," of the rules,
he will find that the more he enforces them, the fewer results he will produce.

One thing is certain. People's actions dictate the end results. But actions
(and the thinking behind them) can be effectively changed if the ultimate
user is trained in the new, improved way of doing things. Renewal ultimately
depends on individuals. It depends on education and motivation; on commitment; conviction; the values men live by; the things that give meaning to
the lives.

Databases offer valuable information for persons in their work. The focus
is everything; and this must be brought into perspective. DBs present challenges and opportunities, but can also turn into instruments of crisis. The
ancient Chinese had two different interpretations (or symbols) for the word
"crisis." One represented danger; the other opportunity.

SETTING PRIORITIES

The DBA's most important function is to work on the organizational aspects
of a project; to instruct the people; to explain; to coinvolve the user; and together with the analysts classify, identify, streamline. He must not become

overly involved with things like the technical details preceding the choice between a relational, network or hierarchical structure of the DB—or blazing audit trails.

This is contrary to what many firms did originally, defining a job that sounds suspiciously like that of a system programmer. But they found out the hard way that priority should go to the true data administration problems we have just defined rather than to the technical software issues which (as far as this job is concerned) are pseudo problems.

Another mistake often made when setting priorities and defining the functions of the job is splitting it into many different responsibilities and assigning each to a different person. That is why we see titles like "data manager," "data controller," "data administrator"—all segments of the DBA. The job is new. Not all of its functions are clear. It is useless to compound the problem by splitting the responsibilities.

We should keep in mind that the potential of what we are trying to accomplish through the DBA is great. And it will be even greater as IS becomes an essential part of management's decision making process, as a true company-wide information system is developed using the database.

We also said that, to perform his duties in an able manner, the database administrator needs a data dictionary more than the DBMS. Practice has taught many database administrators that their database system was relatively useless until they implemented a good dictionary; this is the cornerstone of sound data management.

What shall we include under the data management perspective? The list is long, and it covers: multivolume organization; multiple indexes; the management of files that can be used concurrently by a variable number of tasks; all access on record level; the access mechanism; the access methods (as mentioned: sequential, direct, indexed, dynamic); and functions to process a record (read, write, insert, delete).

Utilities have to be standardized: copy; print; cross reference; debuggers; dumps; etc. Conversational methods have to be developed for the end user. The functions for source, object, load, and user file maintenance must be assured.

A number of other issues must be properly settled in terms of standards. They include interpretive languages; memory optimization; terminal interfaces; editing functions; interactive facilities; screen management and the use statistics.

All these are computer related functions. Yet, the DBA's first duty is organizational. He should give priority to learning his raw material: paper. What regular, or standard, size of paper forms does the organization keep on hand? What are the characteristics and costs of all types of paper used in printing forms?

176

Once he knows the facets of paper, format and costs, it is possible to select the appropriate videoform construction for interactive operations. In other words, extensive knowledge and planning are the key to efficient DB design.

The key to convincing management that such a program is desirable is to point up the possible cost reductions. The facts for such a presentation can be generated through analysis and validated by running selected applications through a pilot program.

OPPOSING VIEWPOINTS

Why should the DBA be involved with videoforms? The answer is self-evident. The data in the DB are there to serve a useful purpose. This useful purpose means *reporting* to either of the three layers we have defined: settlements, optimization, or decision making. If we start with the end user, we will understand what must be put into the DB to satisfy his requirements. When this is completed, we will be well informed on the input (both form and frequency) necessary to update the DB and serve the user.

The reason for a real life test is also clear. It is much easier to gain credibility by processing on a trial basis through a new program. And it is advisable that the items selected are prime targets for cost reduction, and that the goals are obtainable. The DBA can win the confidence and support of management by announcing and documenting significant results.

Assuming that the test and evidence have been quite satisfactory, the next problem which comes up is structural. If the DBA is really recognized as the corporate "master of data," who is his supervisor? Should he be outside or inside data processing?

There is controversy concerning this issue. Both opposing viewpoints have valid references. One says: "I cannot see data management out from under the computer processes that generate the need for it." Answers another: "I think both functions (DBA and IS boss) need to report to the same person. It looks like a chicken-and-egg thing, as far as I am concerned."

Here, again, experience can be a guide. Experience suggests that, when the process of database administration matures, it should be moved out from under the data processing and float to a level within the organization that allows the job to resolve the type of conflict that it was created to deal with. Besides, as we have often stated, the DBA's responsibility is primarily organizational—and the risk is present that, when this function is buried within the larger IS department, it will lose effectiveness because it will be viewed by corporate management as just another technical role.

That is the basic reason why some organizations split the DBA function into two segments: one technical, concerned with the physical aspects of the database, the other handling the logical aspects, along with the business specifications removing the information planning from computer services and turning it over to corporate staff. But we have already cautioned against this split.

Along with organization, the DBA's mission is planning and controlling—except that he is not controlling money but data. He is also planning for data, and it is in this function that he would be required to frequently interact with the users. (Companies put a lot of effort into short, medium and long term planning activity in terms of business operations. They should invest the same effort into planning for the collection, storage and use of data.)

Data is a corporate resource. It is expensive to gather, maintain, organize and use. Let us not forget that most organizations have so far derived minimal return from their investment in data (and in data processing). The job has not been done correctly. Now we understand that the information elements should not "belong" to an application—but instead, should assure access by those applications which require them—we should organize our operations in accord with this new philosophy.

The DBA's job starts at this point. And as he proceeds with an inventory of data and programs, he will be well advised to take account of the age of the software his company is running. Figure 13.1 has been taken out of real life data and documents that there are bound to be surprises.

DATA SECURITY AND THE DBA

This sums up the functions of the DBA under present conditions. But since database systems are evolving, their management is still changing. As more organizations try different structures, we will learn more about how a database system can best be run.

Within this new philosophy the DBA must be responsible for:

1. Projecting, designing, integrating that part of the corporate database which is stored on a computer.

2. Assuring all linkages which should be provided to the not yet computerized procedures and the management of their files.

3. Handling the physical and logical issues associated with the DB, serving as consultant to application and system programmers on the proper use of the database.

AGE OF SOFTWARE
OTHER
INVOICING
PERSONNEL
SALES AND MARKETING
CREDIT CARD MANAGEMENT
CUMULATIVE CURVE
COST ACCOUNTING
GENERAL ACCOUNTING
68 69 70 71 72 73 74 75 76 77 78 79 80
1 2 3 4 5 6 7 8 9 10 11 12 13

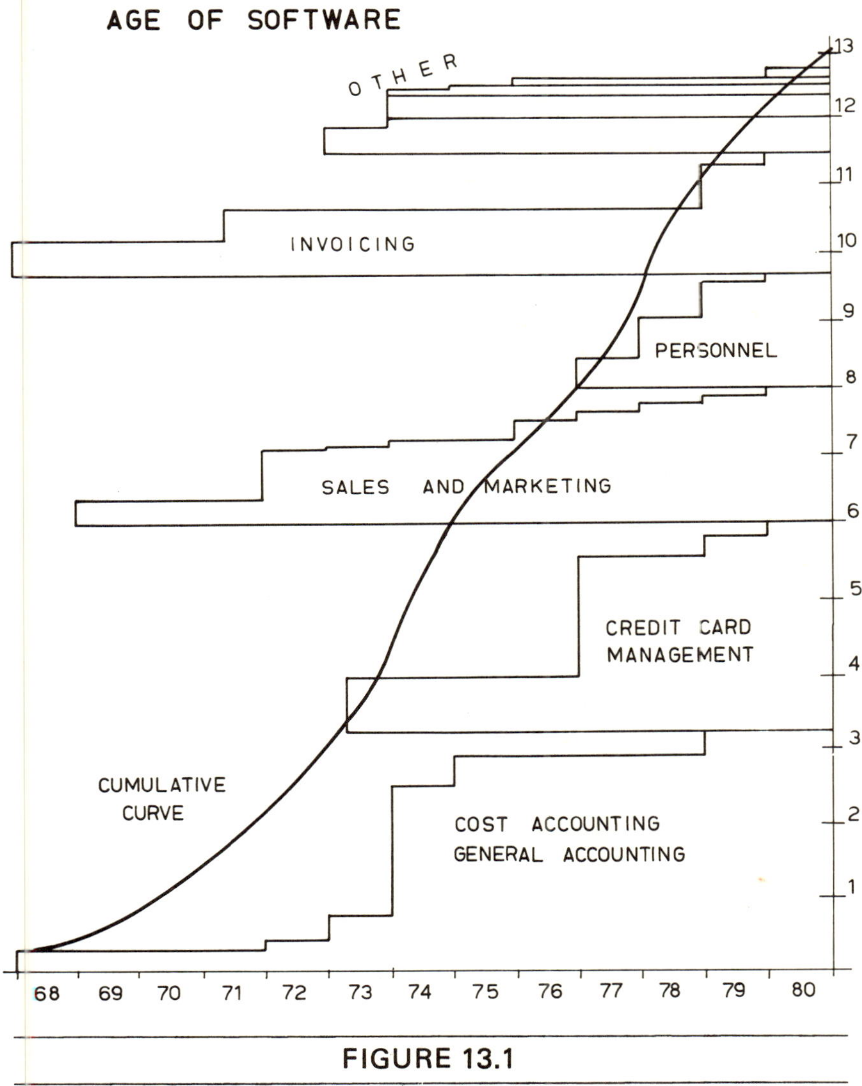

FIGURE 13.1

4. Assuming responsibility for the data dictionary but also have a major role in the selection of a database package, teleprocessing package(s) and so on.

5. Establishing, in conjunction with computer center management, the configuration for DB processing (batch, interactive, etc).

6. Assuming responsibility for the security and integrity of the database (and of the database package).

Here again, the user interaction will be pronounced. *Security* issues are definitely a function of user profile. Handling them calls for a definition of

> logical access,
> negation of access, and
> options.

A competent response to such prerequisites demands both a global view of the DB, and one of greater detail (Figure 13.2). One of the prerequisites is the establishment of field level independence, e.g., giving independence (in terms of handling) at the level of the single field in the database.

Integrity issues suggest other needs. One of the basics is the evolution of the blocking mechanism in the DB. Here, the tendency is to go at the lowest level. The smallest IE is the one which is blocked. Indeed:

> the higher the sophistication of the mechanism,
> the greater the utility to the user, and
> the greater the protection.

Another fundamental relationship is that:

> the more limited the effects of the backout,
> the more detailed the logging must be.

This requires the definition of checkpoints between two lockings as a good means for assuring integrity (Figure 13.3). But even the finer interfaces can have deadlock problems. The latter, to be solved, need:

> forced backout, and
> automatic restart.

But the problems increase in magnitude with a DDB where simultaneous update is applied, as the deadlock problem is much more severe with distributed DB.

SECURITY
GLOBAL
DETAIL
- LOGICAL ACCESS
- NEGATION OF ACCESS
- OPTIONS
FUNCTION OF USER PROFILE

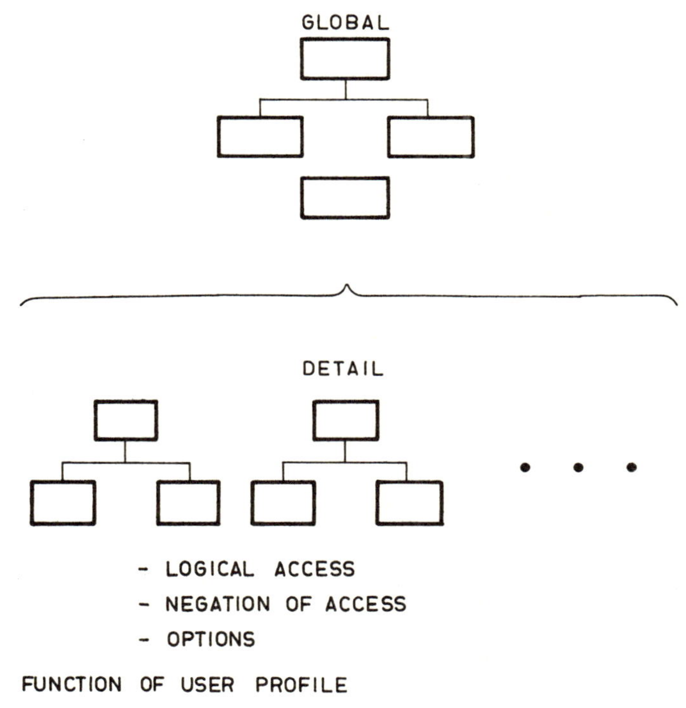

FIGURE 13.2

INTEGRITY

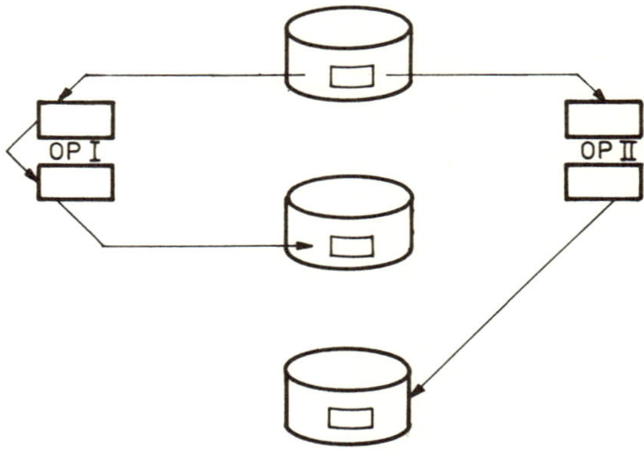

HENCE, LOCKING MECHANISM

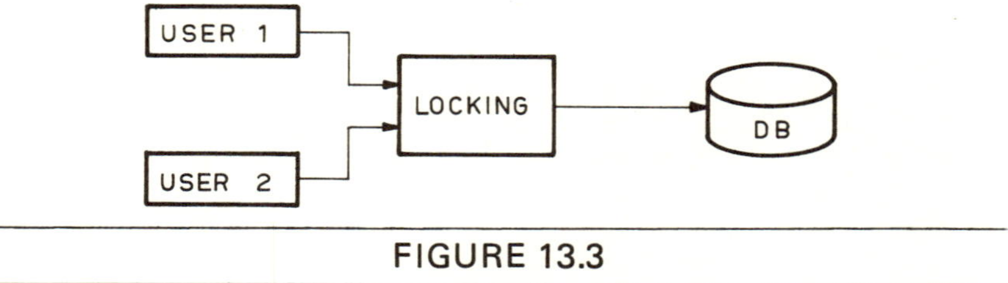

FIGURE 13.3

The general picture of a distributed database with the options in the application of the blocking algorithm is presented in Figure 13.4. Four blocking levels are distinguished going from the total DB to only one file in a single location.

Settling these issues involves extensive preparation: documenting and analyzing existing systems; assessing information requirements; developing new data entry procedures; developing a model of the organization's data; planning for the sharing of data among processes; and working with the users to establish what they really need and when. (This function should not be confused with a management information system task, which is primarily concerned with using the database to develop models and reports for management.)

182

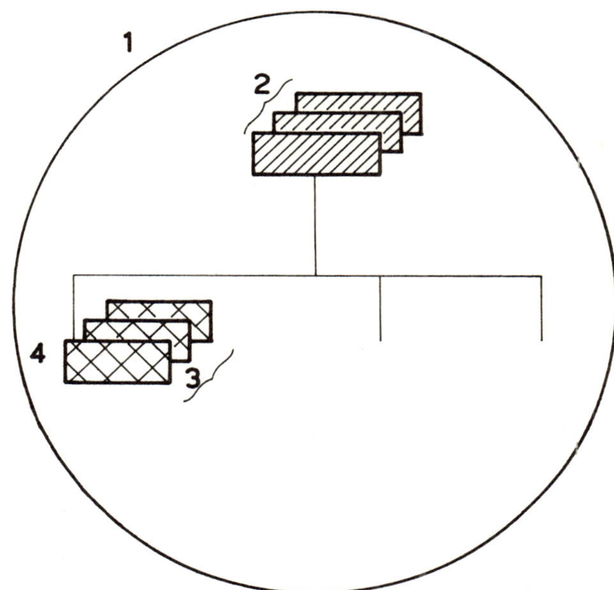

FIGURE 13.4

In other words, the DBA function evolves because there are multiple users for a single resource like a database. This is why one of the primary functions is resource allocation and conflict resolution. (It is also the reason why the ability to sell the DB idea within the organization is essential.)

THE WAVES OF CHANGE

As happened back in the 1950's with the DP manager, the DBA is too often unaware that the procedures for screening, integrating, and standardizing which he develops create waves that disrupt the old operating patterns of the

IS organization. Yet, he should be aware that he is an agent of change. And he should make sure that his innovations are designed to mesh with the current operations as smoothly as possible.

The Chinese have a proverb: "If you plan for one year, plant rice. If you plan for ten years, plant trees. If for one hundred years, educate people." It may sound superfluous, yet it is necessary to emphasize that the man nominated to be a DBA, no matter how experienced, should first educate himself in his duties; then integrate himself among computer experts who will be involved in creating, upkeeping and administering a database; and following this become knowledgeable of the needs of the other computer experts all the way to the end users.

Along with formal seminars, one of the best ways to develop DBA education is to talk to other database administrators who have developed capabilities in their own companies. The DBA should listen to their experiences and pay particular attention to any problems they may have encountered.

A basic prerequisite that a DBA should learn in these meetings is how to prepare a detailed installation plan and how to predict what could go wrong. If he establishes a formal mechanism for solving problems and keeps a log of any difficulties, he will be prepared if the database fails. The DBA should never forget that

> normal operations should be assured throughout the transition time, and
>
> parallel processing should be a "must" prior to giving the green light for a switchover to the new structures.

Still accidents can happen, and to see them through, management must obtain a commitment from all personnel who will be implementing, using and administering the database. Problems should be brought in the open, and superiors should be kept informed of progress (or lack of it) at every step of the installation.

We must always be aware of increasing challenges in this field. That is why, in creating a database, objectives should include planning and implementing an overall information strategy: increasing data utility; and cutting installation costs. These objectives should integrate with the standards to be established.

Maintaining the database environment; providing educational and user-liaison support; establishing and enforcing standards; coordinating application design efforts; controlling and implementing privacy and security mechanisms are activities calling for a steady effort throughout the company operations.

Managing the data assets includes the duties of assigning ownership and responsibility to the users for timely updating and accessing data; establishing and enforcing collection and maintenance schedules; defining needed resources, including hardware, software and personnel; maintaining the dictionary system and the teleprocessing monitor interfaces; and tuning the DBMS for performance efficiency and usability.

Another function which will be marked by constant changes is *coordination*. This was practically unknown when computer programs were discreet islands, but got attention as the different integrating procedures developed. Accounting was pressured by management for reports that required data that was controlled by accounts payable and the material control departments. Who would see to it that the data flow ran timely, correctly and uninterrupted?

Maybe the accounts payable manager refused to work the extra overtime required because his people were already over their overtime budget. And material control had its own priorities to worry about. The frustration created in the accounting would be greater if the IE in the database were common, but there was no authority to coordinate operations. This critical task is a DBA function.

CONVERSION ALTERNATIVES

The development and construction of databases involves conversion of files and programs, as well as many other aspects of the environment. This becomes more apparent as the dual pass is undertaken, not only in terms of databases but also in terms of interactivity.

For example, user data retrieval procedures may change from delayed processing via submission of request forms to immediate processing through on-line terminals. Software design will change from a batch orientation to transaction handling; and from bulk reporting to exception procedures.

On the programming side, the standard input/output commands of the compiler languages will be replaced by data manipulation languages; a considerable amount of classical reporting and updating requirements will be revamped (or replaced) through end user query languages. File and program conversion will be a major task requiring specialized personnel and resources. Typically, it will involve analyzing the existing conventional files and writing a series of ad hoc routines.

Programs will be needed, for any well planned conversion process, to link related records; perform consistency checks; proceed with validation editing; and create records that feed into database formats and specifications. In turn, this work calls for the identification of all data redundances. Only controlled redundancies are admissible, and database design must assure that:

> integrity control fields are interjected, while

> duplicated unique identifiers are kept consistent with their primary image by updating software.

Information on the location of redundant data should be recorded in the data dictionary. This is also true of information relative to file migration, as records formally managed in a "discreet island" approach (inverted files, index sequential, random, sequential, networking and so on) are integrated into the DB in a homogeneous basis (Figure 13.5).

Conversion of database elements necessarily involves examining a number of attributes of information, relating both to the logical handling of data and its physical structure. The logical entities to be studied and renewed include standards for the representation of the IE; the sequencing and representation of information records within data definition and data manipulation languages; and forms of structure representation (hierarchical, network, etc.). Assuming the structure is known, then some form of index or "schema" must be transferred from one system to another—ideally using the same standards.

The conversion job does not end with file handling. As we have seen in preceding chapters, the perspectives engage subjects such as data communications protocols—this broad view includes the line level; the link level; the packet level (if present) and the means to communicate with the end user.

Another issue in the conversion procedures is the codes chosen for coding information: ASCII and EBCDIC which, as well known, are not compatible with each other. Put into that the most likely problem of change in languages to support queries (Cobol 68 to Cobol 74) and the complexity is self-evident. (Figure 13.6 shows a suggested approach.)

Converting programs generally requires one of two approaches: complete redesign; or a more limited conversion of the individual I/O commands to access the data in its new format. Experience dictates that, when converting systems with a small number of programs, redesign should be favored and can be accomplished in parallel with file conversion. However, when working with systems having hundreds or thousands of programs, redesign will call for resources which usually are not available.

A phased approach seems to be a reasonable solution; first converting the I/O commands to their corresponding data manipulation language commands, and then processing the database in an indexed sequential manner just as previous files were handled. Then the programs can be individually redesigned to take advantage of the more efficient access path and addressing mechanisms of a DBMS.

Still, as previously stated, the best solution is to design programs so that I/O is performed in separate functional modules. And the same is true of database access.

Other conversion requirements will probably arise. Existing applications will need to be extended, or integrated. New applications will be added,

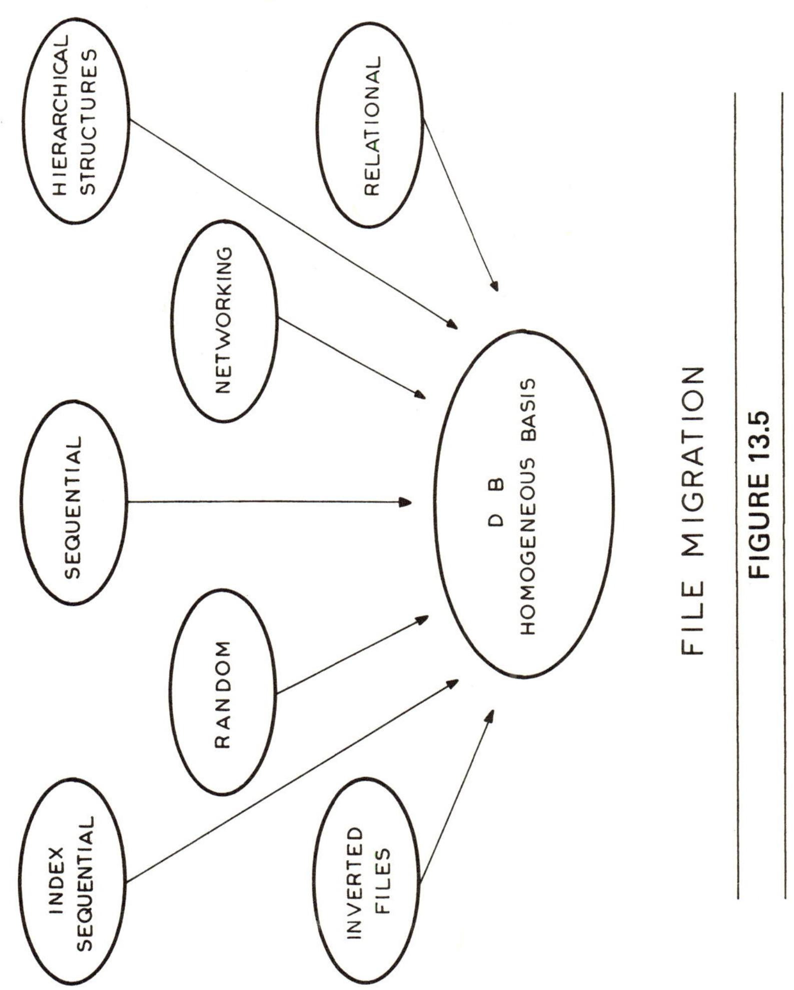

FILE MIGRATION

FIGURE 13.5

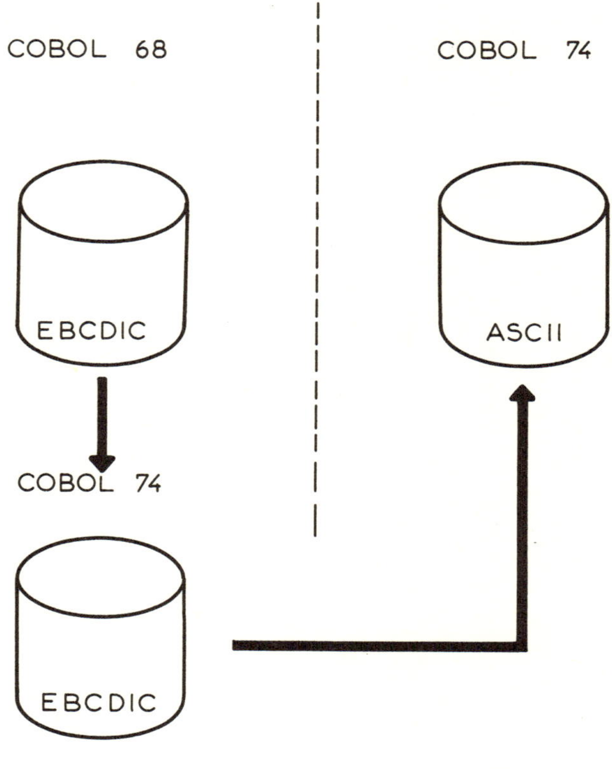

FIGURE 13.6

others will be dropped as obsolete. Transaction rates will change; and this is also true of data volumes and operating modes. Performance must be upgraded; a program of database tuning must be implemented.

This is a steady job and, to be done well, it requires collecting performance statistics; analyzing these statistics; identifying inefficiencies; redesigning, reorganizing, and restructuring the database. A DBA is a living entity, and there must be an ongoing program to refine it for efficiency, scheduling, accounting, and management information requirements. One of the primary benefits from (and objectives of) a database is to support a changing IS environment.

14 The Dimitris Chorafas System

INTRODUCTION

"Guide the people by virtue and regulate them by *li* (sense of propriety), and the people will have a sense of honor and respect", Confucius used to say. He insisted on the rectification of names; calling a spade a spade.

"If the name is not rectified, then the whole style of one's speech is not in form, then orders cannot be carried out; if orders are not carried out, then the proper forms of worship and social intercourse cannot be restored; if the proper forms of worship and social intercourse are not restored, then legal justice in the country will fail; when legal justice fails, then the people are at a loss to know what to do and what not to do."

The people are also at a loss to know what to do or not to do when the resources which they manage are not properly identified. To correctly identify the machines, spares, tools and even concepts which we are using, we must first classify them. This calls for a methodology and for specific examples.

An identification code is a composition of numbers (decimal, binary, octal, hexadecimal, or other), letters, or both, used to identify an item (or data). A classification code enables this item to express its relationship to other items of the same or a similar nature. Identification (ID) should be a short number designed for cost/effectiveness in terms of error free data transcription and transmission. The classification code (CC) should be a descriptive number whose goal is to provide detail and remove ambiguity (Figure 14.1).

Years of experience have demonstrated that one single number cannot perform both functions. It is a problem of specialization. To develop an efficient coding system, experience is required in selecting the most compact, complete and methodological solution and implementing this solution in the population of items (or data) which must be stored and retrieved in mass storage media such as computer memory or microfilm.

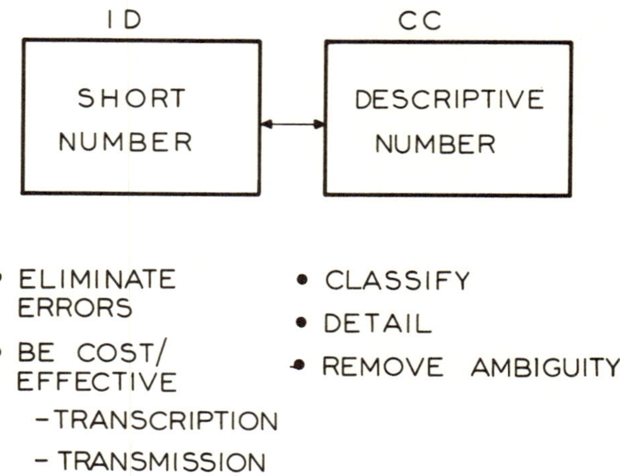

FIGURE 14.1

A computer based coding system able to provide the needed dependability assurances is a difficult and challenging undertaking, particularly as little exists today in terms of a theory able to meet identification and classification requirements. The problem with organizational work concerning data starts exactly at this point, and the following sections will present the solution which I have developed over thirty years of practice.

The principles and applications discussed in this and the following two chapters have been used in working conditions in industrial concerns and financial institutions in connection with the development and implementation of databases. They do not exist only in a test atmosphere; rather they are important facilities that enhance productivity and enable deadlines to be met. The applications have been made available on both large computer systems and minicomputers—standalone and integrated in a network.

In seven years, the services provided by the application of DCS have evolved into general facilities used routinely by administrative and technical personnel. As part of this evolution, it has been possible to take advantage of technological developments and the lower cost they made possible. Lower prices for RAM and disc memories have allowed information to live more freely in electronic form. This has important implications on the nature of the output: *where* it happens, and *when*. But implementation would have been handicapped without a rational database organization.

Rationalization in the internal structure of the database (the identification and classification system) has been instrumental in putting into application the opportunities presented by rapid developments in microprocessors—now cheap enough to serve as control elements for solutions such as logic over data. Furthermore, while network facilities make local document output desirable, and certainly preferable to centralized reproduction and distribution by traditional methods, unless the database is organized in a rational manner (as we will see in the following pages) the benefit will be largely diminished by higher communications costs.

DEVELOPING A CLASSIFICATION CODE

In a classification system, items of similar type must be grouped into homogeneous categories by using their similarities and the relationships developing therefrom. This is primarily a *taxonomical* approach. Different families, groups or classes of items (and data) have distinct classification needs. Therefore, a taxonomical organization may not end in a one-to-one correspondence between the classified items and the corresponding identification code. In this case, the solution is to use *further definiens* to reach the level of detail able to provide an unambiguous link between classification and identification for each and every item.

A collection of sources such as books, drawings, reports or abstracts alone will not originate research or invent anything, but if efficiently classified they will save time engineers and designers otherwise waste in seeking buried or widely scattered information. This is where the economies come in.

The same reference is valid for other data, accounting is a prime example. The handling of accounting data is one of the oldest computer applications. It is also one of the least structured, as client accounts, supplier records, purchased items and inventories (to name a few) have common information elements which are structured at different times and in different ways—being, as a result, incompatible among themselves.

Two issues stand out.

1. We cannot provide homogeneity without identifying the ID which should be homogeneous. This, we said, has a prerequisite: the process of classification.

2. If a classification had to reflect all the special interests of all its individual users, it would have to embody information of no interest to most of them.

The answer to this problem is to have a prime taxonomical classification with the highest common factor of interest, delegating the individual user's special concerns to a secondary classification made by means of further definiens.

The key to a valid classification system design lies in a few rules:

1. Properly define item characteristics so that the resulting codification is tailored to the user's needs.

2. Observe the logical structure of the population under study.

3. Provide for further expansion.

4. Observe a classification rule and the process of ordering which it implies.

5. Provide the right place (and only one place) for each item (or data) in the population being ordered.

Correspondingly, the identification code must be short for economical and transmission purposes; it must distinguish between user requirements (technical, commercial, other) concerning the same item; and it must provide a parity check for error control.

Once properly developed, a classification/identification system becomes a pivot point in management information and control. Figure 14.2 exemplifies this reference, presenting in a coordinate system the ideas we have just discussed. Identification (ID) is the pivot point of a 3-D system which:

1. Supports the classification code and by extension the central information file (CIF);

2. Permits the rearend engine (and data management at large) to run in an efficient manner; and

3. Holds together the geographically or functionally distributed sections of the database.

Without well thought out solutions to the issue of coordination, efforts to weed out unwanted duplications on IE will be futile; database integration a vain exercise; the simultaneous update mechanism impossible to support; and database disintegration a distinct possibility.

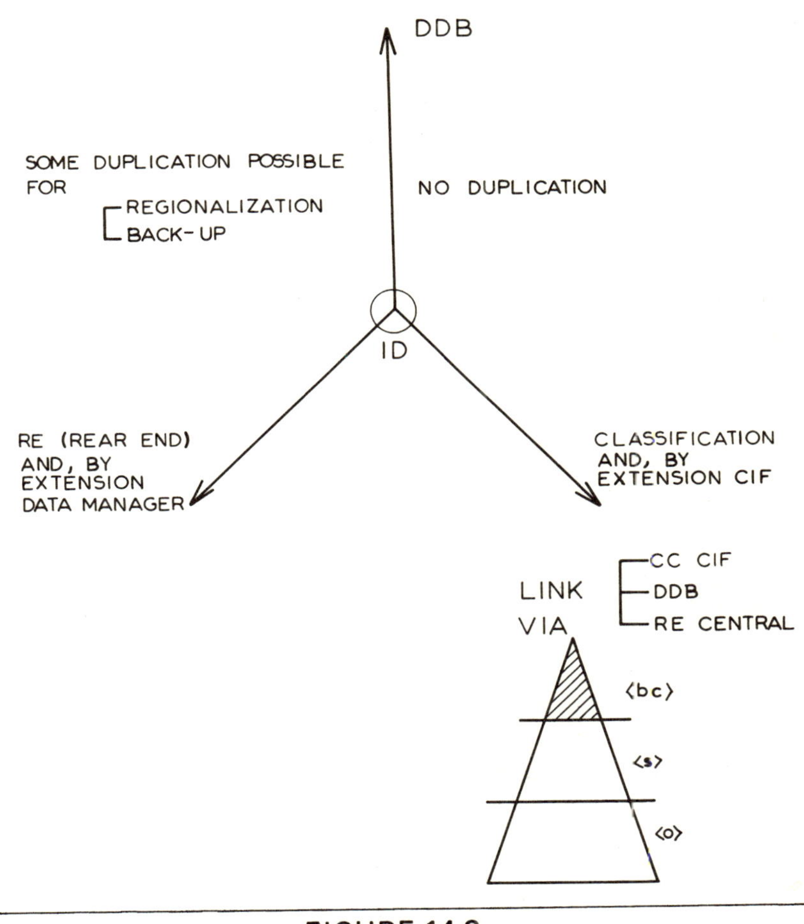

FIGURE 14.2

INDEXING AND RETRIEVAL

A coding system must assure an able answer to data storage and retrieval requirements. Storage and retrieval are a communication process between the user and the database in which information is stored. The interaction of the man/information systems may be threefold:

1. Contribution to the wealth of the database (including update, file addition and deletion).
2. Data analysis and indexing—fulfilling organizational prerequisites.
3. Search for reference by the ultimate user.

In structuring and upkeeping databases, activity "one" is a prerequisite for "two"; and "two" is a prerequisite for "three." Communication is based on an organization of knowledge. A collection of source references such as books, drawings, files, records or abstracts, must be turned into an organized entity where information is added or withdrawn at request. The organization of a database keeping items in properly arranged IE and, subsequently, the search for reference are both essentially concerned with the problem of measuring *similarity* and its opposite, *dissimilarity*. This is basic to all information retrieval systems.

With manual processing, these tasks have been underrated. Given the large amount of available data, it is often physically impossible to search, in terms of overall similarities, a substantial number of related items with many varying characteristics. Computers offer the chance for fulfilling data retrieval objectives, provided that the proper organizational work involving classification and identification prerequisites is completed.

Let us take an example from industry. Two methods predominate in the classification of technological and industrial products:

> one is based on nomenclature,
> the other on design features.

Both start from a recognition of the fact that undisciplined nomenclature causes identical and closely similar parts to remain dispersed and unrecognized. This creates waste in a multitude of ways. To avoid this waste, attempts have been made to establish standards.

Over the last quarter century standardization and streamlining have been handicapped, and methods have proved unreliable, when names, codes and numbers have been allocated by more than one person or department. Efforts to assure a unique name space by leaving gaps in a numbering system to be filled out later (as the need arises) have invariably failed. Furthermore, residual experience from obsolete, manual information retrieval systems complicates the development of universal, analytic indexing and searching criteria.

A serious, fundamental study for indexing and retrieval of IE must consider the existing, incoming and possibly generated information elements. Retrieval needs and requirements derive from this evaluation, but the study should not lose sight of the fact that indexing and retrieval are separate, though closely related activities in an information handling system.

Indexing requires that the facts characterizing an information element are identified, classified and stored in a predetermined fashion. The rules for storing these facts must be recorded with an index and readily available to any authorized system or individual. For retrieval, the general store of data must be searched, and a specific word, topic or subject in a request pinpointed in storage.

For instance, indexing of texts (books, papers, articles, etc.) may be accomplished:

> chronologically,
> by subject,
> by publisher, and/or
> by author.

Inquiries made to the database may range from the form of an exact book title to a loosely expressed subject title or may refer to some ambiguous date of publication. If we have a collection of, say, 10,000 microforms which we want to order in a way enabling us to retrieve any specified document, we have to select an optimal index of classification. If it is possible to express the index or classification in a one-to-one relation between index and document, the latter can be placed in a *linear order*.

This is the classifical approach to indexing for retrieval purposes. Typical cases of such an order are a chronological sequence followed on classifying correspondence, and an alphabetical author index. It is the method used in libraries over the last quarter century, and to a large extent copied by industrial and business processes and for computer handling.

THE PARALLEL CODE SYSTEM

The linear order has a weakness: the difficulty of inserting other items in the list (or deleting them) without upsetting the order. Even if care has been taken in providing spaces for future growth, no one can foresee precisely the number of spaces needed during, say, the next thirty years—the expected lifetime of a new classification system. The solution to this problem led to the Dimitris Chorafas System (DCS).

DCS implies the use of a parallel code along the lines of the principles we have emphasized from our introductory paragraphs. The object of the first code to be drawn is that of classification. Here no linear approach is taken, instead, a relational model which observes a taxonomical order at three levels of detail: family, group and class, as shown in Figure 14.3.

Once this preparatory work is done, a parallel number is associated to the classification to be used in all accesses, transfers and search procedures. This can be a running number of the simplest linear form. We will call this running number the *basic code:* $<bc>$; and to keep it the shortest possible code, it is in hexadecimal (or even radix 32). We will, however, return to this subject to say that within different applications environments the $<bc>$ may not suffice for ID purposes and needs to be supplemented by a suffix and an origin.

Designed primarily to assist in retrieval, this parallel code system meets three objectives:

1. Simplicity.

2. Ability to use statements permitting the retrieval of selected IE, written quite readily with a minimum knowledge of the system.

3. Existence of a formal syntax enabling the retrieval operation to be automatically transformed or translated into a logical sequence of actions.

Since it must be structured by means of syntactical rules and signs, a coding system is a *language*. The ABC of a good language is: that of using a well defined, usually finite set of characters; observing rules for combining characters with one another to form words or other expressions; and of assigning a specific meaning to some of the words or expressions to serve communicating purposes (for people or machines).

Such requirements are met in the design of DCS. The steps characterizing this classification/identification procedure are simple, however, the effort necessary for implementation is substantial. By spelling out the needed criteria, order and selection become feasible.

The organizational effort is quite critical, and different possibilities exist for seeing this effort through.

1. The more general a concept or a criterion, the broader its capabilities to accept items of a wanted information content.

2. The more specific a concept or criterion, the smaller but more precise the information content of a given class, and the more work must be put forward to polish such a system.

The process of polishing is important: the better designed the coding system, the shorter the tracing and the more effective the retrieval. Also, fewer errors will sneak in. Practice suggests that it is better to put in the needed effort at the beginning, rather than chasing after (unpleasant) facts later.

Whether broad or specific criteria are used for classification purposes, it is essential that the terms defining each work criterion are unique, reliable and

196

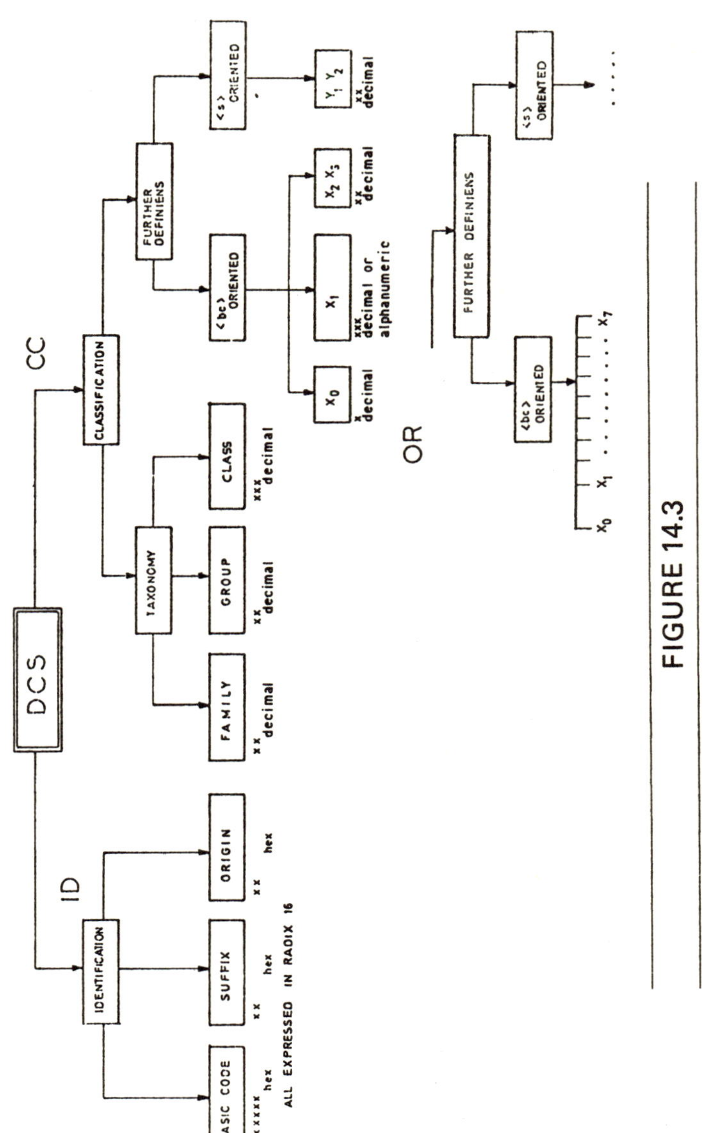

FIGURE 14.3

unambiguous. Inadequacies remaining in the system at the conceptual or applications level can jeopardize the entire classification system. Different prerequisites may, however, prevail, depending on the job to be done. For orderly arrangement and subsequent retrieval, the criteria must display:

1. The kind of information to be revealed;
2. The detail to which this information will be sorted out;
3. The depth of evaluation as to synonyms of cross-referenced items;
4. The purpose this information must serve;
5. The kind of questions which will probably be asked;
6. The structure of retrieval operations;
7. The computer based media to be used in retrieval and their capabilities;
8. The number of possible questions and the acceptable waiting time;
9. The frequency with which these questions will be posed;
10. The numbers of issues which might be involved in each question;
11. The possibilities to be presented in a selection procedure;
12. The outcome of this selection procedure and its impact on further operations.

The kind of questions posed by the end user help indicate whether the organization of the indexing system should be of a general or a particular nature; this influences the procedures of retrieval and selection. If we undertake a simulation of retrieval procedures, a tentatively chosen taxonomy can offer clues on future happenings and support one structure orientation of the projected code against another.

Other issues of importance are: the time span over which this system is projected to be valid; the possible number of items to be added and deleted, in terms of systems upkeep; the need to keep this system as uniform and consistent to early design as possible; this way the system can help promote a better utilization of resources through timely and accurate references and the availability of the necessary talent to perform the required classification functions and subsequent updating.

CODING FOR ORGANIZED COMPLEXITY

A structure specifically designed for information systems usage must be able to cope with the *organized complexity* which characterizes modern business. Organized complexity results from the existence of a large number of information elements which have a meaningful relationship between themselves and their environments.

Data elements are, as a rule, distributed unevenly within the working procedures of an organization, and their characteristics change with use and time. This suggests the need for a systematic arrangement of similar items into suitably selected categories. A coding system able to cope with demands for data storage and retrieval must allow options for the development of methods which would formalize the determination of performance criteria, including efficient search algorithms and cross-indexing.

Flexibility for making alterations can be provided by dividing the classification part into *taxonomy* and *further definiens*. Taxonomical rules are unique for the whole system; more precisely from one *family* (of IE) to the next. Some examples will follow.

As contrasted to the taxonomical criteria, the structuring of the further definiens must consider the fact that an information system contains elements assumed to:

1. Have their own objective function, generally not coinciding with that of the total classification system.

2. Present particular requirements for optimal search; preferably by family of items (or data) and with allowance for expected future activity.

3. Enable a good exploitation of the classification potential by family, if need be, doing this family oriented search better than can be done through a generalization on the basis of the overall classification/identification system.

4. Permit building the overall system step-by-step rather than trying to make everything in one piece.

This approach allows a combination of the interests of an element (or family) to that of the entire system through the development of a plan leading to agreed upon solutions. The basic prerequisites are that: a valid methodology exists, and each analyst understands the potential of the classification/identification system.

Success depends on management's ability to assure consistency in the overall classification program; the researcher's determination to test multiple assumptions with the aim of reaching efficient solutions; the need for effectively planning for future requirements; and the organization's propensity to evaluate many assumptions in a short period of time, thereby assuring reasonable flexibility.

Based on these premises, the design of a rational, compact and compatible coding system can be satisfactorily completed. The system we are about to describe was made possible through the completion of a management research project on a new article identification code for a leading industrial firm. The idea of DCS was advanced and implemented after considerable study and experimentation, to promote records accuracy, improve storage and retrieval perspectives, assure economic data transmission, and guarantee a unique reference to articles and accounts.

As briefly suggested in the preceding sections, DCS consists of two main parts:

> an identification number, and
> a classification number.

The former is binary and can be recorded on hardcopy/softcopy in octal, hexadecimal or radix 32 form. The latter is decimal, "six plus" digits long, and organized in three fields of two decimal digits each:

> family,
> group, and
> class.

One hundred families exist in all—for any and every system. The family layout is in a 10 x 10 matrix form (Figure 14.4). In the application described in this figure, one row is dedicated to top management information; a second row is dedicated to allocation and optimization connected to the sales inventory production system; seven rows are used for the classification of products, machines, services and accounts; and one row is kept in reserve.

Within the DCS family matrix, the seven rows reserved for products and accounts are column-wise distributed by subject:

1. The first column (rows "two" to "eight" inclusive) is dedicated to labor and knowhow (human resources);
2. The second, to assets and liabilities;
3. The following three columns classify information (distinct by family) by raw materials and semimanufactured products;
4. The next three columns concern finished products;
5. One column is used for the machinery families;
6. The last column is held in reserve.

Families twenty-two to twenty-eight, thirty-two to thirty-eight, . . . , eighty-two to eighty-eight, classify and store data on transactional issues, albeit of a predominantly engineering nature.

The files for each product, account or service uniquely coded by the family are subdivided by means of groups, with up to 100 groups existing per family. Greater detail in classification is assured by means of classes: up to 100 subgroups exist per group. To provide a one-to-one correspondence to the identification subsystem, the family-group-class classification is completed with further definiens which reflect on further data (or product) characteristics but are not organized taxonomically.

The following matrix is displayed rotated on the page. Its row axis (TRANSACTIONS-SETTLEMENTS-PRODUCT FILES, Basic-Elements) is numbered 0–9; its column axis (HUMAN RESOURCES … MACHINES) is numbered 0–9.

	HUMAN RESOURCES	ASSETS EXCEPT MACHINES	RAW MATERIALS AND SEMI-FINISHED PRODUCTS			FINISHED PRODUCTS			MACHINES	
			GLASS/CHEM.	WIRE	OTHERS	INCANDESCENT LAMPS	DISCHARGE LAMPS	HYBRID		
	0	1	2	3	4	5	6	7	8	9
0 TOP MANAGEMENT										
1 S.I.P. OPTIMIZATION	(Order Analysis)	(Sales forecasts)	(Transport-Logistics)	(Warehousing-Inventories)	(Customer Records)	(Regional Records)	(Product Records)	(Quality Records)	(Production Plans)	
2	HIRED SERVICES	REAL ESTATE (Land and Buildings)	CHEMICALS (Basic Elements)			STEMS		OTHER ASSEMBLED INNER PARTS	PARTS (Incl. Spares)	
3		FURNITURES AND FIXTURES	CHEMICALS (Derivatives)	OTHER WIRES		INCANDESCENT LAMPS EXCEPT 54 – 59	DISCHARGE LAMPS EXCEPT 64 – 69	OTHER FINISHED PRODUCTS EXCEPT 74 – 79	ASSEMBLED PARTS	
4	SALARIED PERSONEL (EXECUTIVE/GENERAL)	UTILITIES (Electricity, Gas, Water, Information)	FORMATED GLASS	TUNGSTEN WIRES	SHAPED PIECES	INCANDESCENT STEM TYPE LAMPS WITHOUT SPEC. REQUEST TO LO-CATION/MEAS.FIL.	ARC-DISCHARGE LAMPS	ACCESSORIES	MACHINES FOR SEMI-FINISHED PRODUCTS	
5	HOURLY PERSONEL (DIRECT/INDIRECT)		TUBULAR GLASS	MOLYBDENUM WIRES		INCANDESCENT STEM TYPE LAMPS WITH SPEC. REQUEST TO LO-CATION/MEAS.FIL.	GLOW-DISCHARGE LAMPS	LIGHTING FITTINGS	MACHINES FOR FINISHED PRODUCTS	
6		STORAGE AND TRANSFER	FULL GLASS	LEADING-IN WIRES	STAMPS	INCANDESCENT BEAD - MOUNT - TYPE LAMPS			MACHINES AND TOOLS/COMMON USE	
7	QUALITY STANDARDS	CONSUMABLE MATERIALS		COILS	PACKAGING MATERIALS	INCANDESCENT LAMPS WITH QUARTZ BULB			INSTRUMENTS (Measuring, Testing, Control)	
8	KNOW HOW				LAMP CAPS					
9										

Row-axis bands: MANAGEMENT INFORMATION/FINANCIAL RESULTS — SALES-INVENTORY-PRODUCTION — TRANSACTIONS-SETTLEMENTS-PRODUCT FILES (Basic-Elements).

1.4 B

© DNC

FIGURE 14.4

Figure 14.5 exhibits this sequential approach to classification. A population is formed by items which are first sorted into four families which are homogeneous as to item shape. More detailed sorting is based on dimension; up to one hundred groups may be distinguished this way. Still more detailed item sorting may consider materials as the basis for separating goods of the same shape and dimension into homogeneous lots.

The structure of the classification system evolves further as the population within a group is sorted out in accordance with further pre-established criteria, ensuring that input data will find their proper *pigeon-hole* for storage and subsequent retrieval. That is the goal of the preparatory work.

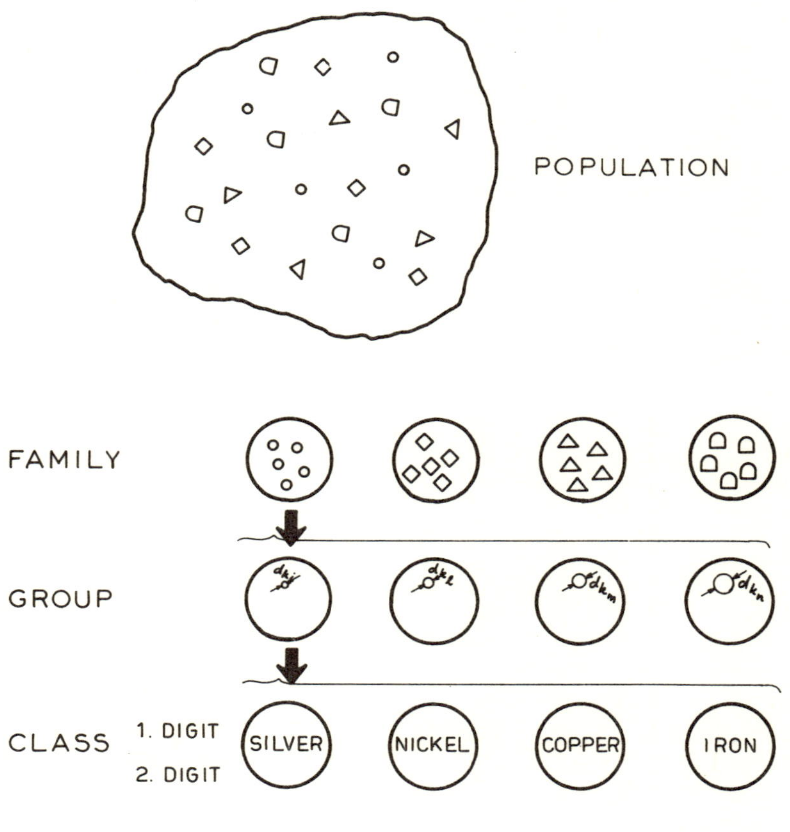

CLASSIFICATION BASED ON WORKMANSHIP

FIGURE 14.5

EXAMPLE OF CLASSIFICATION

The choice of a 6-digit taxonomical number has been influenced by requirements of economy, dependability and the assurance of a short dialing system through interactive terminals. A 6-digit decimal (even a 7-digit) number is quite similar to a telephone number in most cities, the latter giving the first hint as to a possible size of taxonomical code—particularly in the users' ability to retain it in memory.

As Figure 14.6 exemplifies, the family can be located through the KL coordinates in the database matrix of the DCS, the group through the MN coordinates, and the class by means of PQ. Theoretically, up to one million classification possibilities exist. However, because a taxonomical system must allow for expansion, the possibilities are in reality much less, their exact number depending on the population to which this system will be applied and on the objectives to be met.

It is suggested by experience that less than sixty (out of one hundred families) are used in the original design and that, subsequently, no more than thirty to forty possibilities are taken of the one hundred in any given group or class.

Notice that expandability can be insured by converting the classification system's radix ten to, say, radix sixteen, thus making more columns and rows available. However, it would be a poor practice to substitute preparatory work (and the polishing that should follow it) by increasing the size of poorly constructed systems.

An example will show the way this taxonomical classification works. The motor reduction couple demonstrated in Figure 14.7 will be classified within the DCS matrix in that family dedicated to machines (family eighty-six in Figure 14.4). The 10 x 10 matrix of this family might, for instance, be constructed to represent by column electromechanical equipment, and by row reduction gear. This column-and-row intersection defines the group. The two class digits may, for instance, classify voltage and horsepower.

The component parts of the couple will also be classified but in a different family. In Figure 14.4, the family for parts is eighty-two. One group in this family is dedicated to shells; both the shell of the motor and the reduction gear will be classified. The two, however, will be further distinguished by means of the class digits. Should the first of the class digits classify the diameter, at this point the motor shell and the reduction gear will be taxonomically distinguished from one another.

Being assembled parts, the rotor and the stator will also fall into their own groups in family eighty-three. Their place is the column in the group matrix dedicated to electrical components. On the other hand, the gear and the axis will be in family eighty-two; each in its own group. This is the background methodology of DCS.

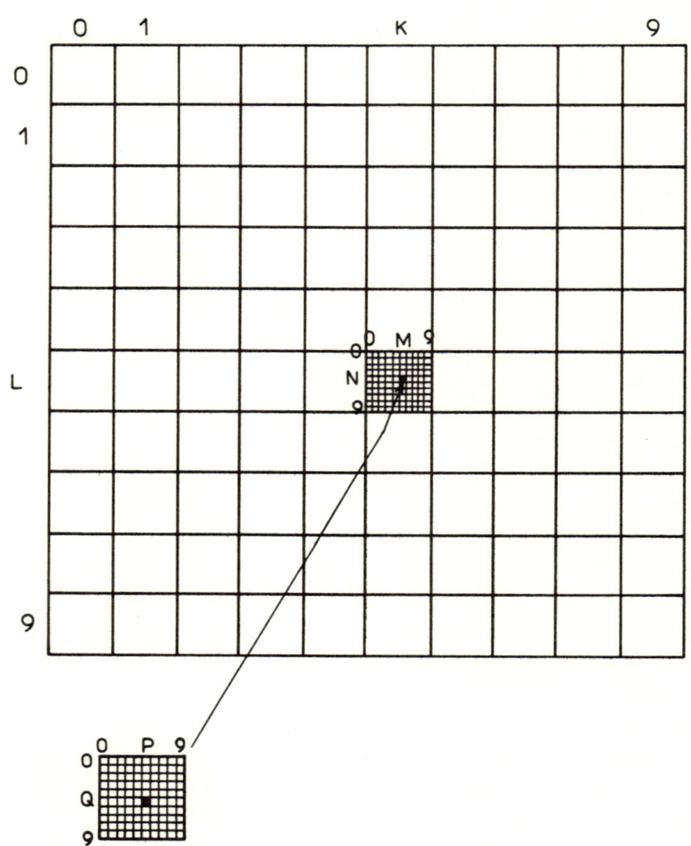

THE CLASSIFICATION (TAXONOMICAL) CODE IS:

KL.MN.PQ

OR, SIMPLY:

XX.XX.XX

FIGURE 14.6

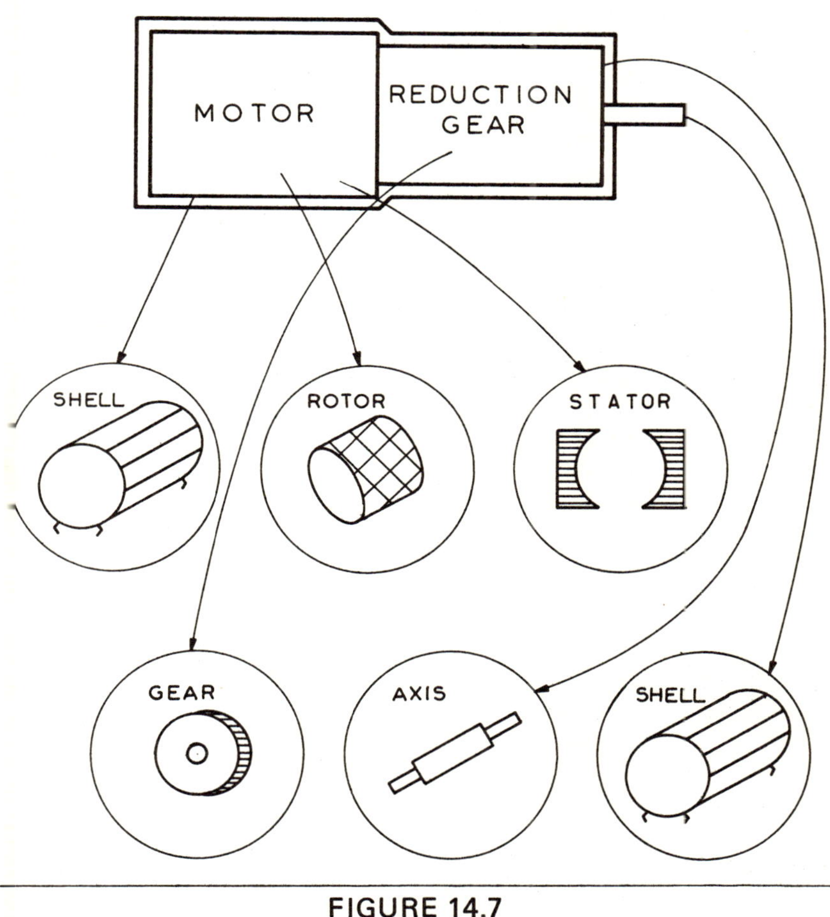

FIGURE 14.7

15 Using DCS

INTRODUCTION

DCS has been designed in full observance of organizational prerequisites in terms of databases and datacomm. Its goal is to classify and identify information elements (and articles) in a cost/effective manner able to serve a variety of applications perspectives.

A code may consist of characters such as letters, punctuation marks or numerals. An identification through characters such as punctuation marks is the least suitable for data communications and data processing. Letters have a greater capacity per character position than numerals because alphabets consist of more than ten different letters. The radix for a numbering system based on the English alphabet would be twenty-six.

Codes composed of letters alone can thus be shorter than purely decimal numerical codes, but even better, we can develop a radix 32 code which is expressed in binary form and uses a strictly numerical basis where the pseudo alphabetic characters A, B, C . . . X, Y, Z serve as an extension of numerical signs. Such solutions adopted by DCS helps shorten the field size in terms of transcription, storage and transmission.

A key advantage of the system rests on the capabilities offered by its parallel code structure. DCS is based on the principle of a one-to-one correspondence between classification and identification. First an item or data is classified (taxonomy: family, group and class). Then it is identified.

So far we have referred only to the basic code. But as we will see in this chapter, identification is made by means of:

> basic code (five hexadecimal digits and one for parity);
> suffix (two hexadecimal digits); and
> origin (two hexadecimal digits).

The basic code corresponds to the taxonomy assured by family, group, class and the < bc > oriented further definiens. (Indeed, the basic code is one of the two pillars of the DCS; the other is the family matrix.) The suffix identifies secondary characteristics still important enough to be carried into the code structure. The origin adds to the latter by focusing on some unique issues such as a given factory or a branch office.

In a typical banking environment, for example, recording and exchanging information are basic to business operations, these functions tend to be cumbersome when the bank stresses diversity of services, and there is an increasing demand for up-to-date management information.

These requirements will not be handled effectively, unless the database is properly organized from the start—this means a rational, taxonomical way to support both geographic and functional distribution of file and database segments. The necessity of this is highlighted by the evolving data communication facilities reflecting the dispersion of banking offices over the country and the need to keep abreast of developments outside the company, such as the advent of Fedwire, Bankwire, CHIPS (the bank clearing center) and SWIFT (Society for Worldwide Interfinance Teleprocessing).

Today, for a financial institution, databasing and data communications are necessary ingredients of most of its evolving classical activities. Because information-based services are expected to keep growing fast, it is good practice to prepare an infrastructure for applications of the present and the future. An integral text and data network is needed, and this means emphasis on classification and identification—and, therefore, on structuring.

UNDERLINING THE CLASSIFICATION ISSUE

Say that a given manufacturing firm is faced with the problem of classifying its spare parts. After having studied the organizational prerequisites associated with this problem, the analysts conclude that the classification code is to be allocated as outlined on page 209. An example is given both with taxonomical considerations and with the allocation of the first digit of the further definiens.

Following-up on the example introduced in Chapter 13, Figure 15.1 illustrates the group matrix for parts, corresponding to the KL positions in the taxonomy. Of the ten columns, eight have been partially used, and two are kept in reserve. One of the ten lines is also kept in reserve, one has been used at eighty percent, and the others at less than sixty percent. The use of the other is only minor. These necessary precautions will allow future growth without upsetting the classifications structures decided upon. This creates no gaps in identification as the latter is a different subsystem altogether.

Figures 15.2 and 15.3 exhibit the class matrices corresponding to the MN positions in the taxonomy. Such matrices carry forward the classification work done in the group matrix; they provide a finer detail. Such detailed items as the shape and, secondarily, function will be classified by *norm evaluation*, as explained in the following paragraph. This explosion beginning with the first digits of the further definiens can be continued by bringing the other digits into perspective.

208

ALLOCATION OF DIGITS IN A CLASSIFICATION

TAXONOMICAL CODE XX . XX . XX

KL: Family (say, mechanical parts)
MN: Group (as in Figure 5)
PE: Class (as in Figure 6 or 7, depending on the part).

FURTHER DEFINIENS: first digit, x_0, allocated to Norm Evaluation.

x_0 = 0; ANSI-norm;

x_0 = 1; ISO-norm;

x_0 = 2; Catalog part without known norm.

x_0 = 3; Reserved

x_0 = 4; ISO-norm, afterwards reworked by this company.

x_0 = 5; Catalog part without known norm, afterwards reworked by this company.

x_0 = 6; Reserved

x_0 = 7; This company's own old product design specifications to which do not correspond cataloged parts.

x_0 = 8; Reserved

x_0 = 9; Reserved

For example, one company which applied DCS divided the further definiens into three groups:

1. x_0 is a 1-digit decimal number that extends the classification capability of the taxonomical code, without belonging to the latter. This gives some families the freedom to drop x_0 while others may need to use it.

2. x_1 is a 5-digit decimal number field. It identifies the company that made the original design of the machine or component. This is vital information for many parts associated with their original manufacturers.

3. x_2x_3 is a 2-digit number acting as a box able to store and retrieve through serial numbering the file for each machine component or part—past the x_1 screen.

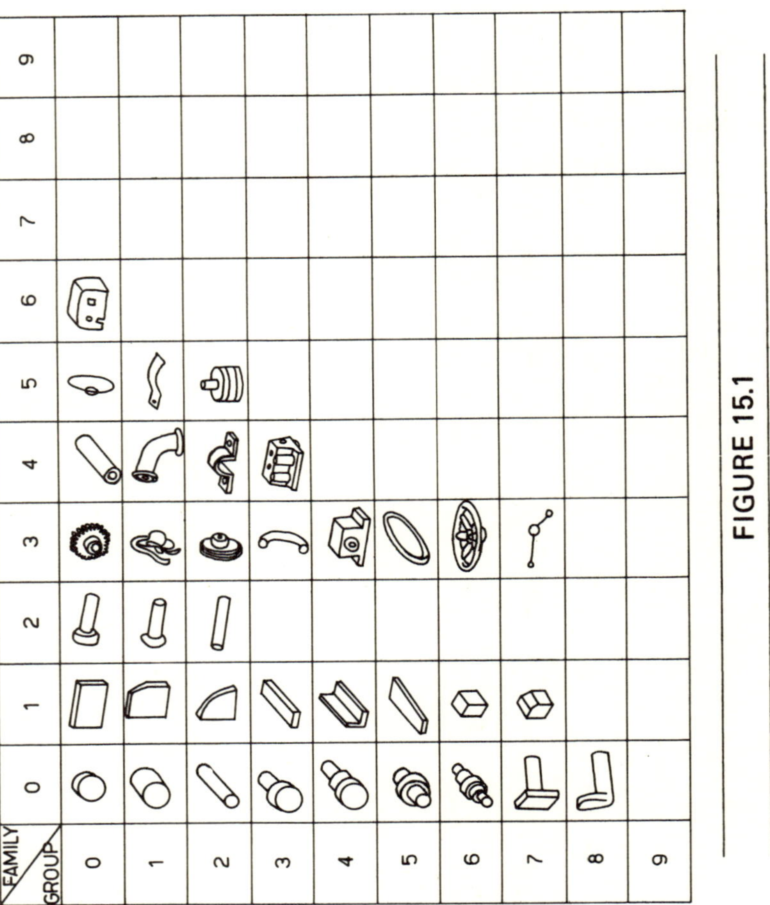

FIGURE 15.1

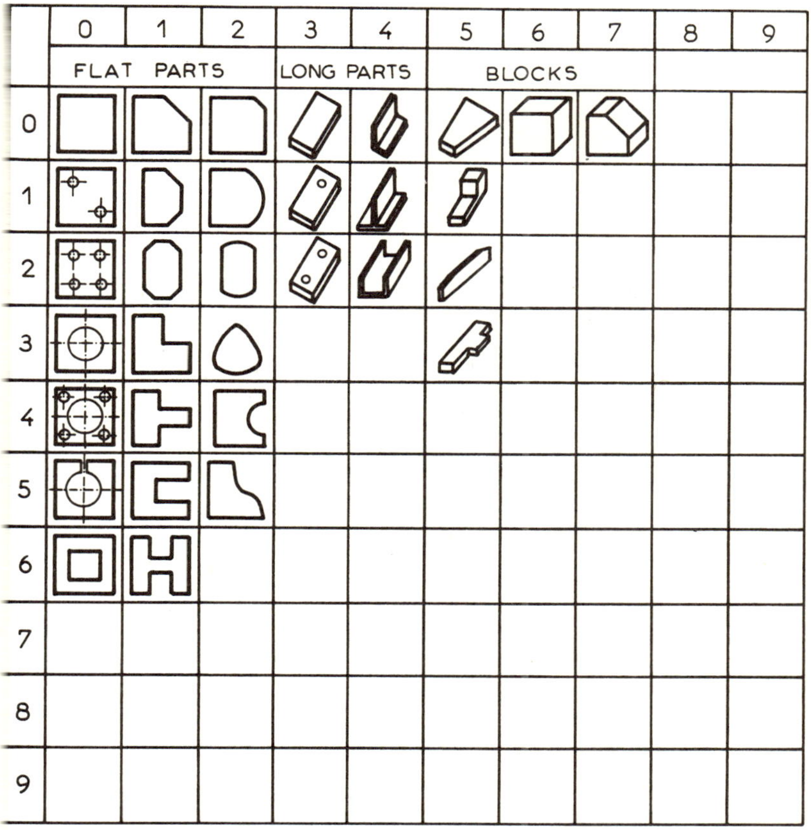

FIGURE 15.2

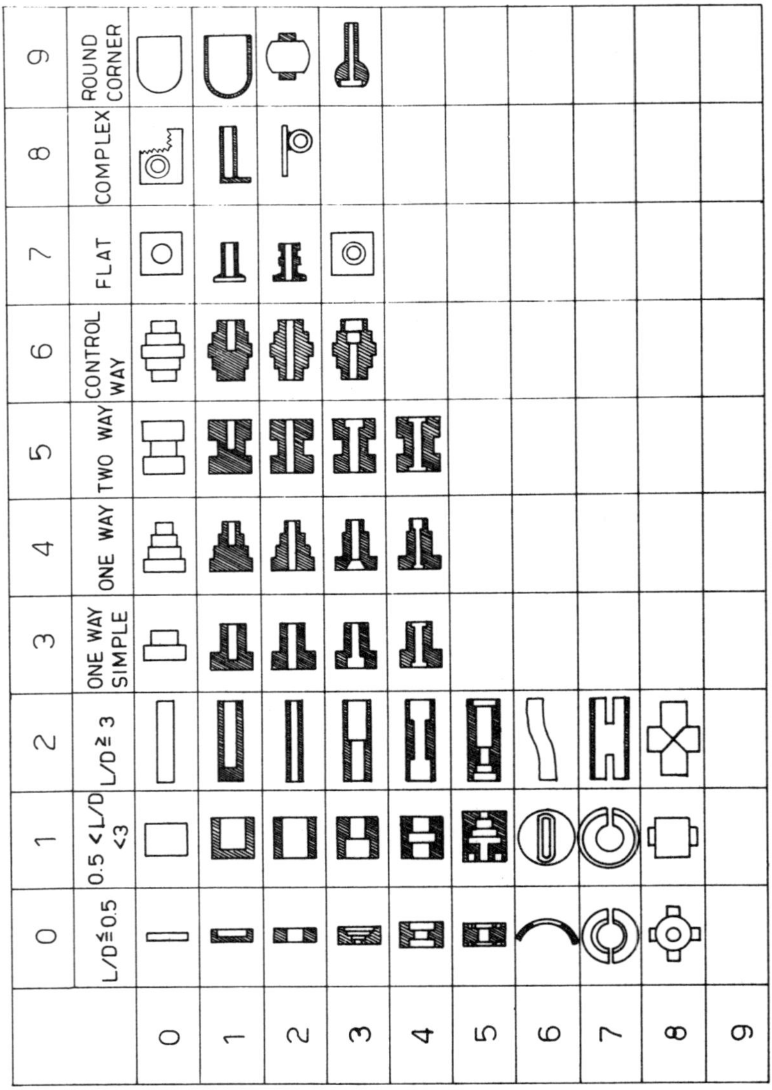
0
1
2
3
4
5
6
7
8
9
L/D≤0.5
0.5 <L/D <3
L/D≥3
ONE WAY SIMPLE
ONE WAY
TWO WAY
CONTROL WAY
FLAT
COMPLEX
ROUND CORNER
0
1
2
3
4
5
6
7
8
9

FIGURE 15.3

The need for this solution has come up as, even though the items on hand (spare parts in this case) have been allocated to pigeon-holes according to a classification and identification code, and the x_0, x_1 digits have been used, more than one item still remains in the classification. Thus, the x_2x_3 field ensures that each file will correspond with one and only one identification number.

The taxonomical considerations and the four digits of the further definiens (x_0, x_1, x_2x_3) help uniquely identify an item in terms of its technical characteristics. A basic code will correspond one-to-one to them; this is a running number allocated on a first-come, first-serve basis.

This provides considerable flexibility. Yet, prior to closing this section, it is appropriate to mention the existence of other further definiens: the $y_0y_1y_2$ which are suffix-oriented, and are discussed later in this chapter. The whole concept has been briefly outlined in Figure 13.1 of Chapter 13.

IDENTIFICATION

As stated in the preceding paragraphs, with DCS each classification number has an identification number in one-to-one correspondence. The identification number is divided in three parts, in order of importance:

>   a basic code, <bc>
>   a suffix, <s> and an
>   origin <o>.

To better follow the rational for this three way division of ID, we should bring it into historical perspective. DCS was first developed in 1969 to serve the needs of Osram GmbH, in Munich and Berlin.[1] When the groundwork was completed, an argument developed between the design engineers and the commercial executives. What is a lamp? or, more precisely: How should a given product be identified?

The most concise answer is through its technical characteristics. But the commercial people argued that issues such as trademark, packaging, and some additional stamps put on a product constitute valid references that must be coded, and cannot be omitted. A system either satisfies every end user's requirements—and thus stands a good chance to be used by everybody—or it does not. In the latter case, it will never become universal.

Furthermore, this distinction became necessary as management research demonstrated that much of today's confusion in item coding by a typical

---

[1] See also "Computer Erfolgreich Einsetzen"; Verlag Moderne Industrie, Munich, 1970.

firm originates the matter-of-fact discrepancy between engineering identification and sales identification of the same item. Translating a given code into another, within a given industrial operation, has always caused delays and mistakes. A new code system should avoid such deficiencies. Figure 15.4 identifies the adopted solution:

1. The <basic code> is allocated on the basis of the technical characteristics of an item (or data) as outlined in the classification code (taxonomy and <bc> oriented further definiens).

2. The suffix complements the basic code; it identifies commercial or secondary characteristics of an item (or data) depending on the family.

3. The origin indicates where an item was made; this is the case with company products. Or, where the item is installed; this is the case with machines.

Both suffix and origin depend on the basic code. Neither can stand on its own. Furthermore, if the origin is to be shown, the suffix must precede it.

In its original design, the basic code has twenty-four binary digits, including four bits for parity purposes. But for man/information communication, it is written in a 6-digit hexadecimal form in order to simplify reading. Suppose that in binary notation, the identification number is:

IOIOOOIIIIIOIOOOOOOI (5 digits) OIOI (parity)

in hexadecimal form it must be written:

<u>IOIO</u>	<u>OOII</u>	<u>IIIO</u>	<u>IOOO</u>	<u>OOOI</u>	<u>OIOI</u>
A	3	E	8	I	5

Selection of the identification number structure reflects a concern for teletransmission requirements: it has been purposely chosen as a short number with a parity check. The use of a 5-digit (plus parity) hexadecimal notation offers the ability to absorb some more than 1,000,000 items in a continuous assignment of numbers, as no classification work needs to be done by the ID structure.

The identification potential is impressive, as in actual application only the difference in technical characteristics is identified through a difference in the basic code. Nontechnical issues, we said, are presented by means of the <s>. Typically, the suffix employs two hexadecimal digits; and so does the origin. (In a hexadecimal code, this assures 256 possibilities for each.)

Furthermore, if necessary, the identification capability of the basic code can be increased in two ways: first, by adding an extra hexadecimal digit to the left, thus bringing the identification potential to about 17,500,000 positions. Second, by switching to a number system of radix 32, thus making avail-

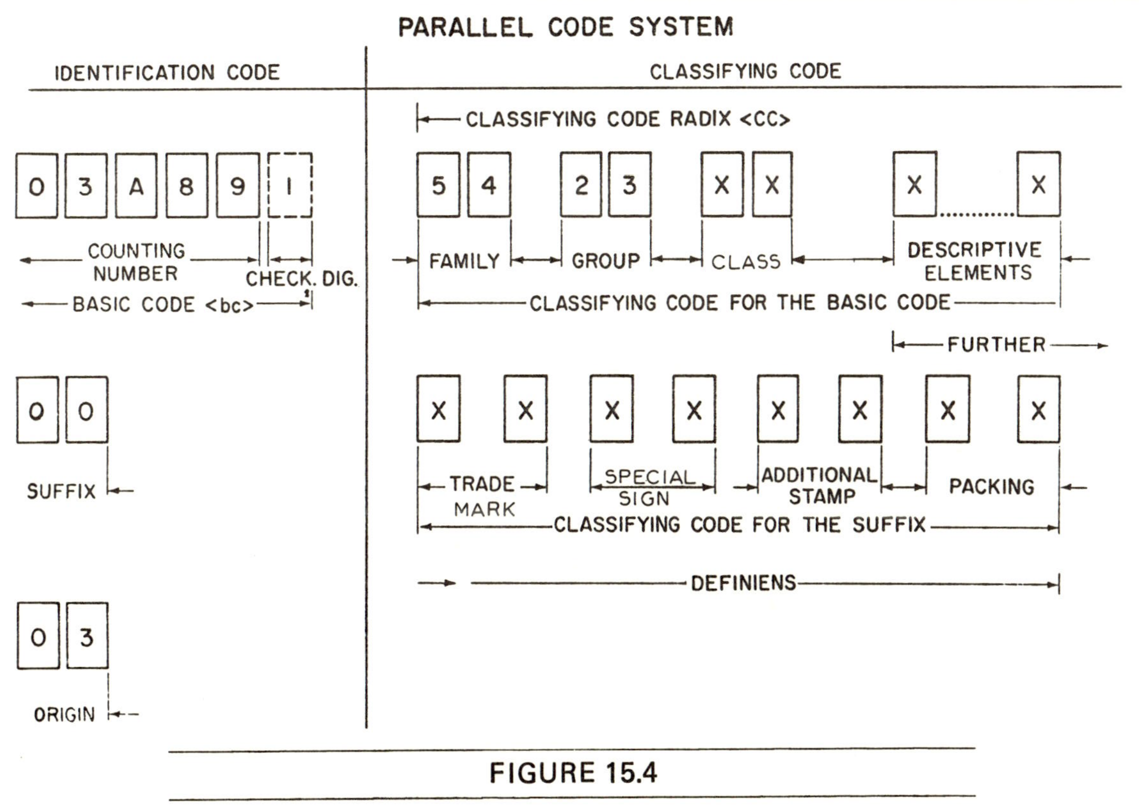

FIGURE 15.4

able roughly 33,500,000 positions. Neither change will upset the numbers so far allocated as either (and both) expansion(s) constitute a system development:

> A 6-digit (plus parity) hexadecimal number is a subset of a 7-digit hexadecimal number.

> A 7-digit hexadecimal number is a subset of a 6-digit number radix 32.

<s> and <o> benefit from the second alternative. The identification possibilities increase for each to 1024, while with the first alternative they remain unchanged. Table 15.1 presents the digit structure for radix 16 (hexadecimal) and for radix 32.

TABLE 15.1*

Digits of Radix "16" and "32"

Decimal	Radix 16 Radix 32	Decimal	Radix 32
0	0	16	G
1	1	17	H
2	2	18	J
3	3	19	K
4	4	20	L
5	5	21	M
6	6	22	N
7	7	23	P
8	8	24	R
9	9	25	S
10	A	26	T
11	B	27	U
12	C	28	W
13	D	29	X
14	E	30	Y
15	F	31	Z

*I, O, Q, V are omitted to avoid confusion: I, O with one and zero; Q with O; V with U.

EXAMPLE WITH PARTS CLASSIFICATION

A case study on the use of DCS will help explain its impact to the reader: highlighting the taxonomical approach taken for the classification of the spare parts. This work was based on two premises: First, the subdivision of the parts was made independent of the classification of machines. The existence of generalized parts useful to more than one machine suggested, based on a study, the importance of instituting a general reference category. Second, group sorting (within DCS) was accomplished along the field of utilization of a given piece. This brought into perspective the different levels of usage the pieces have.

The day-to-day utilization needs (inventories, technical use, accounts) suggested a way of file organization that avoided a complicated memory usage. Efficiency and utility were assured by considering the eventual users of the coding system and by sampling their specific requirements, as shaped in the course of the last five years. The following definitions help explain the approach.

Part (P). Elementary components—or considered as such by convention, a part of machines or other equipment, or becomes a part after simple adjustment or adaptation without changing its fundamental dimensions.

Part of Level "A". PA is a part identified by type and supplier. For PA one envelope is instituted by basic code ("type" part) and one card for the individual part relative to the suffix (in this case, supplier). Being identified by supplier means that it is important to know who the original supplier of this $<$bc$>$ is. The envelope (file) format is shown in Figure 15.5.

Part of Level "B". PB is identified *only* by type. For the parts "B" a card of basic code ("type" part) is established; it includes no individualized supplier sheets.

Part of Level "C". Semi-identified part, classified up to level x_1 (as discussed below) in the further definiens; x_2x_3 are not utilized in many cases. When complete part identification is not necessary, the values $x_2= 9$, $x_3=9$ are used. Part classification is effected in the following manner:

Taxonomy	Further Definiens
KL . MN . PQ	$x_0 . x_1 . x_2x_3 . y_0y_1y_2$

where:

KL = First two digits of classification. Family 82 (Figure 13.1, Chapter 13) is retained for the taxonomical classification of all parts. These find their level of homogeneity in being elementary components.

MN = Third and Fourth Digit of classification, utilized for classifying parts in a characteristic function implicit in KL, as identified by the parts matrix.

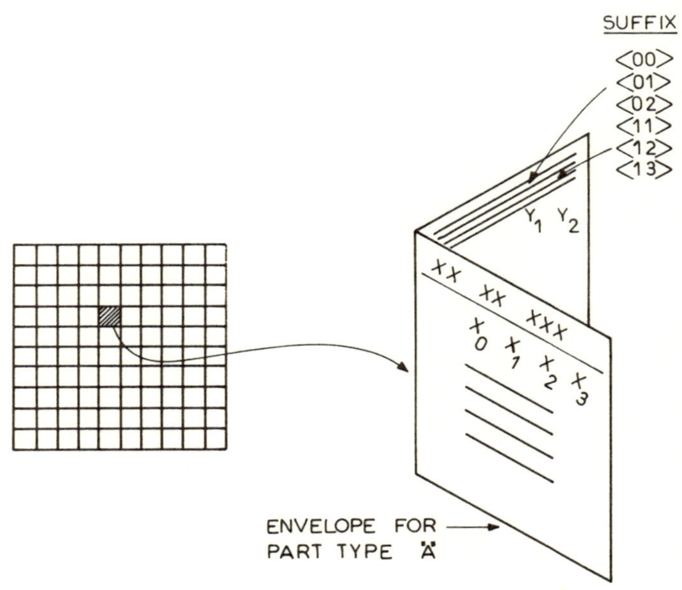

FIGURE 15.5

PR   =   Fifth and sixth digit of classification. Being utilized for continuing the classification of MN. (For instance, Figures 15.1 to 15.3 in
this chapter.)

x_0 =   First *field* (one digit) of the further definiens,

x_0=0 to 8: is utilized as a digit of sorting and as such pursues the
classification of taxonomy,

x_0=9: does not serve any information purpose.

218

$x_1 =$ Second *field* of further definiens (five decimal digits), two cases must be distinguished:

$x_1 =$ 00000 to 99998: supplies the denomination of the catalog(s) of the supplier(s) by referring to the supplier's list.

$x_1 =$ 99999: no information is given by x_1.

$x_2 x_3 =$ identifies a card of basic code ("type" part), thus completing the classification subsystem corresponding to the $<bc>$ in a one-to-one correspondence.

$y_1 y_2 y_3 =$ These decimal digits are associated with the suffix. They provide information on the original supplier source for this part. The values of y_1 do not influence $<bc>$.

Because of the mobility of parts in various warehouses, the study which preceded the implementation of DCS concluded that $<o>$ should not be utilized for supplying information about the specific origin of each part. However, origin identification is followed with the machines where $<o>$ identifies the origin: factory or warehouse. Origin is valuable for the product; it identifies the factory a certain product comes from.

Companies overseeing networks of factories know from experience that the same technical product—hence, the same $<bc>$—may have superficial variations, such as differences in color or packaging; the latter will be given by $<s>$. However, the same technical product in the same package may exhibit process-oriented variations due to the machinery available in a certain factory. The existence of $<o>$ answers this identification requirement; it also permits tracing a given product for reliability (field performance) throughout its useful life.

THE CLEAR TEXT[2]

A *clear text* (descriptive information) designed and built along modular lines was created for each classified and identified part within DCS. It is composed of two sections,

> the first (of fixed length) is forty characters long and rests at the level of the class. In frame presentation this text will become a "heading."

---

[2]Another term is *description*. But the word description has been used for many diverse and incompatible purposes, while *clear text* is a new term to be applied strictly for the work to which reference is made in this section.

The second is of variable length: twenty-five to fifty characters long. It is associated with the <bc> oriented further definiens.

The short clear text requirement has been enforced for two basic reasons: interactive, inquiry necessities and economy in memory usage. These were computer induced considerations particularly at the output (videoform) end. (The adopted structure has been designed to operate in an online realtime environment.) Generally, the advantage in considering them lies in the strict discipline they impose.

In other words, many present-day article names are illogical in length and irrational in structure. A study we conducted proved that a field of eighty characters can contain the clear text of ninety-nine percent of all pieces and materials in stock (some 200,000 of them in this case). A field of forty characters answers a good fifty percent of all requirements, and ninety percent of textual needs find their answer within a field of sixty characters.

To help standardization and homogeneity, a glossary guide was developed for clear text. It carries the abridged words to be used in clear text writing and was made available in two tables: both handled through a data dictionary.

> One sorted on the abridged word basis (argument) with the complete word as a function.
>
> The other sorted on a complete word argument with the abridged word as a function.

The first list was used in retrieving the clear text and in normalization; the second in developing the clear text. Between contracted (abridged) words and full words an unambiguous one-to-one correspondence existed.

Several basic rules have been established to guide the writing of the clear text for machines, parts and materials. For instance:

1. For clear text, both taxonomy and further definiens, the unit of measurement should always precede the numerical value where one value exists: V 110; or fit between the range when a range exists: 220 V 235.

2. The clear text organization should follow the taxonomical sequence of the classification.

3. When the information relative to x_0 and x_1 is absent from the clear text, it must be replaced by the sign "?."

4. For units of measurement utilize the needed number of capital symbols.

5. While standardizing the descriptive information, the clear text should be written in a way the end user can easily comprehend.

System performance was most favorably commented upon by management. The end effect was clarity, simplicity and order—quite a contrast to the multitude of overlapping and (often) incompatible number systems which characterize nearly every industrial concern. Only management's grim resolutions to untangle this situation through radical and imaginative approaches led the companies which applied DCS out of such confusion.

The design and implementation of an efficient coding system can be instrumental to needed classification and identification. This statement is made on the basis of the experience we have had so far with the application of the DCS.

Prior to the institution of this binary computer-oriented numbering system with parity check, one German company was using a 22-digit decimal number (without parity check) to fulfill the same purpose (end product identification for commercial purposes). Furthermore, for different products, seventeen other approaches and numbering systems were used. Error rates in data transcription amounted to roughly seven percent. With the introduction of DCS and the subsequent streamlining, most error sources were weeded out, and the error rate dropped to 0.5%.

16 Case Studies on Database Integration

INTRODUCTION

A general principle exists in our profession—also known (intimately by some, and ultimately by others) as "the law of inverse cost/effectiveness." It simply says this, "What an information system loses in performance and efficiency it gains in uncertainty and added, unnecessary cost."

Information systems can be designed in many ways, but several prerequisites must be met to make them effective to the end user. For the decade of the 1980's, a major effort must be invested concerning the most critical component of an IS—the database. This is why we have placed so much emphasis on DCS.

Figure 16.1 illustrates this point. The parallel code system described is a prerequisite for an effective DB design. A properly projected database is vital for streamlining the IS functions. If all three entities are taken independently, we see that they have common parts:

1. The access to the DB is supported by the DCS.

2. The algorithmic approaches designed to serve the IS feed on the database. (Indeed, eighty percent of the difficulty in using mathematics in management comes from the lack of data; and only twenty percent from model design.)

3. A correctly projected code system is the key to future integration of new applications into the IS.

4. The intersection of the three major areas of interest (IS, DB and code system) provides the basis for access by management, in a user-friendly interactive manner.

The original concept of a computer system as a basic calculator and number cruncher has undergone a profound change. In the past two decades, the development of data processing networks has altered the way we view computers and computing. As systems have become more sophisticated, their ability to process and distribute data has been extended. Remote terminals, and linkages to distributed processing centers brought in new requirements; these are briefly presented in the foregoing four points.

Let us repeat that a major factor in this dynamic development has been the process by which databases can communicate with one another. The significance of interprocess communications is even more impressive when we realize the contrast in requirements between the old and the new approach to databasing—the new being characterized through integrating procedures. But no company can afford to start this work from scratch. The ongoing IS must be kept active and must be able to produce results, until the new structure is ready to take over. With this in mind, let us look at some case studies, from industry and banking, to appreciate the way other organizations have faced this challenge.

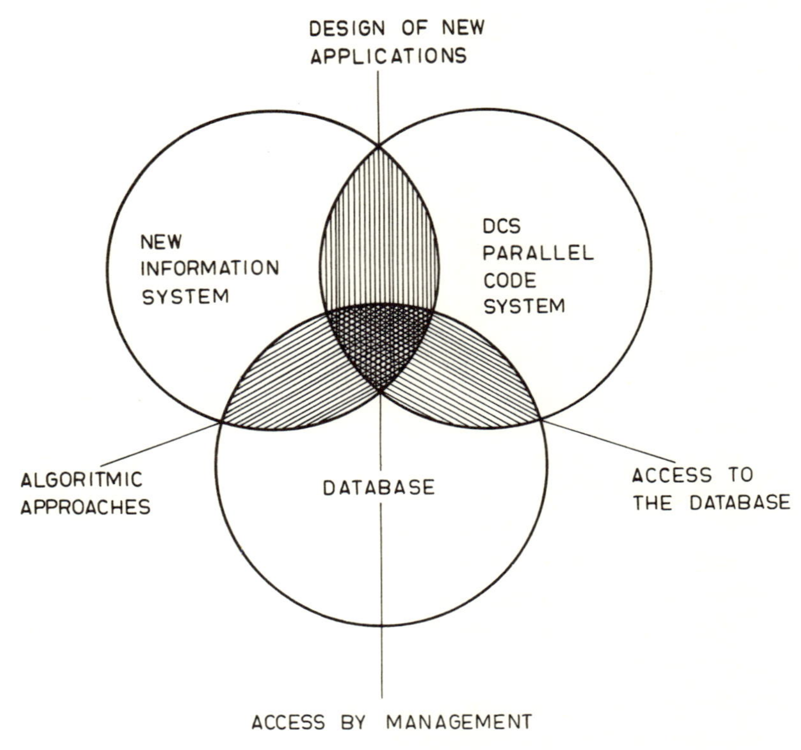

FIGURE 16.1

STEP BY STEP

Suppose that the first mission given to the "new information system" project in the typical industrial firm has been successfully completed. A parallel code system has been developed along the lines suggested in Chapters 13 and 14. Then, a first application has been completed involving the company's product line.

Prior to the clarification and establishment of a single frame of reference, as supported by DCS, senior management has had a rather hazy idea of the company's product line. Marketing was selling some 15,000 products, but some of the people in the division periodically expressed doubt if all these products were different from one another—whether in terms of technical specifications or in terms of sales appeal.

Indeed, the introduction of DCS and its implementation permitted streamlining of the product line, and this was greeted as a major achievement by management. The marketing people applied the system with the help of the system specialists. They established that the truly different products the company was selling were not 15,000 but 7,400.

Significantly, it was found that, with the different old product numbering systems the company utilized for segments of its product line, up to thirty-five different numbers were used to identify (and sell) the same product; while up to five diverse products were coded with the same number. With the application of DCS, the true number of products the company marketed proved to be half of what management had thought for two decades.

Most importantly, DCS helped to clarify a key subject which for years eluded the accountants: "How much profit or loss each product brought to the company." Only when a unique and reliable identification system was implemented was it possible to answer this question in a documented way. It was then found that, of the resulting 7,400 distinct products:

1. 2,500 of the mass produced items made money to cover the losses of the others and leave a profit.

2. 850 articles were manufactured on demand and therefore followed a different procedure in P&L calculation.

3. 370 products broke even but had a good development perspective with the proper promotion.

4. 1,040 items broke even or lost some money, but were needed for the company to present a complete product line to the market; while

5. 2,640 products lost money (some heavily) and were unnecessary to retail.

A decision was made to eliminate the latter not only from possible offerings and future manufacturing but also from stock. Special discounts were offered for items which could sell at a lower price while the remainder (and a good number, for that matter) of the condemned products were literally destroyed (a cost study established that an item carried on the racks unsold for a year represented a cost of $0.50 in carrying expenses).

Management took precautions to insure that the introduction of the new system did not upset the operations. A step by step procedure was chosen, outlined in Figure 16.2. A DCS was the first to be applied (in the commercial operations only). Then, based on the new code system, the IS processes were streamlined, and new AP were added. All of them observed DB prerequisites. The use of database solutions developed as a matter of course.

When the DCS was fully integrated into the marketing operations, a new field of applications was undertaken, that of purchasing, accounts payable, and inventories. Once again, the work was done with a joint group of analysts and users, with the goals of DB streamlining and interactive applications included in the project.

From the beginning of the joint work, going through the purchasing, accounts payable, and inventory control files—which had been handled individually—the analysts were amazed at how many fields the three subsystems had in common. This was not obvious to them during normal operations because the terminology used by each subsystem was different, even if many fields came from the same source documents.

Vendor; vendor address; vendor code; part number; machine number; warehouse shipped from; plant shipped to; etc. are examples on the references which have been given. A procedure was necessary to weed out duplicates and inconsistencies—the one used with the commercial division was adopted.

ORGANIZATIONAL REACTION TO A STREAMLINING PROCEDURE

To make sure where the discrepancies lay the analysts wrote a program to compare the common fields between the three subsystems: purchasing, accounts payable and inventory control. Not surprisingly (given earlier experience) the files did not match. A number of problems were discovered. In most cases field sizes and edit standards were different.

Many discrepancies existed because of the timing differences in update cycles. But that is not all. Error correction procedures differed from one department to another, both in terms of timing and in the way corrections were made. Furthermore, when errors with noncritical data were detected, two of the departments did not bother entering the correction.

Not only conceptual but also organizational differences had to be overcome. The needed solution was to combine the purchasing, accounts payable, and inventory control master files into a single entity. But the three depart-

226

STEP – BY – STEP

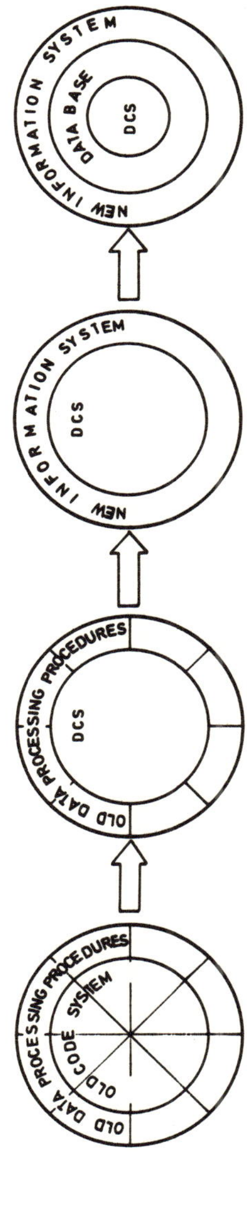

NEW INFORMATION SYSTEM
DATA BASE
DCS

NEW INFORMATION SYSTEM
DCS

OLD DATA PROCESSING PROCEDURES
DCS

OLD DATA PROCESSING PROCEDURES
OLD CODE SYSTEM

FIGURE 16.2

ments reported to different senior executives in the organization, and each was "jealous" of its data—calling its negative reaction "a matter of privacy."

The analysts suggested the integration as a way to greater efficiency. With integrated files concerning the same entities, there would be only one entry for each field, and discrepancies would be impossible. For instance, if the vendor's address was wrong, it would be corrected only once and then would be consistent wherever it appeared. But which one of the three departments would have the authority to enter the corrections?

The analysts answered that the best procedure would be to have the department most interested in an information element be responsible for updating. This way, the purchasing department would update the supplier's names and addresses; and the accounts payable department would be responsible for updating the price field. Most companies have found this to be the field of major discrepancies, and the one where the inventory control file is usually wrong, as stock control people use that field only as a memo item.)

Management answered that the idea was good, but not immediately applicable as it called for some shifts in responsibility and this would take time to resolve. Following an integrated procedure with a system of traffic lights to regulate accesses to the corporate database gave some executives the impression of being deprived of some of their prerogatives. Yet, there is nothing more untrue.

The analysts reacted by pointing to the fact that not only did the suggested procedure mean order, but that there was another advantage: All the duplication of effort would be eliminated, leaving people the possibility to carry on more creative duties. The way data processing worked at the time of the study, for each duplicated field, the using departments had to:

> control the input documents,
> submit data for key punching, and
> process the error corrections.

According to standing company regulations, the data were keyed on tape and the tapes handled. The computer was used to edit and weed out errors; error lists were printed and sent to the use department; they were corrected; then the files were updated. A lot of work done three times instead of one.

Correctly, the analysts searched for approaches which gave the user a tangible benefit to help ease resistance. They found it in the function of the accounts payable manager. He sometimes asked for special reports that included information he did not have, but was in the inventory files—such as the vendor company's parts classification code.

The analysts pointed out that *if* their firm had a consolidated database, they could easily give him reports like that. Better yet, they could give him a terminal and put him online to information. Discrepancies would be eliminated by having only one master; accuracy would be improved; and reaction to queries would be instantaneous.

This argument was agreeably concluded: a single master file was created to serve all three departments and each department was given authorized access to the common database, but at different levels of authorization in accord with the organizational prerequisites of each. Duplication of people and machines was on its way to being eliminated, and each executive was able to receive online on request reports containing data from the common master file.

Figures 16.3 and 16.4 highlight the interactive procedure being referred to. Programs for data security, error diagnostics, program library management,

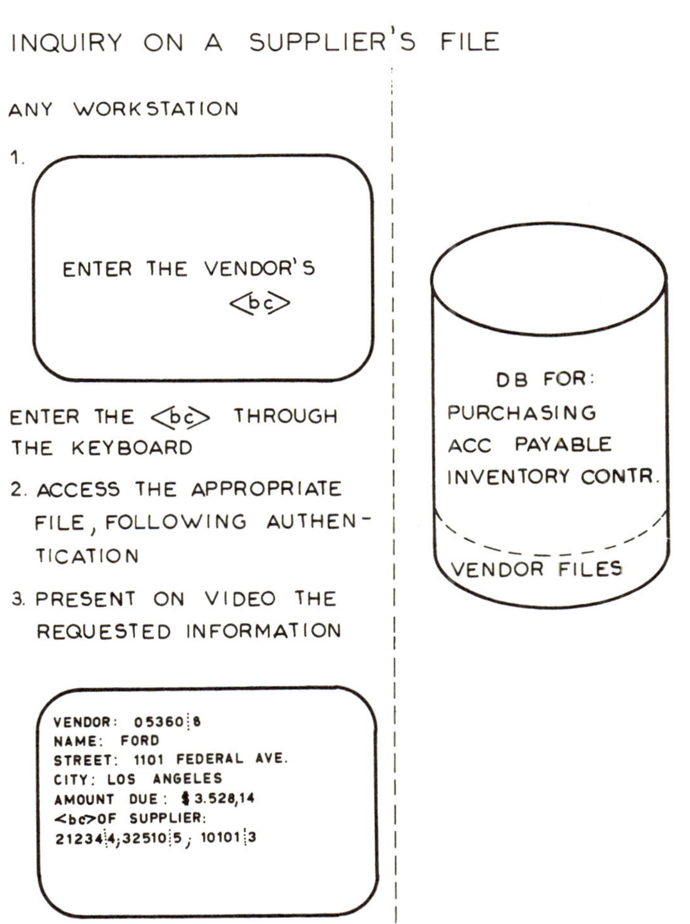

FIGURE 16.3

SIMULTANEOUS INQUIRY ON ARTICLE AND
STOCK LEVEL FILES

ANY WORKSTATION

1.

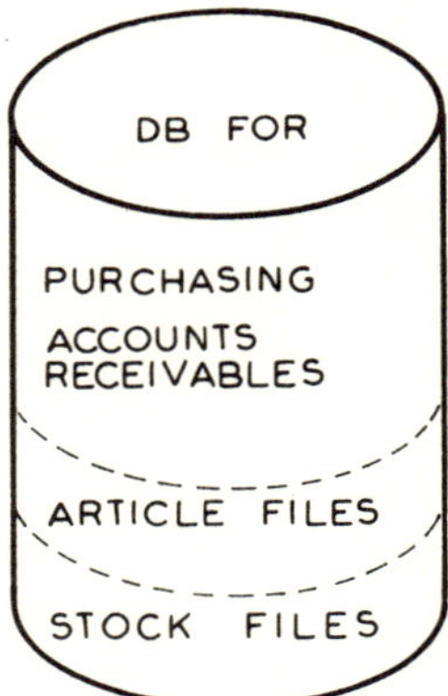

ENTER THE ARTICLE'S
<bc>

ENTER THE <bc> THROUGH
THE KEYBOARD

2. ACCESS THE APPROPRIATE
FILES:
- ARTICLE FILE (DESCRIP-
TION, PROCUREMENT)
- STOCK CONTROL FILES
(MIN-MAX. LEVELS;
CURRENT STOCK BY
LOCATION)

3. PRESENT ON VIDEO THE
REQUESTED INFORMATION

ARTICLE: 12572 1
DESCRIPTION: ....
CURRENT LEVEL IN STOCK: ......
MIN. LEVEL ....
MAX. LEVEL: ....
LOCATIONS: ....
FACTORIES: ....
DEPOTS: ....
PAGE XXX FOR DETAILS

FIGURE 16.4

queuing of requests, and I/O control had been established. The same is true of the needed manuals to help the end users from the three departments getting trained on the job.

EXTENDING THE APPLICATION TO OTHER DEPARTMENTS

Having successfully implemented an interdepartmental solution for purchasing, accounts payable and inventory control, the analysts concentrated on expanding the application. It did not escape their attention that many of the IE fields in the three systems could also be found in the engineering master files; the same problem existed with other systems, too.

For example, the files on employee knowhow and the payroll file had several kinds of duplicated information. Even more strikingly, redundancies existed relative to these files at the level of the manually maintained records which had not yet been converted to data processing.

An overall strategy had to be developed, and this involved several management levels. Once again there were organizational problems to be overcome. For instance, as a condition of joining the common application, engineering wanted to expand the vendor classification code to include a quality rating procedure.

Logically, there were many good reasons for doing this, but the accounts payable people did not agree. The department's employees were used to a credit rating code, and its management was afraid that diverse evaluation procedures would be too much for the employees to digest. They just were not going to go along with it.

The analysts had to explain that videoforms offered the possibility of presenting every user with the information he needed without having to press the forms of one department on the neck of the other. Besides, they suggested that for good order the database administrator must have the power to control either user, from a neutral, company-wide standpoint.

The argument was also advanced to senior management that today integrated databases have become the "in thing." Forward looking companies are using database management software, helping the applications to become more efficient than they used to be.

The main issue in implementing this new mentality is not to consider data as belonging to a given user department and its tailor-made computer application. Data are a company-wide asset; a corporate resource. On the other hand, the analysts said, there is no need to underestimate the fact that DB integration will run into a number of problems—at least in the beginning.

Such problems were both helped and complicated by the fact that company management definitely decided to change the system to an online operation. The example which we followed on an interdepartmental application explains the source of help for the implementation. The complication sprang from lack of the appropriate transactional software package to permit all authorized subsystems to access the DB at the same time and obtain the information each needed in the proper form, without undue delays.

Another technical problem was preventing changes in one subsystem from affecting another. Security was another issue. No department is ever happy about having its data readily accessible to other people, even if all work for the same company.

The turning point in getting acceptance came when the need for database integration caught the eye of the chief executive. Since much of the departmental reaction was psychological, first a program of training courses was instituted covering all aspects of the database, from overall concepts explaining the proper attitudes and responsibilities to the detail level courses discussing the use of the data dictionary, standards, documentation, and interactive requirements at large.

Second, all interactive applications were moved out of the mainframe and onto minicomputers. Each machine was dedicated to one application and, hence, to one department or function. The different minis were linked together through a local network architecture, after the company actively surveyed the market to find one.

The mainframes were kept active for backup purposes and also to extend the life of the existing software (mainly batch). Though the conversion to interactive solutions moved at a reasonable pace it still required two and a half years to complete. Finally, a program was set up to institute the necessary organizational changes, so that the problems encountered during the period of integrating purchasing, accounts payable, and inventory control, could be avoided in the future.

IMPLEMENTING THE <BASIC CODE> IN A BANKING ENVIRONMENT

As is the case with industrial companies, the development of a coding system to serve in banking operations has often taken a twisted path. The client account number is a good example. Client accounts are characterized by different codes, depending on whether reference is made to a DDA, a savings account or to foreign operations. Then the so called "supercode" is introduced to link these diverse codes together, often compounding the confusion.

With such largely irrational approaches, the code varies for the same client from one branch office to another, making a client's consolidated statement a difficult operation; the same is true of the risk calculation procedures followed by financial institutions. Bankers often have to dig out a great deal of information manually. This data is rarely timely; is usually inconsistent from one file to another; contains errors; and often provides little decision support.

DCS, covered in Chapters 13 and 14, can find an excellent field of application among financial institutions, permitting bankwide integration of client files with the proper identification of all accounts through <basic code>, <suffix> and <origin>. In this sense, DCS offers the bank a unique frame of reference:

<Basic code> identifies the client account on a nationwide basis (or internationally);

<suffix> is allocated to the type of account: DDA, savings, portfolio management, foreign operations, etc.

<origin> is simply the branch office code or for large corporate accounts the central marketing service responsible for client handling.

As Figure 16.5 suggests, all levels of management can be served through this solution: <bc>, <s>, <o> will be necessary and sufficient identifiers in handling all settlements involved in day-to-day operation. For loans, investments, and other functions performed by middle management consolidated statements by type of account are what is primarily needed. This can be nicely expressed through <basic code> and <suffix>.

In Chapter 1, Figure 1.4 outlines a management reporting structure which can be utilized through the approach we are outlining up to the senior management level. Top management expresses particular interest not in branch office detail on every single account, but in overall account consolidation. At the request of management, some banks now produce a *customer mirror* report to help judge single client profitability. Such a report can be adequately served through <basic code> since the caller provides the means for a unique customer identification.

Thus DCS constitutes the pivot point for the whole structure of a bank's database, leaving the analysts free to apply themselves to more valuable functions, such as security/protection and risk analysis of the changing context of the DB elements. (This calls for specific studies on the degree the organization fits into that context as the marketplace develops and its requirements evolve.)

Having solved the problem of identification/classification, the database designer can answer this need by listing future steps and available resources on a time scale. The plan for database evolution should have definite checkpoints and target dates to allow constant re-evaluation. Part and parcel of the DB plan should be a phased approach, carving out the most critical aspects within a given operating environment.

Having analyzed the environment and designed the database, the next step is implementation, this has four major phases: conversion into a homogeneous structure; integration; tuning; and steady administration. In time, a bank's database will grow in volume, and plans should have been made from the beginning to provide the IE necessary for

> tests, and
> experimentation;

For instance: risk analysis—to insure that areas of high risk, and/or exposure are systematically scrutinized. This way, a bank's DB, supported through mathematical models, will play a role similar to that of the electron microscope in the physical sciences.

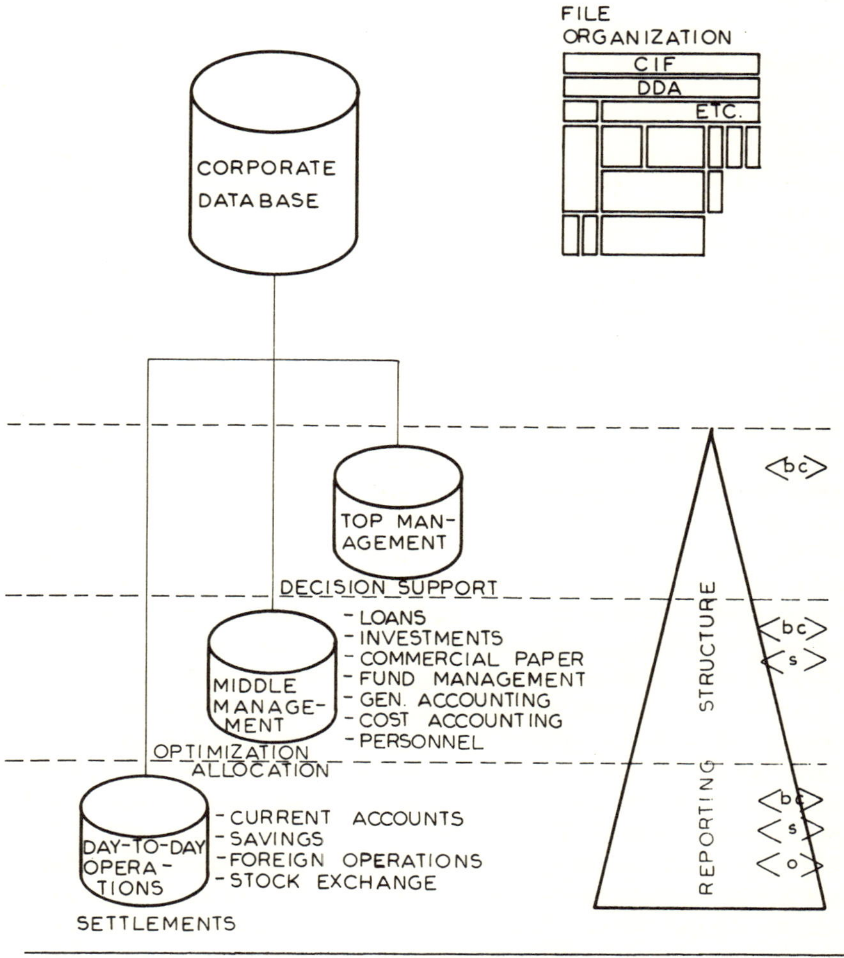

FIGURE 16.5

Furthermore, the database must enhance the capability of management to apply rating schemes and identify, via computers:

> problem operations,
> problem clients, and
> problem managers.

The IE in the DB should allow a sound statistical sampling—and statistical tests of obtained results. This has been a goal long sought by the management sciences, but not implemented because the data were not there. However, just having the data does not necessarily mean obtaining immediate results. A good deal depends on preparation, and DCS is the foundation of this approach.

EVALUATION

The examples considered in this chapter are abstracts from real life applications with industrial concerns and financial institutions. As such, they help pinpoint and integrate the ideas and procedural steps presented in Chapters 14 and 15.

A classification and identification system similar to the one described, handles not only pruning and reorganization of the database but also the on-line handling of transactions—ranging from inquiry through conversational operations to data entry. It allows minicomputers and large computers to be connected to terminal systems with a minimum of complications permitting fairly easy interfacing.

Once the structural aspects have been sorted out, there are no severe constraints on message routing: remember that *any file can be a message and any message is a file in the database.* It is also more easy to cope with an increasing volume of traffic.

Furthermore, a solid classification/identification scheme allows processing distribution in all locations as well as backup processing by process interchange between centers. The storage and retrieval operations are particularly facilitated, as structured approaches permit bulk information (such as data entry traffic) to be effectively handled by the databases in the network.

A good storage and retrieval mechanism allows the originating subscriber to input his data when it suits him. Also, the receiving subscriber can extract this data when it is convenient for him. The service enables the end users to record data on the progress of an applications-oriented process at a centrally located point on the network.

The above references list some of the more important advantages. System dependability is something else that must be constantly kept in mind. Another permanent demand is for system expandability to handle more traffic and new functions. To make this possible, the database must have a modular structure, with each module serving a well-defined and easy-to-comprehend function in the whole system—a reference which highlights the need for proper preparation.

Since the major influence on the next generation of computer systems will come from databases, we must understand clearly what we wish to obtain. What to do should be a function of our objectives. The answer to the question: "How to do it?" (and do it well), will involve a lot of technical problems such as: data definition; data languages; data independence; security; consistency; and integrity.

Many of these issues have been added to the system expert's knowledge and experience over the last ten years to enhance the theoretical background necessary in handling databases. Other basic concepts include:

1. the semantics of the **DB** (conceptual modeling),

2. the inference to be derived from the elements in the DB, and

3. issues of concurrency in DB processing: interactions; deadlocks; synchronization.

Conceptual modeling led to the development of data models. Data models should provide the user with a framework and with formalisms. He needs them to *compute* or *derive* relationships, or facts *not* explicit in the DB.

The capacity of the database manipulation schemes to satisfy the fundamental independence of data and programs largely depends on the logical model adopted in the definition of the image we have of the database, its segments and partitions, down to the level of the single information elements. It is also a function of their interrelationship.

Furthermore, until recently each user had been living in an environment of his own without sharing experience. There was little coordination. Structuring was unknown—and in some places it was almost a dirty word. Yet, as we later discovered, the best effort to provide a common background was to organize and structure: sequential; index sequential; direct (random) or other.

We definitely need valid approaches to data organization, and several solutions evolved to answer structural requirement needs. Slowly, as the idea of a total view of databases and databasing started developing, integrated data storage became the king and many specialists consider that if a DB is not "integrated" it is useless. While earlier integrating was looked upon as a tool, today it has become a DB philosophy.

Then, again slowly, the need for following an integrated approach was followed by other needs, like:

1. *Immediate access*—which led to the research on faster response time,

2. *Virtual storage*—which permits both portability and one-level memory,

3. *Simultaneous update, integrity, recovery,*

4. *Security, protection,* and

5. The task of *database administration.*

The database related functions described here can be expected to become "household words" for all information scientists as, in the coming years, a major part of all operations becomes database technology.

As we said when referring to interactive approaches, the database (or databases) will be accessible from a diversity of end user devices. Routinely, office automation technology will often relate to the same end user machines and to database systems.

End user devices will range anywhere from dedicated minis to intelligent terminals and microcomputers managing data derived from the database system. Such devices will be linked together through a network. But an integrated environment will require well established strategies for handling data, from distributed information systems to office automation.

17 Projecting a Unified Database

INTRODUCTION

Databases for distributed intelligence systems pose problems which must be studied (and solved) prior to segmentation and distribution. DB unification is a necessary prerequisite: to reduce the costs associated with redundant filing; eliminate the sources of mutations and errors; and assure that information is *current* by having a consistent view of the DB.

To fulfill such prerequisites, the preparatory work involves:

1. The segmentation of storage (and probably of the processing capacity) into standardized *modules*.
2. *Linking* these modules together to create a network.
3. Using a *single, dedicated* mini to handle the processing functions in the DB module.

Many of the obstacles encountered in studies leading to DDB unification have to do with ill-defined user requirements (the most frequent case); lack of interface hardware (a problem largely overcome); lack of support software for distributed mechanisms (which is still valid—few if any needed software packages are off-the-shelf); distributed data management software (still in development); synchronization problems for multiple processors; and a still minimal use of microprocessors to carry out architectural functions.

Other problems come up because of poor practice such as custom-made software solutions (also hardware capabilities); minimal vendor commitment to field support; a still high rate of flux in the mini- and microcomputer environment which complicates solution efforts; and once again underscores the requirement for skill and knowhow to satisfy everybody's needs.

CRITERIA FOR DB PARTITIONING

Database usage with distributed systems calls for a very careful definition of the transaction to be handled. Frequency and information content must be established for all messages—including the implied I/O requirements. This will involve the design of logical files; protection systems; I/O dialog prerequisites; communications linkages; and utility programs. But above all, it will require a database integration similar to that discussed from Chapter 11 on in this book.

Only after this work is done, and the applications are defined, can we allocate files and programs to selected hardware to produce an optimum design. Processes must be projected keeping in mind both the conditions of their operation and the transformations to which they will be subjected. Typically:

> processes will be triggered by an input message;
> they will interact with the DB; and
> only then will they produce an output message.

These three steps characterize the interactivity of a process with the database, whether the latter is centralized or distributed. A DDB presents further prerequisites. As stated in the preceding chapter, a distributed database is a DB whose geometry represents an organization and arrangement that support the distribution and separation of application processing. This must be done to a degree necessary to satisfy a specific set of user requirements.

Examples of distributed processes and database elements are the general area of reservation systems; banking applications; multiplant manufacturing control; and utility grids. Whether this distribution is done functionally or geographically, the rule is: "Don't distribute the data unless there is a *reason*." For instance, minis are already installed for DDP purposes, or the network is projected to serve the user through close proximity to the user's own operations.

In studying the partitioning (segmentation) of the database, valid design criteria can be of help. Among them we distinguish:

1. *Natural cluster rule (geography, major function).* Some eighty percent to ninety percent of the "tasks" and the "files" which are involved

should fall within this partition—and, therefore, at the node level there should be a common DB reference such as provided by a directory (which is part and parcel of the data dictionary).

2. *Functional interconnections.* These come into play within the projected applications environment. They are generally supported at the host level; and they should be documented through statistics such as percentage of records retrieved in a "particular" or "typical" files access operation.

3. *Criticality.* This involves issues like: reliability; backup; and the overall management strategy to be served through DDB.

4. *User functions,* for instance: retrieve; read; modify; add; delete—and the authorization levels associated with each function.

5. *DBM* (database management) capabilities: check validity requests; check authorization; locate data; and other functions performed by the DBMS, such as, for instance, lock data; order data; unlock data; map data.

6. *Evaluation criteria,* including function positioning (user level and DBM level); modularity; fault tolerance; and needed control.

7. *Major approach* to the implementation of a distributed information system: general purpose; special purpose.

8. *Technical faculties* to be supported. These largely concern the logical solutions and the software tools available to do the job.

Quite evidently, this is a general expression of evaluation criteria for DDB capabilities. A study performed within a specific applications environment can, however, benefit from rules which, by guiding the analyst's thinking, avoid making repetitive and redundant judgements. Applying these criteria, a leading manufacturing firm designed its minicomputer based distributed system to include the IE identified in Figure 17.1 at the level of each of its sales offices and factories.

Let us recapitulate. To study database segmentation we must consider: the applications; the IE needed to support them; the topology; the functions; the equipment; and the phasing-in of the total system. The best design approach is based on principles and requirements. And the fundamental goal to be served is to bring the DB closer to the end user.

COMMERCIAL / INDUSTRIAL
SALES OFFICES
FACTORIES
ORDER TAKING
ORDER EXECUTION
CHECK
CLIENT FILE
PRODUCTION PLANNING
CREDIT LEVEL
INVENTORY MANAGEMENT
INVENTORY
READY PRODUCTS
PREPARE DELIVERY DOCUMENTS
SEMIMANUFACTURED
EXPEDITE
RAW MATERIALS
COMMUNICATE TO FACTORY
TOOLS, FIXTURES CONSUMABLES
BILL
MAINTENANCE, EXPANSION
CHECK
ACCOUNTS RECEIVABLES
MACHINERY
OVERDUES
HUMAN RESOURCES
AQUISITION
SKILLS
ALLOCATION

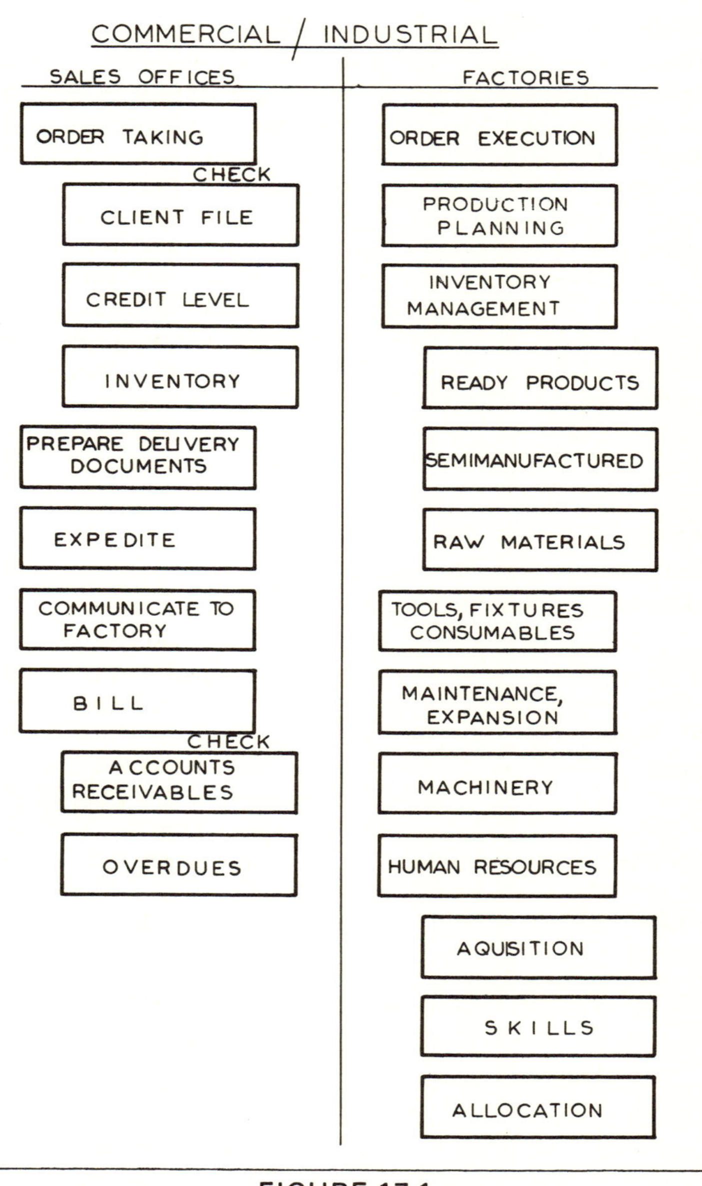

FIGURE 17.1

DDB PROBLEMS AND SOLUTIONS

If a fundamental reason for distributed information systems is placing the computer power in the hands of the user, we must assure the collaboration of the man responsible for this job. He knows his requirements better than any analyst. Let us remember that user collaboration means simplicity in design.

Simplicity also has another aspect. Decentralization and the use of mini-computers means limiting the size of applications; handling one per machine. This, in turn, makes it easier to make or purchase the necessary software. Similarly, decentralized, independent applications simplify the maintenance job.

But the decentralization of the database involves problems that must be faced and resolved—Just as the conversion from paper-based to computer-run data management solutions presented a variety of issues which were not squarely faced from the beginning. The main problems of segmentation and distribution are:

1. The logical grouping of IE,

2. The dynamic aspect of data distribution,

3. Multi-copy update issues,

4. Error control procedures, and

5. The location of the primary file.

If some elements are duplicated, a given update must give all users a consistent view. The update does not have to be current—but it should not be made at the nth time period for some of the elements or locations, and at the $(n-1)^{th}$ for some others.

Further, we must also assure that things cannot happen to throw what we do out of sequence. Even if geographically distributed, a DB should provide a unified system: The DB fractions must be linked together to create a network of DB segments; while, ideally, these DB segments will be linked in a manner resembling connection to a single data bus.

To take a closer look at the multisite problem, we should start with two hypotheses:

1. There are distributed users and each maintains a DDB.

2. An alteration to any IE may originate from any site.

However, all copies must be consistent; any alteration in one copy must occur in all copies; two alterations on the same item must be performed in the same order in all copies; the systems running on each site have a fundamental modularity as reflected in Figure 17.2; the underlying structure has relational characteristics such as outlined in DCS. (This means defining files in terms of relationships.)

SYSTEMS
PROGRAMS
INTERFACES TO DB SEGMENTS
USER EXITS
D B
RECORDS
FILES
FIELDS
BYTES
ITEMS
THE KEY ROLE IS PLAYED BY
DBMS
REAREND ENGINES
INTELLIGENT STORAGE DEVICES

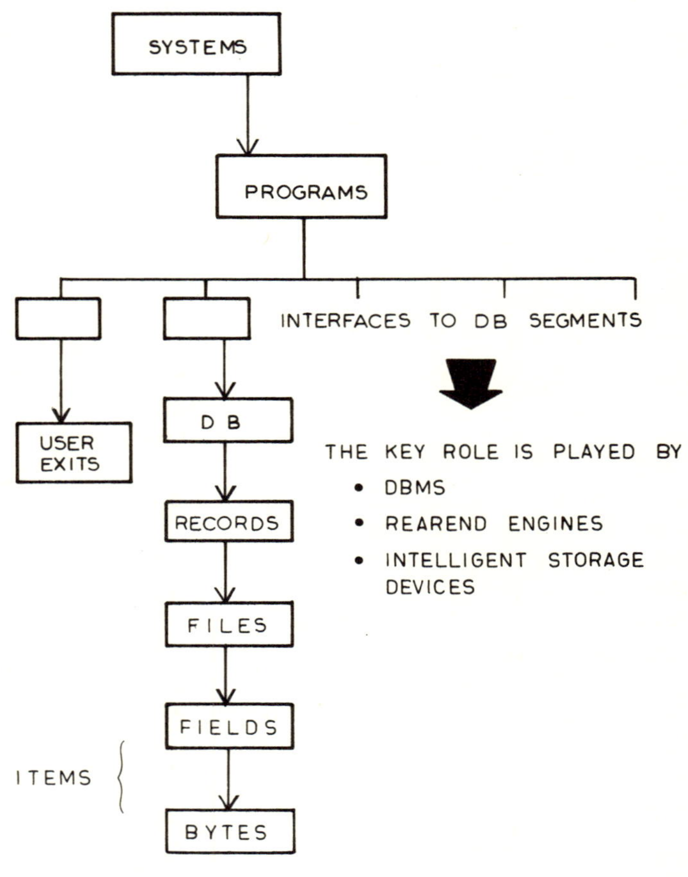

FIGURE 17.2

The relation can be thought of as a record without structure. It will be expressed in a matrix form. This structure has no physical pointers. Hence, the database fractions can be maintained separately. The relation is defined by the matching domain; e.g., the department number. From a distributed viewpoint, relational solutions are the best. (Others will most likely be impractical.)

In fact, chaining, an old approach, will not be acceptable within a distributed environment. Physical pointers from one file to another can be a disaster with DDB. Early experience indicates that we cannot cross-point between machines; what we really want is to establish independence so that the crash of one machine does not shut the network down.

With relational solutions, files will have to be maintained independently. This fits the DDB philosophy. The matrix form we referred to can be served through the directory. This presupposes the need of a directory which tells:

1. Where the files are maintained.

2. Given a node, what sort of files are kept.

3. What is the assurance of consistency and replicated partitions.

Stated in a different way, remote DB access and DDB facilities are not the same thing. For effective remote access to distributed information elements, we definitely need a data dictionary and its file directory. In turn, this will be influenced by the physical media to be incorporated into the network as a DB support and by the logical solutions to be adopted.

The latter bring to the foreground the capability to define a logical file and tell which partitions exist and how they are maintained. The real questions now become:

1. How do we manage the directory?

2. How do we implement the internal access method?

3. And how do we follow-up on the DDB updating method?

These questions bring up the issues of replicated files, and the synchronization of the replicated files—including the synchronization of the database in its totality.

Different mechanisms exist for updating the replicated copies: primary—secondary definitions; locking mechanisms; polling alternatives; and bringing together the different copies of the same IE managed through the database. Each of the possible solutions must be examined in terms of the amount of network overhead; the risk of desynchronization; the possible crashes; and the institution of a central authority. We will treat these problems in the proper sections.

THE MECHANICS OF STRATIFICATION

We said that a distributed database is one logical DB created in the form of a number of nonredundant partitions, each located at different processors.

A database can be partitioned for several reasons. Ease of use and immediate direct access is fundamental. Another reason may be to separate sensitive data from public access. Security/privacy protection can then be concentrated at the sensitive partition(s) of the DB.

Whatever the reason for distributed databases, and whether or not replicated solutions are adopted, the mechanics must support seven basic activities, and these should be assured network wide:

1. DB integration;
2. DB segmentation—by geography, function, and major issue such as client handling;
3. DB distribution;
4. DB update;
5. DB integrity;
6. DB management systems;
7. DB administration.

In deciding among the choice of goals, the designer must understand the costs and the timing of those costs—both for the distribution of the database and for its steady maintenance to meet specific application processing requirements.

Database costs are sometimes high, especially in the areas of personnel education and reorganization. But only if a long range plan for the database has been established can the organization look forward to profits from this effort.

We cannot repeat too often, in a distributed database not all elements exist on the same machine. However, a DDB is one logical DB placed at multiple physical locations—which may or may not be physically distributed. To have a DDB, we must partition the elements of the DB into subsets—with regard to the defined relations—observing criteria on:

> performance (cross reference),
> accessibility,
> efficiency (duplication),
> timeliness, and
> cost

to minimize the cross-system access in regard to requests.

A number of technical questions call for answers: Is the DB integrated, global, or networkwide? Should the programmer know where the data is? For instance, is one network worldwide schema to be identically implemented in

all machines in the network? If a company is engaged in international operations, what about multiple descriptions (clear text)?, e.g., should we allow
local options?

Such choices have enormous impact on design and performance. Particularly in the banking sector, the classical approach has been to keep the main
DB centralized (as a master database) taking subsets to the periphery—but as
secondary DB partitions. Then plug the segmented DB in strategic locations
to reduce communications costs.

In fact, this has been the key reason for DIS—which in this aspect, is no
new sophisticated or exotic approach. Of course, the flaw has been that it
tends to keep the applications in the image of the old batch solutions.

A rational organization along the lines suggested in Figure 17.3 slowly be-
gins to evolve as experience accumulated. *Stratification* becomes the architectural standard. Six different strata are distinguished, largely associated
with the DB capability attached to each DP center:

1. Strata zero is the host level usually with greater than one GByte storage
   availability.

2. Strata one and two distinguish among themselves in the sense that the
   former supports (under present conditions) more than 100 MBytes of
   local storage.

The emphasis is on the capability to locate entire files and offer services
which go beyond what can be done with some file extracts as they have been
used within predominantly batch environments.

> just the same, Strata three, four and five range from a minimum of
> cassette recording for local journaling and/or local, controlled data
> collection, to capabilities up to, say, ten MBytes.
>
> finally, Strata six is reserved for unintelligent terminals whether con-
> nected to a local mini, a network, or directly to a central resource.

The goal of this organization is to take a fresh look at the DIS benefits
and capitalize on lower mini costs and the falling prices for data supports
(and, as well, the direct, immediate accessibility of databases).

Decisions have, of course, to be made, a key issue being how we look at
the integrated database which has been copied (entirely or partially) with
each copy placed at a different data processor. Another key question is
whether both database partitioning and replication should be adopted.

An example on stratification, partitioning and replication is given in
Figure 17.4. The full customer record identified by $<bc_1>$ is stored at a host
residing at Strata zero—which may be at the headquarters. For operational reasons,
this information element is totally replicated at Strata one (for instance, a
major company division). However, at the sales office level (Strata two) only

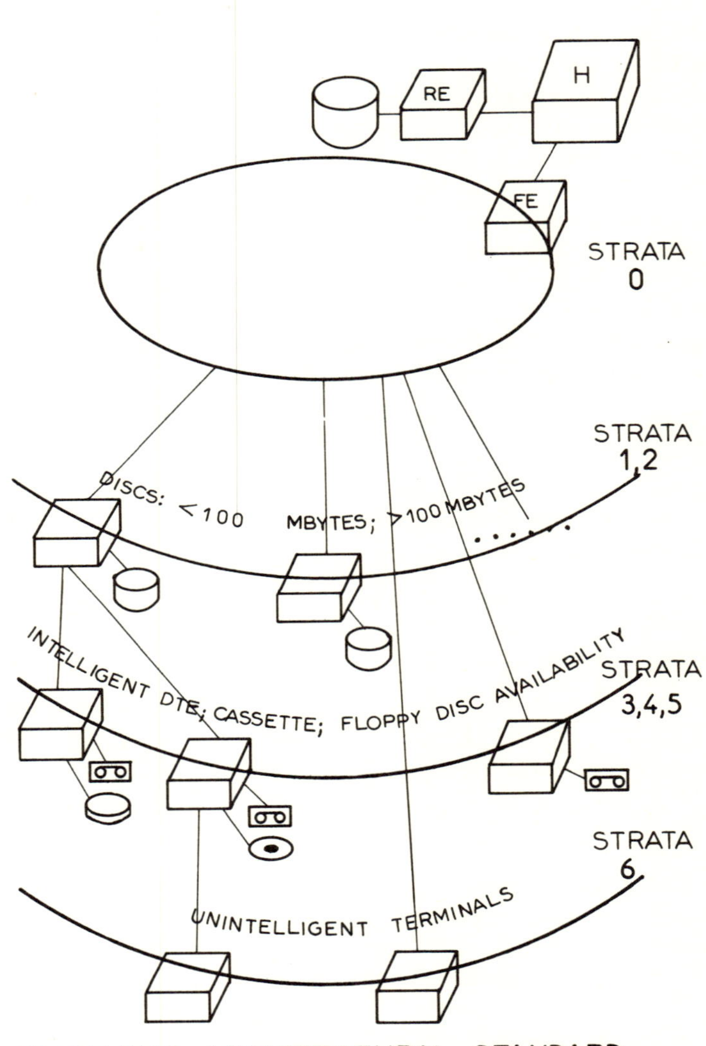

EVOLVING ARCHITECTURAL STANDARD

FIGURE 17.3

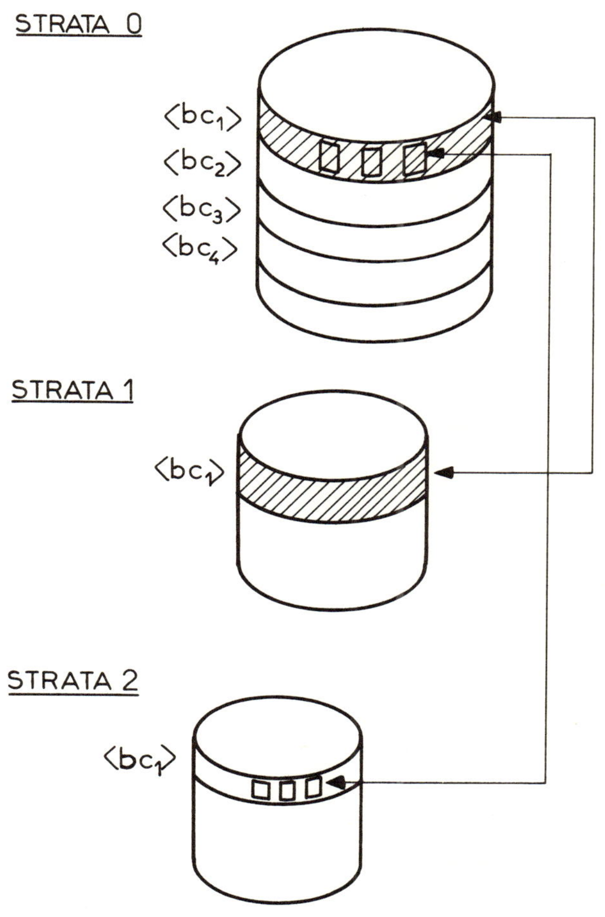

FIGURE 17.4

a subset of the record is kept, such as customer number, customer name/ address, and line of credit.

This is the logical solution. The physical solution will be influenced by the media available, the relative costs, the company philosophy concerning information systems, user requirements, past experiences, etc. Only a thorough study done with skill and dedication can chart the path to follow for the best interests of all concerned.

As is nearly always true, the right systems study calls for a generic approach to applications: What is the product? How far can we go in improving the information services? What kind of support is necessary? What does the end user really need? As transition will be gradual, a timing plan is very important.

CONSIDERING THE APPLICATIONS ENVIRONMENT

We have underscored the fact that distributed database systems extend the capacities of a computer to give access to a wide range of applications. We have also insisted on the fact that DDB share many design problems with both one machine databases and computer networks; as well as with data transfer possible among any nodes in the network.

It is exactly because of this kind of supported facility that distributed database systems provide a solution to real problems for the geographically distributed organization which needs to preserve unified information sharing and processing. Or, alternatively, for the organization whose functions are better handled on a "one machine per application" basis.

Technical, managerial and economic reasons may be in the background of a distributed approach. On the technical side, the data load might suggest the need for a data volume distribution. If this is the case, then the approach should be sensitive to the work load; most likely it can be functionally oriented; ignore organizational boundaries; and go beyond the formerly sacrosanct geographic limits.

Most likely, solutions of this type will be transaction-oriented and performance and growth capabilities will be prime considerations. This means that design must:

1. Be volume sensitive,

2. Reflect the number of transactions (both current and projected),

3. Account for file location and distances, and

4. Take account of the limits minicomputers can serve.

Still on the technical side, the logical distribution of IE may involve: different functions at the different distributed points; some sort of centralized processing (backup or other), and an application-oriented processing within the distributed system. Data traffic must be considered; the number of accesses to each DB segment measured to avoid contention; the location of the DTE properly considered, and solutions such as the direct attachment to the network or rear-end computers examined as to their applicability (Figure 17.5).

Possible bottlenecks should also be considered. A leading American bank, for instance, calculated a load of 150 transactions per second. No single maxicomputer could effectively handle this volume, and such statistics were instrumental in switching to DDB.

A major department store computed 200 transactions per second in data load necessary to answer: sales; billing; online inventory control; and client file inquiries plus continual updating. (The generic name of the functionally distributed systems able to handle the rate of transactions referred to is: *power through parallelism.*)

Given "typical" requirements, performance and growth are key considerations. But typical requirements for DDB can only serve as a frame of reference. We have no unique solution. For a serious and documented implementation, we must study case by case according to real requirements. Sales, inventories, and marketing have specific needs which a distributed system must answer.

Cost considerations are evident from inception and help shape decisions. This issue has become important as information processing and storage costs have been dropping at twice the rate of decreases in data communications costs.

This difference in savings between centralized and distributed solutions made DIS increasingly attractive in substituting lower cost local processing and storage for (relatively) more expensive data communications. There are also advantages in system reliability and system performance for those applications where distributed databases are appropriate. But there are limits, most of them have to do with knowhow.

To be cost/effective, the effort to proceed with a distributed environment requires a very high level of capability on the part of the users. This is important as DIS design is not standardized; there is no typical node because of the applications dependent nature of the configurations. It is a good idea to take a prudent approach to DDB until internal company experience becomes available.

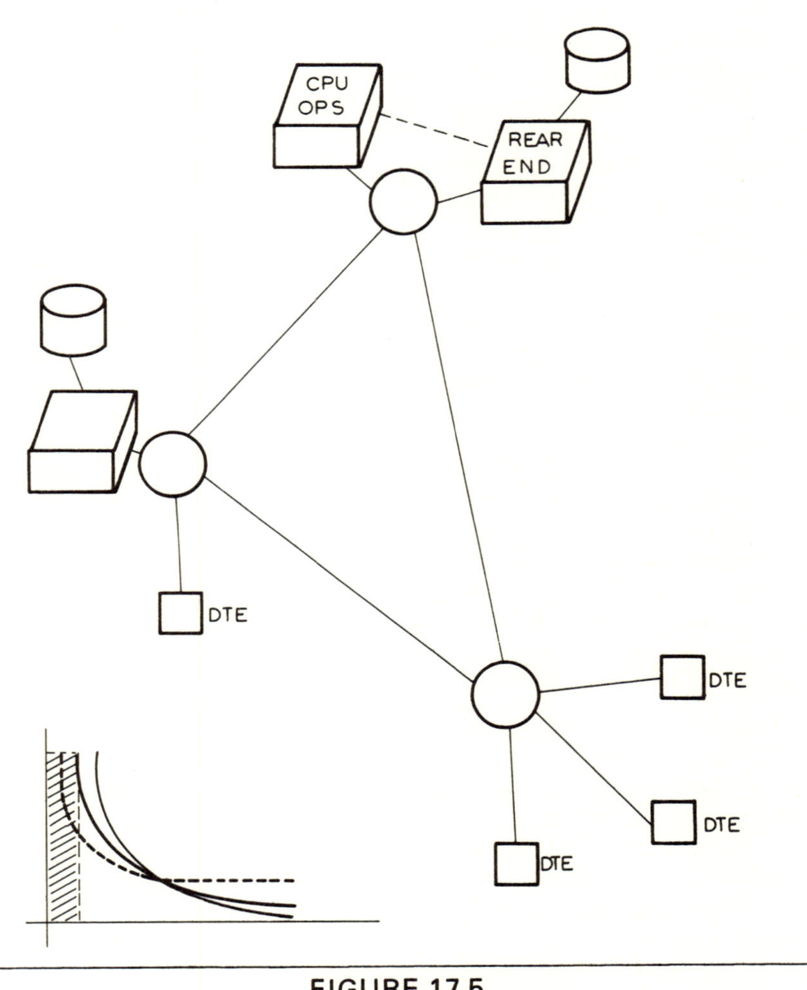

FIGURE 17.5

18 Managing the Operational Parallelism

INTRODUCTION

Two critical subjects with distributed databases (whether topologically, functionally, or by task) are the problems of the multicopy simultaneous update; and a database temporary partition. The latter is created whenever two sites are unable to communicate with each other. Such partition can occur:

1. In space; when communications failures split the network into two independent subnetworks; or

2. In time; when all the spoolers for a site are down when the network recovers.

DB partitions cause serious problems because it is impossible for sites to coordinate and thus ensure correct update synchronization. Failure recovery in a DDB environment (Figure 18-1) requires a mechanism able to provide and maintain guarantees regarding network failures, and site failures. Both issues impact on the intersite message transmission system, and involve:

    lost,
    duplicated, and
    out-of-sequence messages.

A possible serious failure is the crash of one or more of the sites maintaining a copy of the DB. To prevent system capacity from degrading, it is necessary to restore crashed sites. Mechanisms are being developed for performing such restoration—both in the case of temporary failure and for complete loss of the database.

A POSSIBLE DB ENVIRONMENT
DB 1
DB 2
DB 3
DB 4
NODE
NODE
NODE
NODE
NETWORK SUPPORT
AP 1
AP 2
WITH PARTLY REPLICATED DB

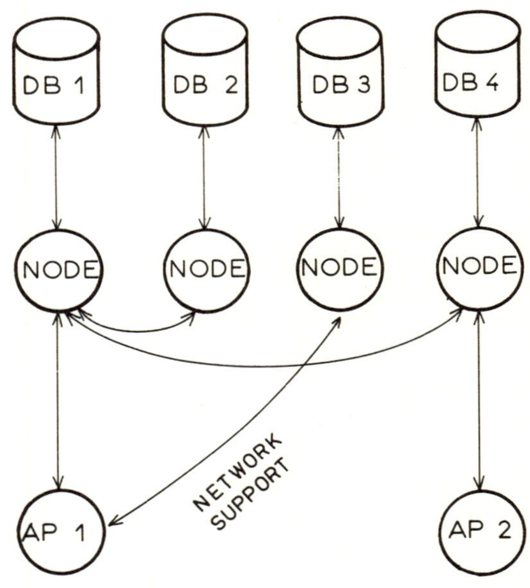

FIGURE 18.1

CONSISTENCY

Suppose, for example, that there are multiple sites, each maintaining a segment of a database; and that an alteration to an IE can originate from any site. We require that the copies of the database be "consistent":

> any alteration to an item in one copy of the database is performed in all copies, and

> two alterations to an item are performed in the same order on all copies.

A synchronization mechanism for maintaining such consistency must be provided; and it is not true that the most "evident" or "classical" solutions can do the job. A classical solution, for instance, is interlock. We have been using it since the 1950's. But it will not work in a distributed information environment. In fact, its effects can be disastrous.

A distributed synchronization engine that comes quickly to mind is one which locks all copies of the database for the duration of the update activity (Figure 18.2). Yet, since the operation of such a mechanism requires every DB partition (functional or topological) to be accessible to process and update, it is highly vulnerable to component outages.

What are the possible solutions? To start with, we must realize the magnitude of the issue. The new, online applications perspectives present unique problems, and have many areas to investigate. Such as:

1. File allocation,
2. File distribution,
3. File location,
4. Interlocks,
5. Deadlocks,
6. Structural optimization,
7. Concurrency,
8. Reliability.

Some problems, like concurrency, are particularly acute in the case of multiple storage of the same file structure—whether we talk of different physical media only, or different sites.

To look at a possible solution to the concurrency problem, let us go back to the situation presented in Figure 18.1. Four DB segments and two AP (applied programming) procedures are involved. Assume that several information elements in these DB are replicated. Each AP indicates a DB access: read or write (update; add/delete).

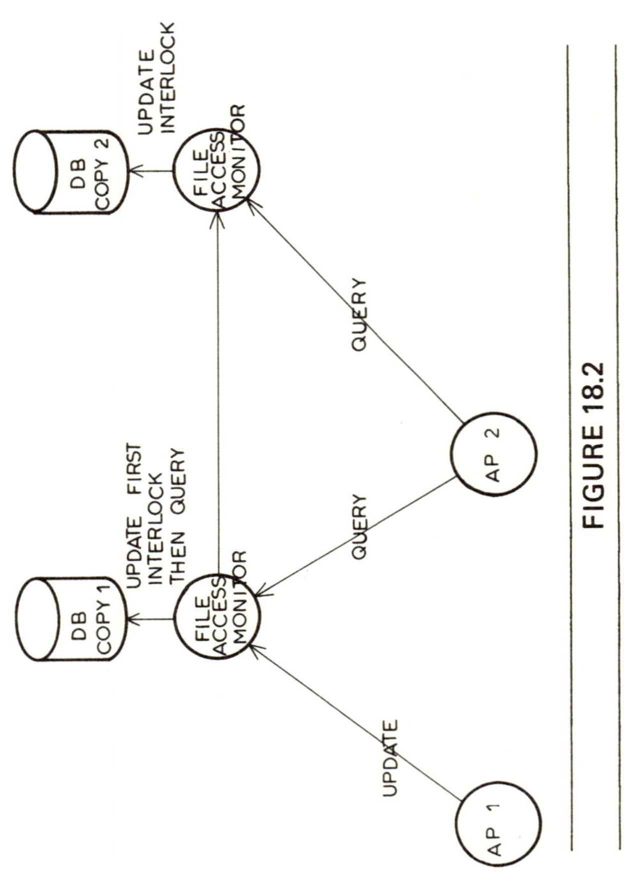
UPDATE
INTERLOCK
DB
COPY 2
FILE
ACCESS
MONITOR
QUERY
AP 2
UPDATE FIRST
INTERLOCK
THEN QUERY
DB
COPY 1
FILE
ACCESS
MONITOR
QUERY
UPDATE
AP 1
FIGURE 18.2

The DB/OS must assure that *internal consistency* is *not* violated. Possible unwanted outcomes in a DB update are those resulting from a lack of coordination. Such as: proceed with the updates at a different order each time/each site; or update IE "A" at the one DB and IE "B" at the other (same files).

A system solution must assure that all DB copies converge to same value, and that these values are identical if internal delays are accounted for. This calls for algorithms able to preserve both *mutual* and *internal* consistency. (This is a different way of saying that all IE, wherever stored, preserve their preestablished, internal relationships.)

Seen at the level of the IE, the efficiency of a solution for distributed database(s) can be measured on the basis of the following factors:

1. All IE carrying the same information are standardized;

2. All handling processes appealing to the same IE are homogeneous;

3. Unplanned duplications of IE are avoided;

4. The multi-copy update problem is faced in an able manner;

5. Security/protection measures are taken;

6. The DDB is periodically pruned;

7. All discrepancies are registered and traced to their origins.

This is a more detailed way of expressing what we have repeatedly stressed. Implementation and operation of DDB requires extensive preparation. This effort has two basic characteristics, fairly independent of the type of the application: it is to a very substantial extent procedural and organizational; and it must be carried at the IE level in order to be successful.

Furthermore, such goals must be achieved through *decentralized control*. This is a prerequisite for both distributed and replicated databases.

A REPLICATED DATABASE

The existence of multiple copies of the same record in different physical or logical locations identifies a replicated database. Consider a banking environment where selected client files are held, for instance, at five different locations. Such files include: account number; name; last deposit/withdrawal; and balance. New transactions update the DB. Consistency demands that all five copies are updated. While talking of internal consistency, we considered some alternatives. These included: centralized locking; a backup policy with a central controller; and a decentralized locking solution—an example being the voting algorithm. (The problem with this approach is that even if one gives permission to update, the transaction must wait. Furthermore, this solution results in a lot of message traffic in the network.)

Let us look more carefully at the voting algorithm. In applying it, use is made of a time stamp:

$$t_i; \; s_i$$

where t_i = time of last update

s_i = local site number.

Then an update is a sequence of read, process and write operations, which have to follow general form: First, a request is made. Second, it is accepted *if*: all the base resource time stamps are current and another request is not trying to modify a base resource. Third, the update is performed if a majority of sites accept the request.

This leads to a daisy chain solution and poses further problems:

> time stamping needs secondary memory bytes—and this on a distributed basis;
>
> lock tables call for central memory capability; and
>
> there is a degree of rejection, I/O overhead, CPU overhead, implementation costs.

This is the current status of research, and it suggests that DB update technology is not yet stable and it is advisable to avoid multiple sites with distributed IE which pose simultaneous update problems. Currently, multiple site storage of the same IE is not a realistic requirement for applications-oriented installations.

Databases can be developed without replicating IE; with the exception of backup/security, which can be handled as a separate issue using the *n-1* copy and the nth transaction journal. Or, still better, rather than father-and-son approaches, producing a "brother image" preferably on a different storage medium which can be accessed on request.

Let us also remember that replicated databases pose a number of other issues at specific levels of reference:

1. At the query level the challenge is query decomposition;
2. File level subjects include file placements; migration; and data compression—the way we have already spoken of;
3. Task level issues center on task scheduling.

Other critical references include logical organization; user interfaces; overall architecture; operations control and future systems evolution.

We should remember that simplicity is at a premium. Complex solutions are not efficient. As previously stated, they require more resources for housekeeping than for the productive work which needs to be done. To simplify,

258

we must decompose a multiple relation to as many single relations as possible. The overall data transfer will be less than handling a fairly complex system.

Let us repeat this last reference. To achieve a solid DDB design, a basic objective must be to minimize complexity—both logical and physical. To do this we must establish in valid terms the types of problems we are presented with; their frequency (by type); the IE involved in a DDB access; and the overall efficiency model to which the projected use requirements lead. Furthermore, data redundancy must be transparent to the user.

APPLYING AN UPDATING ALGORITHM

Assume that DDB update is performed through the following five step algorithm:

1. Read (query) DB,
2. Compute update,
3. Synchronize update,
4. Implement update,
5. Notify AP.

This very simple procedure identifies three types of communications: First, between the AP and the IE in the database; second, among the AP; third, DDB to DDB. Either operation can be: interhost, or intrahost (Figure 18.3.)

The correct performance of the forementioned operations calls for the definitions of: update variables; basic variables and their timestamps. Timestamps are used in two ways: to determine the currency of update request base variables; and in the update application rule, to guarantee that recent updates supersede older ones.

In both cases, timestamps reflect sequence numbers to order events. Their properties are:

> *uniqueness*: no two update requests should have the same time-stamp, and

> *monotonicity*: successively generated timestamps should increase.

All timestamps ultimately come from update requests which are assigned timestamps by a DBMS when they are initiated. (The DBMS is assumed to have access to a local, synchronized monotonically increasing clock.) As a rule, update requests must be communicated, screened, accepted and *then* processed. Two possible communications disciplines are:

> broadcast, and
> daisy chain.

SIMULTANEOUS UPDATE MECHANISM
DB 1
DBM
FE
DB 2
DB 3
AP1   CURRENT   ACCOUNTS
AP2   LOANS
AP3   FOREIGN   OPS.

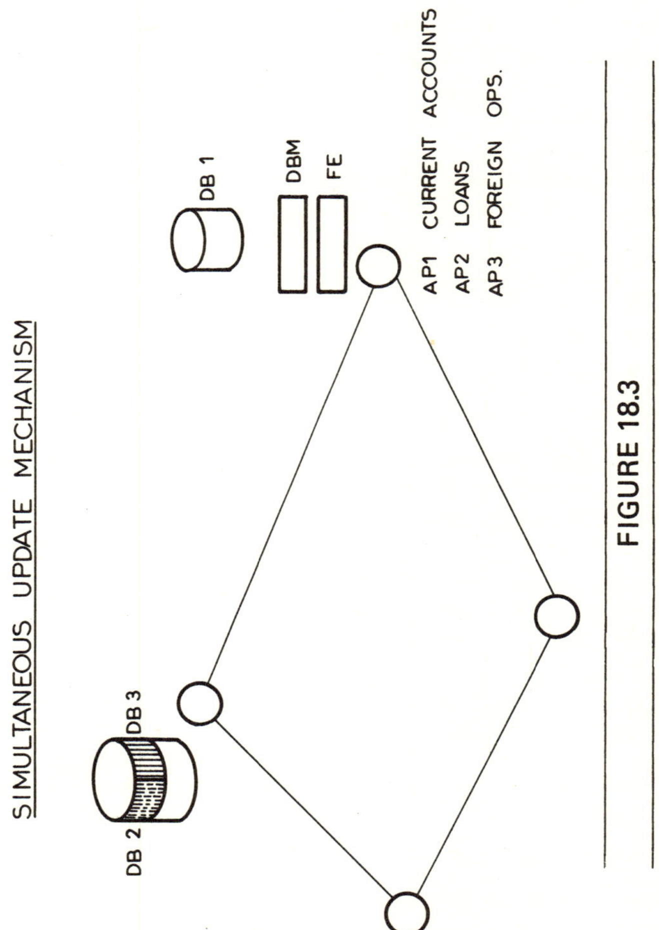

FIGURE 18.3

In a broadcast solution, the DDB receiving an AP update request broadcasts it to the other DDB. The latter sends its reply to the original DDB for request resolution. With the daisy chain, the DDB receiving the request forwards it along with the proposal to another DDB. In turn, this one forwards the request and its proposal to another DDB that has not voted yet. (See also the discussion on the voting algorithm.) This procedure continues until the request is resolved.

The broadcast discipline allows requests to be resolved at shorter delays within the possible expense of extra messages. Daisy chaining results in resolution with the minimum number of messages at the expense of relatively higher delay. In practice, the choice of a communications discipline should be based upon performance requirements for the database system as well as the characteristics of the underlying communication system.

As a third example, the object of a voting algorithm may be maintaining multiple copy databases with distributed control. That is the sense of the *majority consensus* considered here:

1. The DDB vote on the acceptability of an update request.

2. For a request to be accepted and applied to all database copies only a majority need approve it.

3. The voting procedure followed by each DDB allows it to approve an update request only if the information upon which the request was based is valid when it votes.

This algorithm, too, needs to employ a timestamping mechanism used both in the voting procedure and in the application of accepted updates to the database copies. The operation of the algorithm can be demonstrated to preserve internal consistency and mutual consistency of the database copies. But there are prerequisites.

The application of this algorithm suggests the need for: a unique request ID—to which the <basic code> solution can be applied (see Chapters 13 and 14). It requires unique timestamps; and calls for the observance and maintenance of a *voting record*. It also requires DDB-to-DDB communications rules.

ORDER KEEPING MECHANISMS

An order keeping mechanism is necessary to assure a system of traffic lights in a simultaneous update implementation. An example of such an engine can be the following: If not satisfied, the update requests are maintained in FIFO for later consideration. This is a simple way to look at order keeping, but some solutions must be used to avoid deadlocks and inconsistencies:

1. Vote by DDB on requests transmitted by AP (if needed, give priorities to the requests).

2. After "voting ok" and there is a majority consensus: accept requests and notify the other DDB and AP.

3. If voting rejects the request, again notify the other DDB and AP.

4. If a request is accepted by some DDB, but not by all, then introduce the idea of *conflict*. Conflicting requests must be reconsidered.

5. Provide for internal consistency to assure that there are no conflicting updates.

This, in turn, means that a DB/OS function must be assured, at least in terms of supervisory activities. The reliable operation of a database distributed along topological or functional lines can thus find an efficient solution. And like any solution, the one just described obviously entails costs.

The cost of the subject algorithm can be divided into three parts: communications; computational; and storage—both dynamic and long term. To calculate storage costs, the amount of time things will have to be remembered is a fundamental decision. To look into computational costs, we have to ascertain the algorithm's simplicity. Finally, communications costs will be a function of housekeeping traffic. A compromise has to be reached.

Preference, performance and advisability can play a role in reaching the right compromise. The objective should be to show the combination of possibilities which can occur—and to capitalize on these possibilities. Some rules can also help.

Perhaps the most fundamental consideration when projecting an order keeping mechanism is to avoid scrutinizing physical details (like disc access) and logical issues simultaneously. This dual preoccupation will complicate an already complex problem. It is advisable to first attack the logical issues: frequency of updates; types of queries; needs of nearby IE; adopted updating algorithms; policing action which is necessary.

The search for an efficient solution to the problem of the simultaneous update is like an insurance premium. The best case suggests: no conflicts; no DDB failure. This does not happen as a matter of course. The proper fail-safe algorithm must account for the worst case. And that is what we are discussing in presenting a methodology for order keeping and safeguards.

RESTORING A CRASHED SITE

There are different levels of recovery and restart to be studied: system level; node recovery; local process; the individual transaction; the level of the single information element. Furthermore, to implement recovery in an able manner we should project valid solutions at the original design level of the DDB. Stated a different way, before we segment files and decide what data we put on which DTE or DDB, we must study how the system will handle recovery and restart. Without a clear definition of these two subjects, it is impossible to tackle segmentation.

To bring a crashed site back into the group of live sites, we must make its database consistent. There are two cases. First suppose that the copy has not been destroyed by the crash. Then the question arises: Is there any way of defining the set of possible inconsistencies? Potential inconsistencies are of two types:

1. Changes, originated by the sites that did not crash, that may not have been carried out at the crashed site. These changes include those in progress at the time of the crash as well as all those changes that occurred subsequent to the crash.

2. Changes, originated by the crashed site, that may not have been carried out by the crashed site. This possibility arises if an update is broadcast before the local copy of the database is altered.

Let us recall that each live site should be maintaining a journal of recent updates originated by every live site, forgetting updates that are "older than n." Suppose however, that instead of simply being discarded, old updates are recorded on some medium such as a disc. An update history produced in this way would then contain a record of any changes of the two types just described.

Have all possible inconsistencies been covered? No, another problem remains. Say, the crashed site modified its database, but no other site received the broadcast update message. Then, for consistency purposes, the modification must be "undone" when the site is restored. The only record of such modifications that could exist is one made by the site itself. We must guarantee that this record is made before the database is altered—and that it is preserved if the DB survives a crash. If this is insured, then the contents of this record, combined with the disc history, include all possible inconsistencies. Furthermore, the recent update list of the crashed site should be used to identify those updates performed only locally and received by no other site.

Since the update history identifies all those updates performed by the other sites and possibly not performed by the site that crashed, to be reactivated, a copy of the update history must be sent to the site starting at the identification mark that specifies the configuration instance at the time of crash. As an example, let Figure 18.4 reflect the topology of three sites: A, B, C; respectively depending from the Nth, M^{th}, and L^{th} nodes.

"A" broadcasts to "B" and "C." Say that A crashes. What will happen if B has received and processed the update—while C has not yet received it? The

MULTI – COPY   UPDATE

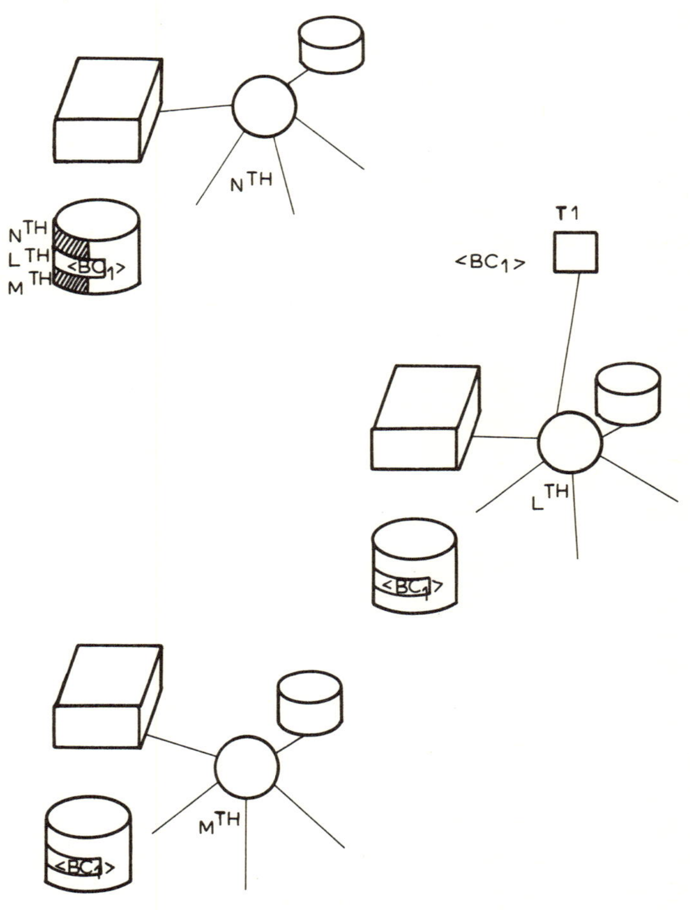

FIGURE 18.4

procedures established must make the restoration process possible. The rules are simple.

1. Previous updates must be kept on history tape and disc;

2. Current updates must be on the recent update list;

3. Realized updates must be carried on the history tape.

For multicopies, within a network, the *potential inconsistencies* should be studied in advance, and a restoration procedure established. Restoration often involves: undo all entries on the recent update list; process the history data, starting from appropriate identification mark; after pruning and synchronizing (within the network) join the multiple copies together into one system.

Finally, a distinction should be made between bringing up a new site, and restoring a site from catastrophic failure. To help the process of restoration: all active sites must write an ID mark; one site must make a copy of the DB on the fly; new sites should be established with a copy of the DB and a copy of the history data.

This procedure is applicable to both the introduction of new sites and recovery after failure. However, for the latter case, it is better to follow a fail-safe approach from the start. This way, concurrency control and recoverability can become one integrated process rather than distinct facets of a loosely coupled procedure.

AN APPLICATIONS EXAMPLE

For an applications example, suppose that "A" sends an update message to sites "B" and "C." Say that: the update message worked at "B" and "C," but "A" crashes. A mechanism is thus necessary, and this can take the form of a two-phase operation:

Phase 1: send messages (B, C, send ACKs) but do not update till phase two.

Phase 2: send from A "commit" messages.

In this case, if it crashes, there is no half-baked operation in process. However, there is an ACK problem. If *no commit* order is sent, B and C must throw away the updates. There is also a problem that if "A" and "B" crash, "C" has done the update. For synchronization purposes, a rollback is necessary when A comes up. This leads to a three-phase commit:

Phase 1: save.

Phase 2: send commits not to B, C . . . but to other DDB, for instance, X, Y, and wait for ACK from them.

Phase 3: then send commit to B, C.

In this case, even if A, X, Y fail, the system will work overall. (But this solution involves complex features which increase overhead costs and delays.) The function of phase two is important: to assure that, when the "commit" goes out, all locations have received the update.

An improved two-phase operation is *not* to execute (change the DB) upon receipt of "commit"—but wait a while "t_o" then procedurally require that sites consult with each other as a means for failure detection. For most practical purposes, this two-phase solution is sufficient. Another possibility advanced by ARPA is to skip phase-two but keep the improvements it has brought forward. Namely: allow time for consultation among sites, prior to updating the DDB.

In conclusion, as an overall evaluation of crash/restore capabilities: alternative solutions exist; all carry a price tag; and choices have to be made. In making a choice, and prior to finalizing it, it is important to establish failure statistics; study how vital the recoverability is; examine recoverability worths vs. the cost involved in different algorithms; then, and only then, choose one alternative.

Both the mechanism for reorganizing the crash and the recovery procedures are important and subject to tradeoffs. A main difficulty is the fact that the statistics needed for evaluation and decision are *not* always available. Furthermore, there are really two reliability issues at stake: *local* and *global* reliability. Their interplay points up the need for a dependable concurrency mechanism—this should be one of the goals with DDB.

19 Supporting a Distributed Environment

INTRODUCTION

Which elements define a distributed information system? Five basic aspects should be considered: distributed processing at the transaction level; distributed communications (not only transmission requirements); distributed databases; and procedures restructured to fit a distributed organization and the new technological realities. Standards represent the fifth critical issue.

Diverse organizational goals and decentralization have led over the years to a lack of standard references. Hence, the need for a company-wide distributed environment concept, and the normalization and administration this entails. Many of the DB problems, for example, exist largely because of inability to respond to diverse requirements by kingsize organizations. Even with "centralized" operations, DB coordination has been an illusion.

As time went by with computer usage and the exploding applications environment, the only thing that remained centralized was the computer utility itself—because the software was there. This is a different way of emphasizing the fact that an IS philosophy is just as necessary with centralized operations as with distributed processing and databases. Such a philosophy must be able to cover: management needs, applications requirements, overall network structure, and source and destination perspectives.

A number of design criteria have been discussed as we examined the subject of distributed databases and the associated communications support. If the same distributed environment is to serve many, diverse applications, it must be applications independent. If the aim is to support many hosts, it must be computer independent; the same is true of intelligent terminals.

Furthermore, an online system must answer the criterion of standardization—if it is designed to talk to other networks. And it must provide vital housekeeping services—both to itself and to the computer gear it supports.

(Indeed, the most useful networks are those which can be assembled through standard hardware, software and communications modules.)

THE NEED FOR STANDARDS

Standards play a very important role in distributed data networks. For private solutions, interface and protocol standards can allow users to connect terminals from different suppliers. Here, the observance of the standards must come from the supplier and from the user.

For public networks, interface and protocol standards allow the telecommunications agency to connect many end users with different equipment. The carrier, however, will not get involved with the standards which should concern the database construction of the user. In this, apart from the design standards which we have considered, a basic decision concerns the choice between centralization and distributed control.

The advantage of a centralization of the DDB control procedures is to avoid having to frequently tune the database because of mutations, deviations and inconsistencies. As Table 19.1 demonstrates, company organization as well as resource management may be hierarchical. But, within this structural solution, data processing may be either centralized or distributed; while the database is hierarchical and centralized; hierarchical and partitioned; or fully distributed in a logical sense.

Fully distributed databases can be networked, this brings the issue of structural (hierarchical) dependencies into perspective. There are several options to choose from. A given company may decide to implement independent databases at each user end; with protocol choices able to determine if replication is appropriate; there may be more than one copy of the IE on a functional or geographic basis; and the DBMS itself can be located in one node or can be spread among different nodes, as usage demands.

But the point remains that, whatever solution is chosen, it must become a company-wide standard to help support the distributed environment in an efficient manner. Several factors must be taken into consideration in establishing the standards which best fit an industrial or financial organization: configuration dependencies; the actual end use requirements; the choice of DBMS; the data dictionary usage; the design of intersystem IE; the interface mechanism(s) to be adopted; security/protection; interrupts, deadlocks, interlocks; recovery and restart necessities.

Quite often, the latter is lost from sight. Yet, we should always ask what the user will be getting for his money. How can the DDB services be better tailored to his needs? to the evolution of his needs?

Designers of database systems are faced with conditions, not with theory. The most severe conditions result from the current immaturity and inexperi-

TABLE 19.1

Company Organization	Resource Management	Data Processing	Databases
Hierarchical	Hierarchical	1. Centralized 2. Distributed	———— 2. Partitioned 3. Fully Distributed

Design standards are necessary to:

1. Determine the size of the final system and its functions;

2. Estimate the time required to produce and deliver the data in the DDB;

3. Reasonably forecast the cost of the system;

4. Project data quality—what constitutes a good DDB solution?

5. Establish reliability: uptime and maximum acceptable number of errors;

6. Outline test procedures—including when, where and how;

7. Project on maintainability—including shutdowns for maintenance, MTTR, ease of needed modifications and retrofitting;

8. Outline the user's convenience.

ence in this field. To meet valid objectives, we need efficient planning and control plus devotion of time and resources to estimates, feedback and corrective action.

Tradeoffs will have to be made, and they will most likely be operational, technical and economic. Invariably, they will involve software support, hardware configuration(s); suppliers' volatility; database design; DBMS considerations; conversions; system capacity; and life-cycle costs.

DOCUMENTATION

When we talk of rational design procedures, we certainly mean that errors committed in the past with data processing should not be repeated. For instance, underestimating the size and complexity of a system; production delays; deficient documentation; and cost overruns. Effective procedures should be laid down and followed with an iron hand in order to obtain valid solutions.

Choices must be made between simplicity and sophistication, depending on the best method for fulfilling objectives within available time and resources. This is attainable only through precise formulation of system design specifications. One of the critical issues is documentation.

Whether we talk of transaction handling or of DDB, documentation must play a prominent role, including:

> rigorous releases,
> review procedures,
> uniform terminology, and
> standard formats.

Technical reports and documents are in a very real sense the only tangible products of a database system development process. Only the computer can read the magnetic disc which stores the special software, the IE and the messages.

Let us emphasize that documentation is not a subject to be handled at the end of DB design, after all issues have been settled. Quite to the contrary, the documentation accompanying a system project should consist of:

1. Administrative progress reports (plan vs. actual for cost and time; manpower issues);

2. Technical progress reports (soft points, strong points, deficient specs, lack of precision);

3. IE design and standardization;

4. The design of the input and output videoforms and hardcopy alternatives,

5. Operational manual;

6. User's manual;

7. Maintenance manual (including design specifications, amendments, upkeep, and detailed hardware/software description).

The computer should definitely be called upon to help with the production and upkeep of the documentation. Both progress evaluation and the proper description of the database system will be found in this documentation, in enough detail to permit understanding and comprehensive evaluation. Figure 19.1 suggests a procedural outline and a graphic model for implementation.

Documentation will be the link between the developers of the database system and the users. It will also help in interfacing old systems; in the definition of system boundaries, between subsystems which perform the same or similar functions; and in the overall evaluation. After all, the best test of any system is: does it work?

GRAPH MODELS FOR DATABASE DESIGN
REQUIREMENTS
MISSION
SYSTEM ENGINEERING
SYSTEM SPECS
REQUIRED SPECS.
DB DESIGN
OVERALL PERSPECTIVE; INTEGRATION
IE DESIGN
DETAIL AT INFORMATION ELEMENT LEVEL
DDB ORGANIZATION
DECISION ON PARTITION; DISTRIBUTION; REPLICATION
IMPLEMENTATION
ACCESS CAPABABILITIES; SECURITY; RECOVERY; JOURNALING; MAIN-TENANCE
FAILURE STATISTICS DUE TO REQUIREMENTS AND DESIGN
SOLUTIONS SHOULD BE KEPT AT EVERY STEP OF THE PROCESS
% OF COPIES EXAMINED
UNCLEAR
UNRELIABLE
MISSING
AMBIGUOUS
CONTRADICTORY

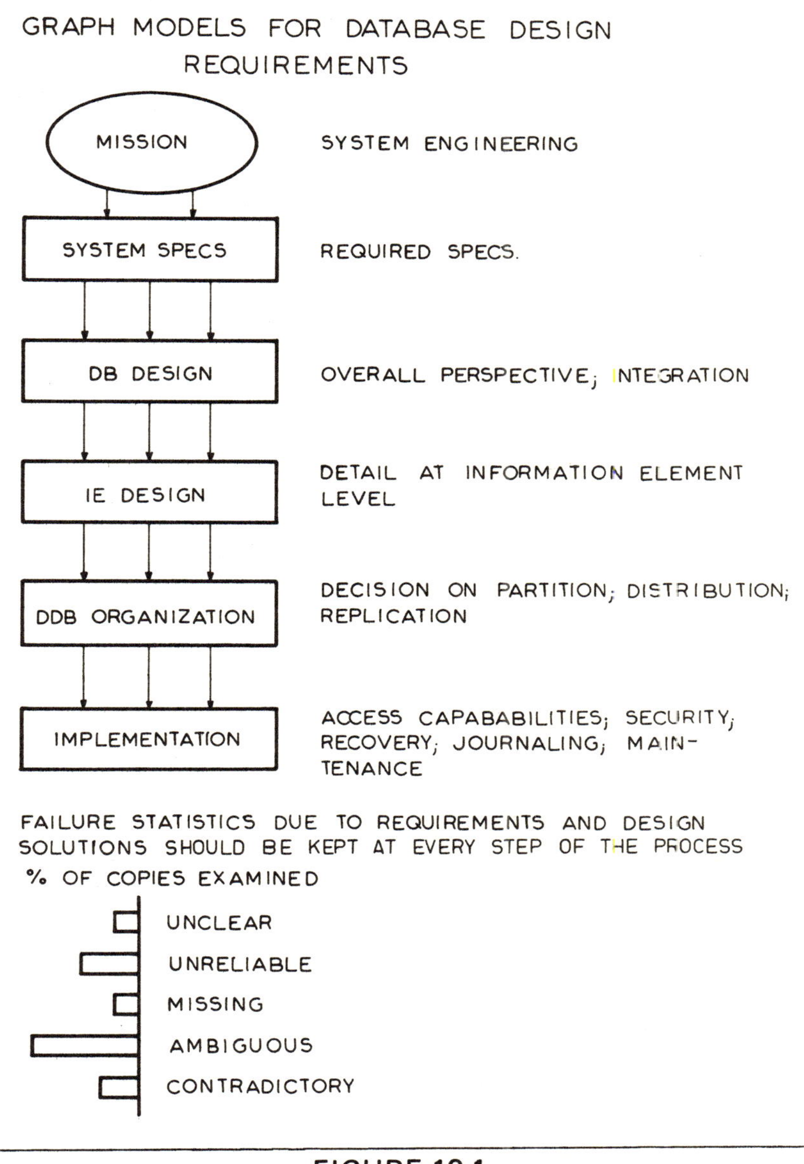

FIGURE 19.1

COORDINATION

During the past fifteen years, as the terminals connected online to a computer user started increasing in number, first slowly, then rapidly, the geographically distributed system user had two approaches available for implementing a unified data system. First, the files were centralized, with access by remote terminals assured through communications lines.

Almost from inception, this approach provided for economy of scale and for easy central implementation and control. However, communications costs were often high and the system proved to be quite vulnerable to a failure at the central site or in the communications system. Furthermore, the economies of scale were only valid up to a point. Increased size and complexity made them uneconomical.

Second, systems were implemented with a number of minicomputers at the various locations, each with its own mass storage and terminals. Several options were, and still are, available with this approach.

For instance, there may or may not be a nodal network with private lines. Figure 19.2 outlines an approach chosen by a leading French bank: the DDB is both functional (at the headquarters level; H_1, H_2, etc.) and geographic (branch offices; B_1, B_2, B_3 and so on). A controlled replication exists between the functionally and geographically distributed IE, and the entire system is coordinated through an ingenious procedural solution and the use of public lines at preferential (evening) rates.

Having the database elements distributed while keeping the coordination and control action centralized has given this bank considerable advantages. There is a communications failsafe capability; lower communications costs; dual: distributed and central failsafe assurance; configuration flexibility; high system performance; fast response for the end user; modular implementation and modular upgrade.

The following situation was identified at an early time for a distributed database implementation: large volumes of data generated at many locations; fast access required by the end user; some of the data, and summaries of all of the data needed at the central site in a timely manner; remote locations generating large volumes of data for fast response and immediate inquiry.

The system study properly documented that the majority of the inquiries were local, fast response was needed infrequently from other locations. This led to the establishment, after experimentation, of the "80/2" rule: eighty percent of all data born in the periphery stay in the periphery; and only two percent of the inquiries made in branch offices do not find an answer in the local DB—if its component elements are well chosen.

When an access is made to data not held locally, the transaction is treated as an exception, and at least two options exist for handling it. The transaction

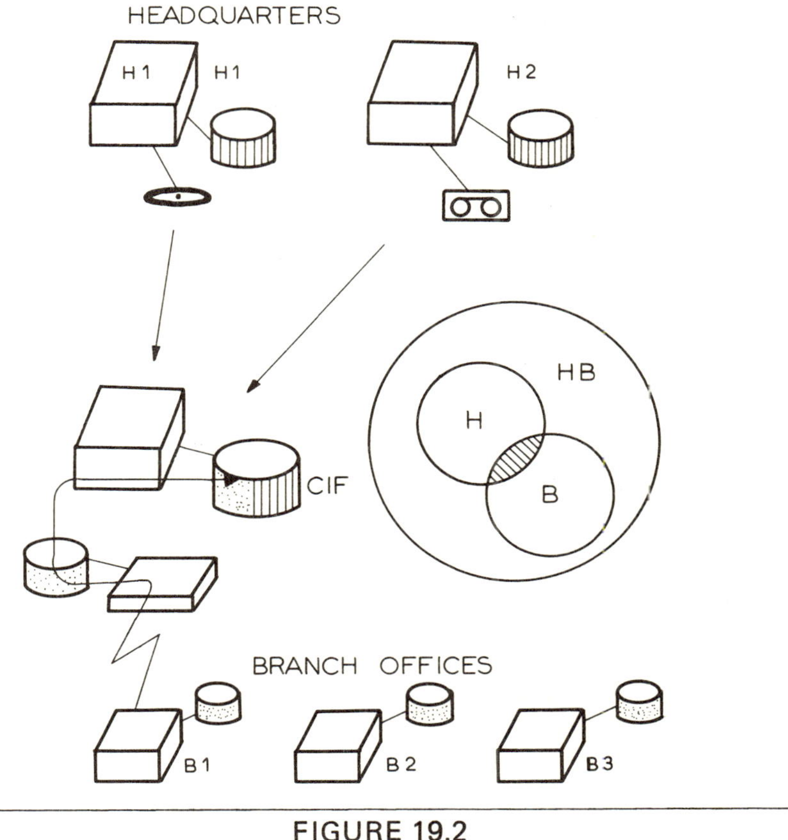

FIGURE 19.2

can be forwarded (through a public line, using automatic modems) to a central node where a master directory exists to forward the transaction to the proper location; or a phone call is made to the other eighty so that the transaction can be handled there directly (provided that the risk of the money involved justifies the expense).

After the system was deployed, central coordination was assured for all vital issues. No minicomputer centers were allowed in the old sense of "EDP." The whole system was run as a utility. The system was put online at selected time periods, but file storage and file search were kept in the periphery where they belong.

The planners carefully avoided creating a large architecture. They made the system modular and picked up minicomputer based applications points as they ran through the usage requirements. They evaluated the alternatives;

defined the problems; kept the proper statistics and made documented decision making.

They simplified; broke down complexity; standardized the hardware, software and procedures; trained the local users on how to apply the system—and found out that with minis they could standardize and still be flexible. Simplicity offered another advantage: experience documented that, if we kept the machine simple, we could keep the software management; the IE visible; and the maintenance costs low.

We should also keep in mind that, currently programming has not been very helpful. About eighty percent of the application programs in use today in a typical installation were written within the last fifteen years and, though they may still be serving the functional procedures of corporate departments, they are mainly batch and do not observe DB prerequisites. Programming languages do not provide reliability and have not been designed with interactive approaches in mind—yet, programs and DB management are highly interrelated activities.

The purpose of coordination becomes more important as a host of new problems have been encountered with DIS: the duplication or replication of databases between the central and the distributed sites adds system control and security problems. Just the same, the interaction of a mini of one manufacturer (or even the same manufacturer with incompatible hardware) presents problems of language translation and communications protocols.

When establishing proper coordination perspectives it must be kept in mind that, with DDB, centralized control of the database can be weakened and the problems of the audit function possibly increased substantially. So much the better if the DBA who handles the job of coordination has the ability to be forcefully convincing.

JOURNALING AND STATISTICS

The typical transaction will impact the database by demanding the execution of specific tasks such as capture; receive; storage; call-back; and it will also keep system statistics. It will call for system missions, one of the most challenging being to get the different tasks talking among themselves within a specific operating environment.

Without getting involved in the detail of DBMS, Figure 19.3 presents the main functions of a database management system. Note that the supervisory program performs both a coordinating and a control function. Control must log system activity, and the available software must include on- and offline diagnostics.

The hardware must permit modular troubleshooting, repair and replacement. The communications capability must accept the advanced, standard protocols. The database perspectives must incorporate not only the IE in storage but also at the points where information is collected and delivered: that is, where it enters and leaves the DB.

Surveillance and controlled access must be maintained at all times. A DDB function should include the data flows and the paths they follow to interconnect the various segments available online on the network.

Let us remember that in DDB design, in any given firm, data is as much a resource as are people; money; machinery; and products. With online systems, the database is not only the most valuable information warehouse, it is also the framework for supporting the applications' distribution; it is highly functional; can be designed with IE identical in structure and type; and if properly planned and followed up, can assure the greatest flexibility.

Journaling should be projected to protect this flexibility. The user communicates with the DB supervisor. The latter takes the necessary action to activate the journaling routines. However, a logical (and sometimes physical) distinction must be made between:

> a user journal, which can be interrogated at all times, and

> a supervisor (or internal) journal whose functions are needed to keep the system running.

The management of the DB and, especially recovery and restart procedures, and file protection prerequisites demand the maintenance of the journals "before" and "after." The breadth of the journaling function will include: network assignments; control duties; and DB oriented approaches.

The network functions must identify the source station, the destination, the hardware and software interfaces, the communications links, the virtual circuits (if any), and the network routing.

The DB prerequisites can be served through the identification of author, sender, and station of origin; receiver and destination station; operation per se; operating data; file(s) which is (are) addressed; the distribution list (if any); and other important statistics such as unusual events, time in and time out; exercised control (for instance, stop action), restore and recovery.

Lots of valuable data can be compiled from the DB journal for example, frequency by type of request, by sender, by receiver, files addressed, amounts handled, stop action, and frequency and recovery procedures.

Some of the control functions journaling must answer in an able manner include, overall supervision, integrity identifiers, data security, operating statistics, and lots of utilities. For instance, format control, code control, transcoding, data on timeliness, accuracy, failsafe, backup, backout, and the handling of such overhead items as time of operation and type of transaction.

More specifically, operational statistics should involve: the line load, volume analysis, possible bottlenecks, (by hardware, software, or for operational reason), queuing delays, overall response, turnaround, uptime availability, error references by type and time of happening), and whatever else is neces-

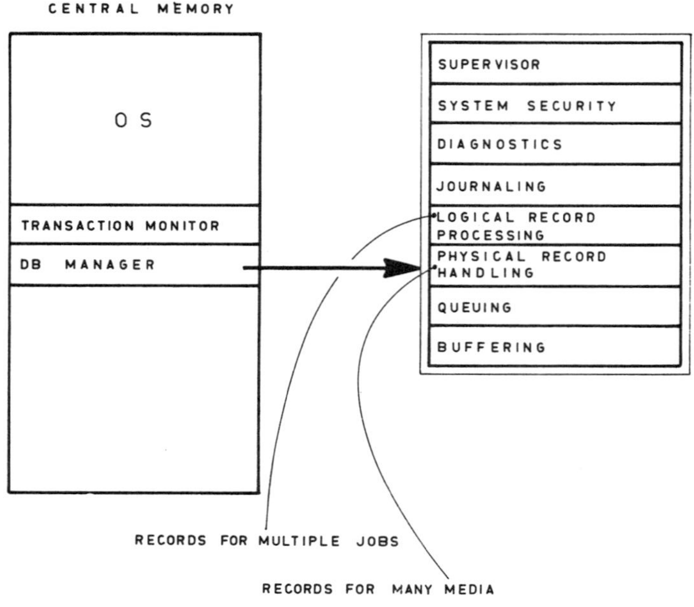

FIGURE 19.3

sary for final billing. The provisions of these functions bring a unifying approach to the procedural solutions which have been discussed in considerable length throughout this book.

CONCLUSION

The excessive centralization and development of very large computer-based systems encouraged an uncritical escalation toward exploding files which lacked organization, integration, and auditability. The steady increase in the size and complexity of the file aggregates created an unavoidable increase in the size and complexity of both hardware and software. As a result, there has been a tendency toward loss of flexibility and reliability of the information contained in these aggregates.

Companies looked toward the creation of a database as a means for overcoming this obstacle. Ideally, this should be designed to support all applications programs: no AP should carry its own files anymore. But the conversion of file aggregates into a coherent, homogeneous, solid database has not been the easy process DP management thought it would be. And the new trend toward minicomputers and networks (in short, the distributed databases) has aggravated this task.

Advances in computer, communications and database technology steadily emphasize the advantages of dedicating applications to self-standing minicomputers with or without the benefit of a private network. This provides the end user with the ability to control his own resources and service levels, isolating him from effects of unpredictable blackout in central computer capabilities, or changes in priority beyond his control.

Indeed, distributed processing has been the first great departure from the centralized mainframe complex, with its ever increasing costs. On several occasions with maxicomputer systems, a loss of control has resulted from the increasing number of software, hardware and applications components that must coexist on the same mainframe. As a result, in industry and banking, a DIS experience has already been acquired, using mini and microcomputers able to stand alone and to be linked to a network.

The second great departure has its origins in the impossibility of managing in a growing data communications environment the transport (networking) mechanism with the same machine which runs the application programs. Hence, the concept of frontends; data communications engines; and network protocols.

The third departure from the established ways of the 1960's and early 70's is in the way we look at the administration of large, complex databases. Complexity led to the need for separating the application processes from database management, creating a rearend engine. Slowly, this led to revamping the way we view information elements: their structure, standardization, and distribution among partitioned or replicated databases.

Such experiences have led us toward an integrated approach to database design, implementation and upkeep. The point is, once the DB is projected, it must be described through a database description language and processed to create a dictionary. This is a fundamental procedure in a DB definition process. The data dictionary serves as a common point and source of the information about the elements in the DB; and the directory tells where to find the data within a distributed environment.

Such developments have evolved out of necessity. Computer-run databases are getting increasingly sophisticated; demanding; and expensive. Online computer systems have helped to open these frontiers. As a function of time, the overall computer-based system becomes more user-oriented, interactive, and DB-intense. That is why databases constitute a prerequisite to the efficient usage of computers.

A number of critical factors have come into play during the last three years, their impact mainly felt by the distributed systems: rising communications costs, but falling processor and memory prices; a growing users' demand for processing power and databasing capability; the growing inefficiency of overcentralization: poor response time, longer time leads for applications development, incompatibilities in file design, and so on.

User demands and the threat to go along on a microcomputer basis (personal computers, the so-called "gorilla computers" in organizations) has had an impact on distributed perspectives: from processing to databasing and network design. At the same time, experience created an evolution in our concepts concerning partitionable and replicable databases; better defined network and DB structures; new applications capabilities and a new look at applications and databasing requirements.

Suddenly, organizational and procedural prerequisites became a capital subject—but the task became complicated by the fact that information systems must continue providing service to the present users, while planning and implementing the future capabilities.

Current objectives and future goals are not necessarily the same thing. As far as we can see today, the objectives to be served through properly designed, distributed and interactive databases range from a reduction in personnel costs, to higher productivity, to the control of communications costs and an increase in computer availability to the user.

Computer professionals are steadily on the look-out for solutions which might simplify management and control tasks. And they know very well that the requirements of the 1980's will go beyond DIS. Such requirements will stress data quality control and computer and microform based paperwork conversion. Many organizations have established peer review groups to look into office automation—a desktop computer at the work place.

This is not only required for cost-control purposes, but also because new services to be offered in the 1980's will be IS intense. They will involve: telecommunications; electronic mail; EFT; viewdata; broadcasting; direct input by the customers into the database; each and every issue calls for computers, databases and communications.

The dedication of database segments to business functions, while keeping the whole database integrated, accessible and reliable, makes it possible to reduce response time and provide higher availability. These advantages can be realized if database sections can be placed at or near the point of work. Then access prerequisites are less susceptible to disruptions due to outages and component failures. (Typically, such databases have been based on minis, because minis are inexpensive. Given their cost/effectiveness, they are perfectly suitable for multiple computer sites—and, unlike mainframes, they have been designed for interactive applications.)

Projecting database systems, organizing the information elements, pruning the files, are functions which must necessarily take into account the general applications perspectives to be served by the database. Productivity, cost reduction, security/protection, availability, data quality control, and the new information services are component parts of the picture. *But the most vital ingredient is knowhow.*

Index

interactivity, *see* environments,
  interactive; system, interactive

J

journaling, 275-276

M

machine, virtual, 141-142
mainframe, 37-39, 41, 42
management, database, 18, 77-79
mechanism, order keeping, 261-262
memory, recognition, 80
memory, virtual
  goals of, 136
  and microcode, 134-135, 139
  and pages, 137-141
  and simplified programming, 135
microcode, 134-135, 139
microfiles, 34-35
mini (minicomputer), 39-43, 49,
  129, 278
minicomputer, *see* mini
multiaccess, 90
multiprogramming, 84, 91

N

networks, design elements of, 9-10

P

page, 137-141
partitioning, *see* database; database,
  distributed
pipelining, 139
priorities, database
  data volume, 83-84
  goals, 74-76, 80-81
  migration, 85-86
  software for, 81-82
processes, communicating
  configuration of, 98-99
  critical factors, 109, 111-113,
    115

  design parameters, 99-101
  interactive, 101-103
protocols, 4, 38, 87-88, 90-96

R

rate, low bit error, 2
realtime, 29, 129
REM, *see* memory, recognition
retrieval, *see* system, coding
RT, *see* realtime

S

S+F, *see* software, store and forward
services, computer communications
  media
    fiber optics, 8
    microwaves, 7
    satellites, 8
  supported services
    internetworking, 8
    network control centers, 8
    network population, 8
site, crashed, 262-263, 265-266
software, store and forward, 2
storage, virtual, *see* memory, virtual
stratification, *see* database
synchronization, 255, 265
system, coding, 194-195
  see also code, classification;
    Dimitris Chorafas System
system, interactive, 40-41

T

telesoftware, 138
time stamp, 258, 259, 261

V

videoform, 177-231
VM, *see* memory, virtual
VS (virtual storage), *see* memory,
  virtual